A STRANGER IN EUROPE

A Stranger in Europe

Britain and the EU from Thatcher to Blair

STEPHEN WALL

OXFORD
UNIVERSITY PRESS

This book has been printed digitally and produced in a standard specification
in order to ensure its continuing availability

OXFORD
UNIVERSITY PRESS

Great Clarendon Street, Oxford OX2 6DP

Oxford University Press is a department of the University of Oxford.
It furthers the University's objective of excellence in research, scholarship,
and education by publishing worldwide in

Oxford New York

Auckland Cape Town Dar es Salaam Hong Kong Karachi
Kuala Lumpur Madrid Melbourne Mexico City Nairobi
New Delhi Shanghai Taipei Toronto
With offices in
Argentina Austria Brazil Chile Czech Republic France Greece
Guatemala Hungary Italy Japan South Korea Poland Portugal
Singapore Switzerland Thailand Turkey Ukraine Vietnam

Oxford is a registered trade mark of Oxford University Press
in the UK and in certain other countries

Published in the United States
by Oxford University Press Inc., New York

© Stephen Wall 2008

ISBN 978-0-19-928455-9

For Catharine and Matthew, with love
For Sir Nicholas Henderson, with admiration

Preface

This book is not a memoir. But it draws on my memory and experience.

From 1983 to 1988, I worked in what was then known as the European Communities Department of the Foreign Office, ultimately as its Head. I was involved, in the backroom, in the negotiations in which Margaret Thatcher secured a budget rebate for Britain: the famous "I want my money back" row with our European partners.

Thereafter, until 1993, when I was sent as Britain's ambassador to Portugal, I was Private Secretary to Geoffrey Howe, John Major, and Douglas Hurd—the successive Foreign Secretaries at that time. When John Major became Prime Minister, he asked me to join him as his Foreign Office Private Secretary. Today, the Prime Minister has an entire foreign policy team. In 1991, as before, there was only one person: me. Like my predecessors, I did everything from record taking, to advising, to negotiating late at night with the National Security Adviser of the United States. I was with John Major at the Maastricht European Council which launched Economic and Monetary Union and at which John Major secured the British opt-outs from EMU (Economic and Monetary Union) and the Social Chapter.

In 1995, John Major sent me as the United Kingdom's Permanent Representative (or Ambassador) to the European Union (EU) in Brussels. I was there for five years, including the change from a Conservative to a Labour government, and helped negotiate the Amsterdam and Nice Treaties.

In 2000, I came back to London to head up the European Secretariat of the Cabinet Office (which coordinates the Government's EU policies across Whitehall) and to be Tony Blair's senior adviser on the EU. I left Number 10, and the Diplomatic Service, in 2004.

The title of this book, *A Stranger in Europe*, mirrors the title of the book, *A Stranger in Spain*, written in the 1950s by the great travel writer, H.V. Morton. It is not a title that needs much explanation. A number of people have told parts of the story. This too is part of the story. It concentrates on a period of some twenty years, beginning in 1982 and ending with the negotiation of the ill-starred EU Constitutional Treaty in 2004.

I chose this period because it is the period when I was intensively involved in the EU policy of successive governments, and could therefore write from experience. It is also the period that saw the negotiation of *all* the significant changes to the European Treaties which have been made since the original Treaty of Rome was signed in 1957. For between 1957 and 1985, the year in which the Single European Act was negotiated, virtually no changes were made to the original European treaties. Since then, we have had the Maastricht, Amsterdam, and Nice Treaties and the draft Constitutional Treaty. All of those institutional changes posed serious substantive and political problems for the British governments which had to wrestle with them. It seemed to me worth telling the story of that period and of the big negotiations within the EU from Margaret Thatcher's day to Tony Blair's. I have sought to explain why successive British governments took the decisions they did. I have also tried to paint a picture of the issues which dominated the relationship between British Prime Ministers and their German and French opposite numbers.

The book starts in 1982, when the argument over Britain's contribution to the European Community (EC) budget was coming to a head, and concludes with the negotiations on the EU draft Constitutional Treaty in 2004. It is not a history but it attempts to be an accurate account, albeit of course a personal one. The Foreign and Commonwealth Office kindly gave me permission to look through relevant documents to support my recollection of the period. I have consulted the memoirs of political leaders from the time and drawn on the advice and judgements of colleagues. But the account, its conclusions, and its judgements are mine.

The bulk of this book covers a period which, if not quite history, is anyway an era of governments no longer in office. In so far as my memory, aided by the official records, has added to the sum of human knowledge, a good deal of that knowledge had already been widely promulgated in the memoirs of what Douglas Hurd used to call "the great ones", his own compellingly among them.

I was a privileged insider during part of Tony Blair's time as Prime Minister, first as the British ambassador to the EU until 2000 and then as Tony Blair's official adviser on EU issues from 2000 to 2004. There are plenty of blow-by-blow accounts of the period already in the public domain, written by journalists and historians who were, unlike me, not signatories of the Official Secrets Act and who were not working for the government as I was. Given those constraints, I have not, in the chapter on Tony Blair and Europe, attempted to follow them but, instead, to analyse, against the background of what is already in the public domain, the nature of the issues Tony Blair's government faced, the pressures they faced, and the positions they took.

I am convinced that wholehearted participation in the EU is strongly in Britain's national interest. Few of the politicians who have exercised power in our country in the years covered by this book would disagree with that view. Yet, in different ways, they have all wrestled with the EU as a *problem* in British politics. From the viewpoint I had as a civil servant, and from the archives, this book is an attempt to describe at least some of what happened, and why.

Acknowledgements

This book is not the story of my career, but the story it does tell dictated much of my life in Her Majesty's Diplomatic Service for 35 years. I frequently sacrificed family life to work and this book is dedicated to Catharine, my wife, and Matthew, my son, who bore with me and sustained me. It is also dedicated to Sir Nicholas Henderson, who was successively Britain's ambassador to Poland, Germany, France, and the United States of America. I worked under his leadership in Washington and he was the model of the very best of British public servants as well as a passionate advocate of wholehearted British commitment to Europe. "What would Nicko have done?" is the question I often asked myself as I tried to wrestle with difficult issues in later years.

I learned a lot from the many colleagues, older and younger, with whom I worked in the Foreign Office, in overseas posts, and in the Cabinet Office and Number 10 Downing Street. This book is an inadequate reflection of their dedication, talent, and human qualities. For their comments, advice, and help in filling in the blanks in my own knowledge, I am especially grateful to Sir Michael Butler, Lord Hannay, Lord Kerr, Lord Renwick, and Sir John Grant. They were all outstanding public servants for, or with, whom I was privileged to work. Robin Renwick generously allowed me to draw on his own, as yet unpublished, memoir covering his work in Europe for Margaret Thatcher. I am also grateful to John Newhouse, who covered much of this period in depth for the *New Yorker*, for permission to quote from his article in the issue of 22 October 1984: "The Diplomatic Round: One Against Nine".

I was Private Secretary successively to Lord Howe, Lord Hurd, and Sir John Major. They all generously read, commented on, and improved the manuscript, as did Anthony Teasdale, who was Geoffrey Howe's special adviser when he was Foreign Secretary. I did not work directly for Baroness Thatcher, who dominates a chunk of this book, as she did the history of this country. But I was a backroom boy during the struggle over the British budget and even if you were not in her presence, you felt the power of her will. I am grateful to the Thatcher foundation for their *nihil obstat* to what I have written.

Lord Jay, then Permanent Undersecretary at the Foreign and Commonwealth Office (FCO), generously agreed that I could look through relevant FCO documents to check my recollection of the period. I am particularly grateful to Patrick Salmon, the chief historian at the Foreign Office, and his colleagues, Chris Baxter and Alastair Noble, for their advice and patience.

I was encouraged to write this book, and helped in framing its structure, by Professor Anand Menon, Director of the European Research Institute at Birmingham University. It was Anand who pointed me in the direction of OUP, who introduced me to Dominic Byatt, their chief editor, and who gave rigorous comment on my draft. I would not have got there without both of them. Dominic realised very quickly that I was enthusiastic but inexperienced and I owe a lot to his expert, generous, and kind guidance.

I hope this book conveys something of the way British politicians and civil servants work as a team. I chose, by chance, a career which brought me into contact with some of the most able politicians of our day. I hope I have done them justice. I will not have done justice by name to the many colleagues and friends in the Diplomatic Service and in other government departments with whom I worked and who contributed hugely to such successes as we achieved within the EU. Nor will I have done justice to the colleagues from other EU member states with whom I worked, negotiated, and sometimes battled. Negotiation in the EU is always intense and frequently rough. But everyone round the table has a sense of an interest greater than the lowest common denominator of inter-governmental agreement: that of a peaceful, prosperous, and democratic EU.

Contents

Abbreviations

ANC	African National Congress
BSE	Bovine Spongiform Encephalopathy
CAP	Common Agricultural Policy
CBI	Confederation of British Industry
CFSP	Common Foreign and Security Policy
COREPER	Committee of Permanent Representatives
CSCE	Commission on Security and Cooperation in Europe
DEFRA	Department for Environment, Food and Rural Affairs
DM	Deutschmark
EBRD	European Bank for Reconstruction and Development
EC	European Community
ECB	European Central Bank
ECJ	European Court of Justice
ECOFIN	Economic and Financial Affairs
EEC	European Economic Community
EFTA	European Free Trade Area
EMU	Economic and Monetary Union
EP	European Parliament
ERM	Exchange Rate Mechanism
EU	European Union
FCO	Foreign and Commonwealth Office
GATT	General Agreement on Tariffs and Trade
GDP	Gross Domestic Product
GDR	German Democratic Republic
HMG	Her Majesty's Government
IBRD	International Bank for Reconstruction and Development
IGC	Intergovernmental Conference
IMF	International Monetary Fund
IRA	Irish Republican Army
MEP	Member of the European Parliament

MOD	Ministry of Defence
NFU	National Farmers Union
NHS	National Health Service
OPD	Office of Public Diplomacy
POCO	Political cooperation
POW	Prisoners of war
QMV	qualified majority voting
RAF	Royal Air Force
SDP	Social Democratic Party
SEA	Single European Act
TUC	Trades Union Congress
VAT	Value Added Tax
WEU	Western European Union

1

The Start of a Troubled Relationship

*"I am not puttable offable": Money, the Veto,
and European Union*

In 1963, General de Gaulle issued his first veto of Britain's application to join the European Community (EC), the Common Market. "Take your dreams of independent power, and stick them up your Eiffel Tower" were the concluding lines of one popular British retort to de Gaulle at the time. But the humour was a characteristically British attempt to disguise the hurt of the humiliation.

My own family's background and attitudes were probably not untypical. My father fought in France, as an 18 year old, in the last year of World War I. He had benign memories of the German prisoners of war (POWs) over whom, as a young subaltern, he had held authority. He and my mother spent holidays in Germany before World War II. After that war, their view of Germany did not readily recover. I recall, on holiday in Cornwall in the early 1950s, the Latvian refugee who worked in the boarding house where we stayed telling tales of the horrors she and her family had endured. My aunt had Dutch friends whose parents had died in German camps. For most of my early childhood, the war was the main topic of conversation between my mother and our daily help in middle-class Epsom where we lived. For much of the cold war, my parents remained more frightened of Germany than of Soviet Russia. Yet, for that very reason, they welcomed the EC as something that made war less likely. I was 16 years old at the time of de Gaulle's veto and I cannot remember a time from then on when, despite the irritations and frustrations, membership of the EC did not seem to me the right decision for Britain.

Our country had declined to join the original Six founders of the EC. Even in the early 1950s, it had been, as Harold Macmillan confided to his diary, the British "functional" versus the Continental "federal" approach. For much of the 1950s, the economic case for joining the Coal and Steel community and then the embryonic EC was not self-evident: Britain's trade with the Commonwealth was much more significant than our trade with the countries that were to form the Common Market. And, even when the balance of economic argument began to change, the political problems associated with joining a "federal" project kept us out. After the debacle of Suez in 1956, however, our self-image of great power status could no longer be indulged. And the new Common Market, established by the Treaty of Rome in 1957, soon began to outstrip our economic growth.

It is often argued that the British people were deceived about the true supranational nature of the EC by Harold Macmillan who was the first British Prime Minister to apply for membership, by Ted Heath who led Britain into the EC in 1973, and by Harold Wilson who called the referendum on our membership in 1975. But Macmillan did set out the argument in a pamphlet entitled *Britain, the Commonwealth and Europe* published in September 1962, and he addressed the issues with more candour than has been common since. "We in Britain are Europeans", he wrote:

We have to consider the state of the world as it is today and will be tomorrow and not in outdated terms of a vanished past. There remain only two national units which can claim to be world powers in their own right, namely the United States and Soviet Russia. To these may soon be added what Napoleon once called the "sleeping giant" of China, whose combination of a rapidly multiplying population and great natural resources must increasingly be reckoned as a potent force in world affairs . . . It is true of course that political unity is the central aim of those European countries and we would naturally accept that ultimate goal. But the effects on our position of joining Europe have been much exaggerated by the critics. Accession to the Treaty of Rome would not involve a one-sided surrender of sovereignty on our part but a pooling of sovereignty by all concerned, mainly in economic and social fields. In renouncing some of our sovereignty we would receive in return a share of the sovereignty renounced by other members . . . The form which political unity of the Community should take is now under active discussion in Europe, where opinions on it are strongly divided. There is a school which ardently believes in the unitary concept of a European federation, a new European state. I myself believe that the bulk of public opinion is firmly against the extinction of separate national identities and would choose a Europe which preserved and harmonised all that is best in our different national traditions. We would, I think, favour a more gradual approach worked out by experience, instead of a leap in the dark, and this is a view shared by many leaders of opinion in Europe.

Macmillan made no secret of the federal ambition of some members of the EC. His argument, that most wanted something that fell short of the suppression of national identity and were more in line with our own thinking, is an argument made since by most of his successors in Downing Street. That tension, compounded by specific policy differences and, especially, by the argument over the British financial contribution to the EC budget, dominated the Thatcher years and set the tone of Britain's relationship with her partners for the past quarter of a century.

The seeds of that scratchy partnership were possibly sown as long ago as the Reformation, with Henry VIII's assertion of Englishness and resistance to continental encroachment. They grew in the blood-enriched soil of numerous conflicts up to and including the two world wars. Macmillan was obliged to defend his decision to apply for EC membership against the charge laid by Opposition leader Hugh Gaitskell that he was playing fast and loose with "a thousand years of history", a charge that resonates in Britain to this day.

There was a brief honeymoon. In October 1972 in Paris, Ted Heath attended his first meeting of EC Heads of Government. Britain was not set to join until January 1973, but Heath signed up to a communiqué in which "the Member States of the Community, the driving wheels of European construction, declare their intention of converting their entire relationship into a European Union before the end of this decade". What that statement meant to the member states was to become a source of friction between Britain and her partners—one that remains unresolved to this day.

Ted Heath was probably the only British Prime Minister to have shared the view of the original Six that the destination of the EC might one day be a federation: something different than the sum total of the component member states, albeit not one that would necessarily replace the nation state in all its forms. Heath certainly shared the vision of the European project as a dynamic one, evolving constitutionally as well as pragmatically. That view was not shared by the British public at the time, or by any of Heath's successors since. But the search for political union in Europe has been the quest of most of the European Union (EU) member states throughout the project's history, and the bugbear of British governments over the same period.

In December 1974, with Labour Prime Minister Harold Wilson back in power, the EC Heads called on one of their number, Belgian Prime Minister Leo Tindemans, to make a report on what European union would involve. A year later, Tindemans concluded that European union should include Economic and Monetary Union (EMU) but that the process should be "gradual" and "progressive". The other Heads of Government agreed. They said in a communiqué:

European Union will be built progressively by consolidating and developing what has been achieved within the community, with the existing Treaties forming a basis for new policies. The achievement of Economic and Monetary Union is basic to the consolidation of Community solidarity and the establishment of European Union. Priority importance must be given to combating inflation and unemployment and to drawing up common energy and research policies and a genuine regional and social policy for the Community.

Already, in that communiqué, there was evidence of British influence and hesitation, with the implication that EMU would involve no new treaty and the emphasis on practical, immediate economic and social policies. Fear of treaty change was to be a prevailing theme of British policy towards the EU. Britain had accepted the sharing of sovereignty implicit in the Treaty of Rome. After much hesitation, the British people had voted in a referendum (and in the end by a majority of 2:1) to stay in the EC. But successive British governments were to be nervous of press, parliamentary, and public scepticism about Europe, and to frame their policy responses accordingly.

To these seeds of future aggravation was added dissension over Britain's financial contribution to the EC budget, a story whose first chapter was vividly told in the official report on Britain's negotiations to join the EC, written by the senior official in the negotiating team, Sir Con O'Neill. In brief, the terms of the definitive arrangements for EC finance were set by the original Six before the final, successful round of negotiations with Britain began. That indeed was a condition set by President Pompidou: the financing of the EC had to be settled before serious negotiation with the British could start.

Sir Con O'Neill attributed at least part of de Gaulle's effective veto of the Labour government's membership application of 1967 to France's determination to sort out Community finance on terms favourable to her before Britain was in a position, as an EC member, to influence the outcome. Those financial arrangements set by the Six in 1969 transformed EC financing into what is still known as the "own resources" system whereby the EC was funded by a mixture of levies and duties on imports into the Community. Those levies and duties were to accrue not to the national exchequers of the countries in which they fell, but to the Community as a whole. To them was to be added an amount equal to the yield of up to 1% of a Value Added Tax (VAT). As Con O'Neill put it: "Under the finance regulation, we should have to pay 90 per cent of all our import levies on foodstuffs and animal feed, and 90 per cent of all our customs duties, to the Community budget. As a large food importer...the levies we should pay on agricultural imports would be far higher than those paid by any other member." The problem was compounded by the fact that some 90% of the Community's budget was, also at French insistence, absorbed by subsidies to agricultural exports from the Community. "There was bound", according to O'Neill, "to be an equally profound bias against us on the expenditure side. The sum of money we could hope to recover from the Community budget in respect of agriculture was certain to be small, mainly because, since we had no major agricultural exports, we should enjoy no major export restitutions."

The detail of the negotiations for entry is beyond the scope of this book. Suffice it to say that the British delegation foresaw a problem that could become serious once the transition to full financial contributions came to an end in 1979. Its prior resolution would have depended on a shift away from agricultural expenditure in the intervening period. In a concluding chapter of his history ("Did we get a good deal?"), O'Neill, writing in 1972, talked of "a reasonable chance that the Community's expenditure on agriculture . . . will tend to diminish rather than increase as a proportion of the total wealth of the Member States including ourselves".

In the short term, that hope proved unfounded. More significantly, he also referred to the Community's assurance, enshrined in the British government White Paper of July 1971, that "if unacceptable situations should arise [on the budget] the very survival of the Community would demand that the institutions find equitable solutions", as well as to "the rather rash and sweeping predictions made by the Commission that the burden on us of our contribution to the budget would be very much less serious than we had claimed".

In an editor's footnote to O'Neill's account, which was published by the Foreign and Commonwealth Office (FCO) in 2000, Sir David Hannay, who was one of the original negotiating team and later UK Permanent Representative in Brussels, noted that

in the event, this issue did have to be addressed again. The first attempt was in the renegotiation undertaken by the Labour Government which came to power in 1974, when the Corrective Mechanism which subsequently proved to be of no significant use, was agreed; then again in the long series of negotiations which began in 1979 and culminated in the Fontainebleau European Council in 1984 when an abatement mechanism which reduced the United Kingdom's net contribution to the budget by two thirds was agreed.

That paragraph encapsulates the most long drawn out and bitter battle yet fought in the EU. Its repercussions continue to this day. The British government of the day had done a deal on finance as part of our entry negotiations which may have been unavoidable in the negotiating climate of the time but which, as the negotiators themselves had foreseen, would prove inequitable. By the time Margaret Thatcher came to power in 1979, the transitional period for Britain as a new member state was coming to an end. The budgetary inequity was becoming more pronounced. Britain was one of the poorer member states in terms of relative prosperity, but the second largest net contributor to the EC budget after West Germany, by far the Community's richest member. Officials were acutely aware that the problem was an imminent one for Britain and would have to be tackled. Yet, interestingly in the light of subsequent developments, the issue got only a low-key mention in the Conservative manifesto for the 1979 election. "It is wrong to argue, as Labour do, that Europe has failed us," said the manifesto. "What has happened is that under Labour our country has been prevented from taking advantage of the opportunities which membership offers." The manifesto went on to offer policies for the reform of the Common Agricultural Policy (CAP) "which would reduce the burden which the Community budget places upon the British taxpayer" and to propose that "national payments to the budget should be more closely related to ability to pay".

Sir Michael Butler, Britain's Permanent Representative to the European Communities at the time, recalls that at his first briefing meeting with Margaret Thatcher after she had become Prime Minister, the issue of Britain's contribution was not on her agenda; she had to be briefed about it. That soon changed. One month after the British General Election, Margaret Thatcher attended her first European Council, which took place in Strasbourg under French chairmanship. Some who were present recall that President Giscard d'Estaing treated Mrs Thatcher with condescension. At the formal dinner of Heads of Government, he did not put her at his right, though she was the only woman present. She had to press to get Britain's budget contribution given the priority she believed it merited. "It was at Strasbourg", she later recalled in her autobiography, "that I overheard a foreign government official make a stray remark that pleased me as much as any I can remember: 'Britain is back', he said."

Worse was to come. Margaret Thatcher was by now fired up and determined to secure progress. France and Germany were equally determined to resist. There was a stand-off at the Dublin European Council in December 1979. The European Commission put forward proposals designed to help: shifting expenditure away from agriculture and towards structural programmes; more spending in Britain; and a continuing correction mechanism. But these were not enough to prevent Britain remaining almost as significant a net payer into the EC budget as Germany and twice as big a contributor as France, even though the UK's relative prosperity was much lower than either.

At Dublin, Margaret Thatcher said two things of significance. She told her partners that the financial arrangement must last as long as the problem, that a continuing series of ad hoc fixes would not be the answer. And she told the Press: "I am only talking about our money, no one else's." This utterance, which has gone down in history as Margaret Thatcher's "I want my money back" demand, caused what Sir Michael Butler called "some genuine, and much spurious, outrage in other Community capitals". Britain's partners, more than capable of calculating that Britain's gain would be their loss, maintained that the money, being the Community's *own resources*, was not Britain's to argue over. Britain was accused of demanding the so-called *juste retour*: we expected to get back what we had put in. This was an unjust claim as Margaret Thatcher always maintained that she was prepared to see Britain remain a net contributor to the EC budget.

In May 1980, Britain's negotiators, led by Foreign Secretary Lord Carrington and his deputy Ian Gilmour, secured a three-year deal for Britain and the establishment of a mandate for the negotiation of a long-term settlement. "My immediate reaction was far from favourable", Margaret Thatcher noted in her autobiography. That was an understatement. Ian Gilmour's Private Secretary at the time recalls the Prime Minister, on the front step of Number 10, positively fizzing with outrage. I was working as Assistant Private Secretary to Lord Carrington at the time, albeit on other issues. But I remember his mixture of exasperation tinged with reluctant admiration that, after he and Ian Gilmour had negotiated for days and nights, and secured a deal which gave Britain a refund of some two-thirds of her net contribution, Margaret Thatcher should treat them as if they were schoolboys who had failed to produce their homework to the standard required. For the deal that Carrington and Gilmour had brought home was, in reality, a good one The payment of lump sums to Britain for the EC budgets of 1980–1 that they had secured meant that Britain ended up paying almost no net contribution at all for those years. Even in 1982–3, when the repayments to Britain were much smaller, Britain made a net contribution of about a third of what we should normally have paid. One reason for Britain's success was that she had held up agreement to the annual round in which agricultural prices were set in the EC. In other words, the CAP was held to ransom for the sake of the British refunds. Two years later, we tried the same trick, with much less happy consequences.

Money was not the only troublesome issue facing the British government in its relationship with the rest of the EC. On 29 January 1982, Hans-Dietrich Genscher, the German Foreign Minister, travelled to the Economic Forum at Davos to set out his views on Europe. "Economic constraints are not a uniting force", he said. "Rather, they are pulling us apart into the dead end of a short sighted national egotism. And, in its never-ending debate on agricultural prices and surpluses, or national balances...the EC is running the risk of forfeiting the support of its citizens." New life must, he warned, be breathed into the European idea. Hence, the plan conceived by Genscher and his Italian opposite number, Emilio Colombo, for a European Act "intended to integrate what has been achieved so far in every sphere of the European unification process in a high level political document". That document would encompass what Genscher called the "great goal of political unification: the European Union".

The plan had first emerged in November the previous year. Peter Carrington, the Foreign Secretary, explained to the Prime Minister in a memo what he thought British tactics should be:

As regards its substance, the draft is long-winded and Germanic. But the proposals include nothing strikingly new...Our overriding aim in Europe at the moment is a satisfactory outcome on the Community budget question. For this we need German cooperation. We shall also find it easier to persuade our partners to make the substantial moves we need from them if we can provide them with evidence of simultaneous progress on the wider, vaguer and more theological issues addressed in the German proposals.

Margaret Thatcher was not persuaded. She was prepared to welcome the initiative. She was not prepared to welcome the proposals themselves. She feared that the reaction among the government's supporters would be very negative, and indeed that there would be a risk of another split. She thought that the House of Commons would react negatively to the emphasis on the European Parliament (EP) and that those views could not simply be ignored. As a result when, in January 1982, the Genscher–Colombo proposals were first discussed by officials in Brussels, the Foreign Office brief set as the "fundamental UK position" that Britain would accept no proposal which would require treaty amendment of parliamentary ratification. That was to remain a constant preoccupation and requirement.

Genscher in the meantime was encouraging members of the EP of his own party to produce a draft constitution for Europe, as the focal point of the 1984 European elections. Faced with this initiative, the Foreign Office instructed its European embassies to point out to their interlocutors that Britain preferred to make progress pragmatically. Britain doubted whether the Community needed a written constitution. The UK had, after all, "always managed without one".

British tactics were to stay constructively engaged and even to keep consideration of the Genscher–Colombo proposals alive until the outcome of the negotiations on the British budget contribution was clear, particularly since the UK would need the support of Genscher and Colombo for that issue to be settled. Lord Carrington wrote again to the Prime Minister on 25 February: "The proposals amount to very little in substance and in many cases simply reaffirm existing arrangements and commitments...I think it important that we should continue to appear willing to examine the proposals constructively while naturally resisting any detailed suggestions which we do not like." Carrington was supported by Henry Plumb, Leader of the British Conservatives in the EP, who warned the Prime Minister that there was a new and pervasive sense that the EC was in crisis: the negotiations on the restructuring of the budget were widely seen as putting the basic principles of the CAP and the Community's financing at risk; the Iberian enlargement was approaching; recession was promoting economic nationalism; and the post-war consensus on European security seemed to be deteriorating.

The Prime Minister agreed with Carrington's approach, though her earlier fears of adverse reaction in the House of Commons were reflected in a letter from Douglas Hurd (Minister of State at the Foreign Office) to the Leader of the House of Commons, Francis Pym, warning that the Labour Opposition were likely to maintain that the proposals amounted to a major step in the direction of federalism, involving erosion of national sovereignty and the powers of the Westminster Parliament. For its part, the government would need to emphasise that the proposals did not involve treaty amendment or change in the existing powers of the institutions.

None of this was happening in a period of calm. Three issues were to dominate the spring of 1982: the row over the British budget contribution, a crisis over the so-called "veto", and, on 2 April, the Argentine invasion of the Falkland Islands. EC Foreign Ministers had met in January to try to resolve the British budget issue, but, on 25 January, the talks collapsed. Lord Carrington told the Press: "I could not persuade my other nine colleagues of the justice of the case [for a long term solution], although they agreed on the logic ... The ministers of finance in some countries see that there is going to be a bill to be paid if Britain contributes less to the Community."

Carrington also made clear that there was a linkage in the mind of the British government between the issue of the British budget contribution and the forthcoming annual negotiations to fix EC agricultural prices. The agricultural price-fixing package that was on the table in Brussels implied a large increase in Britain's overall net contribution to the EC budget. So Carrington explained that he did not see how anything could be settled on agricultural prices until there was a solution on the budget. The atmosphere was fraught, *The Times* reporting on 29 January that "anti British feeling among other EEC countries is so high at the moment that even the two men chosen as persuaders [Leo Tindemans, the foreign minister of Belgium, which held the EC presidency, and Gaston Thorn, the President of the Commission] are not prepared to make any open effort to solve the basic problems". A month later, Lord Carrington said in a speech in Hamburg that Britain was not asking for a permanent system of compensation, but, in the longer term, for "a better balance of policies ... that reduces and eventually resolves the need for financial adjustments". Nor was Britain seeking the so-called *juste retour* whereby each country got back from the European Community as much as it put in. "We are", Carrington said, "happy to see a transfer of resources from some member states to others; but it would seem more reasonable that these flows should go from richer to poorer member states rather than the other way round."

By the time the EC leaders met in March 1982 to celebrate the 25th anniversary of the Treaty of Rome, the friction between Britain and her partners was becoming ever more scratchy. "Mrs Thatcher all in deepest black would not have looked out of place at a state funeral", said *The Times*. The Commission President, Gaston Thorn, summed up the mood in his speech at the "celebration": "Europe's achievement was under serious threat from nationalist and protectionist tendencies and from the short view taken by member states." "The European idea", said Thorn, "was losing popularity as the feeling grew that Europe served no purpose, that it could do nothing to resolve the economic crisis or to relieve international tension."

Earlier in the month, Margaret Thatcher had told Thorn that Britain wanted an equitable solution to the British European Economic Community (EEC) budget problem, once and for all. In response, Thorn proposed a five-year deal consisting of a lump sum for Britain for the first three years, with a separate negotiation to take place in 1984 on the last two years. At the 25th anniversary summit, Mrs Thatcher said that she would accept a five-year deal provided it was for five years and the last two of the five did not have to be separately negotiated. But French President François Mitterrand said the Thorn formula could not be accepted as it stood. Mrs Thatcher told a press conference at the end of the summit: "I am stubborn and I intend to go on being stubborn. I have much to be stubborn about." Asked whether she would be put off by opposition, she said, "I am not puttable offable."

Reporting to the House of Commons on the summit, Mrs Thatcher stressed that all parts of the negotiation on European financing were linked:

Only last week some £813 million of refunds were returned to this country in respect of last year's budget. More will be coming. That is our money which the previous government would have left us to pay to Europe but for our negotiations. They talked a lot about it but did absolutely nothing...We regard it as urgent to achieve a full and satisfactory solution but it has to be on all three parts of the mandate at the same time.

Mrs Thatcher also told the House: "During our discussions I laid particular stress on the need to complete the common market in the services sector." The attainment of that goal, laid down in the Treaty of Rome, would take another twenty-five years.

The British determination to block the annual agricultural price fixing until a deal was done on the overall issue of Britain's budget contribution was becoming increasingly public. On 19 March, Margaret Thatcher had invited German Chancellor Helmut Schmidt for talks at Chequers, telling a Press Conference afterwards that Britain would block that year's EEC farm price review until a satisfactory solution was found to the budget dispute. Schmidt responded that there were greater issues at stake, such as the continuing world recession.

The Lord Privy Seal (who was Carrington's deputy and the Foreign Office's spokesman in the House of Commons) had told the House on 24 March that the negotiations between Britain and her partners covered three issues: the development of Community policies outside agriculture [so as to increase the likely British receipts from the budget], the reform of the Common Agricultural Policy (CAP) and the budget itself. He claimed that it had been accepted all along by all the EC governments that the three chapters should be carried forward in parallel. His stance was commended by one of the leaders of the Social Democratic Party (SDP), David Owen: "We appreciate the government's determination to secure a fair deal for Britain and their determination to link the budget contribution to reform of the CAP."

While the British government was convinced that it could veto the CAP deal, others were signalling the exact opposite. The French agriculture minister, Edith Cresson, said on 17 March that France would try to force a majority vote on agriculture prices if Britain were isolated in the negotiations. President Mitterrand was reported in *The Times* to the same effect: France could not allow one government to obstruct the implementation of the fundamental Community rules.

In threatening to "veto" the agricultural price settlement, the British government was relying on the Luxembourg Compromise. In the 1975 referendum on British membership of the EC, the Luxembourg Compromise had been presented as being a "veto" and it is probable that many who took part in the campaign had convinced themselves that it was indeed just that. But the compromise was in fact a political understanding reached in January 1966. It followed a year in which the French government had boycotted meetings of the Council. France's empty chair policy was based on her discontent at the imminent move to majority voting, especially in the field of external trade, presaged by the end of the first phase of the transitional process laid down in the Treaty of Rome and by European Commission proposals to give budgetary powers to the EP. The compromise said that "where, in the case of decisions which may be taken by majority vote on a proposal of the Commission, very important interests of one or more partners are at stake, the Members of the Council will endeavour, within a reasonable time, to reach solutions which can be adopted by all members of the Council". So much—or so little—was agreed between the Six. It is for that reason that the compromise was always described by British officials as "an agreement to disagree". The French government added its own understanding that "where very important interests are at stake the discussions must be continued until unanimous agreement is reached". It was this French view, shared by Britain, that led British officials and ministers to believe that if they invoked the Luxembourg Compromise no vote on the agricultural price-fixing package would be taken.

The "veto" was an issue not only on the table in the Agriculture Council but also in the negotiations on the draft declaration on European union. One idea being canvassed was to require countries that invoked the Luxembourg Compromise to state their reasons for doing so in writing. The Foreign Office was prepared to countenance the idea. In similar vein, the European Secretariat of the Cabinet Office produced a note in April 1982 which argued that a national veto was likely to be regarded by ministers, pressure groups, and public opinion in the UK as an essential safeguard of British interests in the Community for the foreseeable future. That national veto was, said Cabinet Office officials, protected by the Treaty of Rome, which laid down substantial areas of Community business on which decisions had to be taken by unanimity. Over equally wide areas where the treaty prescribed majority voting, the national veto was in practice safeguarded by the consensus approach, bolstered by the Luxembourg Compromise.

The issue came to a head in the Agriculture Council in May. Before that, on 2 April, Argentina had invaded and occupied the Falkland Islands. Within a very few days, the Foreign Secretary, Peter Carrington, had resigned and been replaced by Francis Pym. Pym was a hugely experienced politician, but his immediate attention had to be given to the Falklands War and he inevitably knew much less about European business than the Prime Minister who, according to one well-placed observer, did little to ease his passage. On the contrary, she sought to use her greater knowledge to cow him during meetings on EC issues in those early days.

On 11 April, at British request, EEC Foreign Ministers agreed to ban all exports of arms to Argentina and all imports into the EEC from Argentina. "We were extremely pleased with the solidarity the member states have given us", said a British spokesman in Brussels. But the support was fragile. When EEC Foreign Ministers met on 20 April their short statement laid emphasis on the urgency of finding a peaceful solution to the Falklands dispute. Throughout the crisis, Ireland, then a member of the United Nations (UN) Security Council, waved her neutrality like a placard. In early May, foreign ministers were unable to agree to renew sanctions. According to *The Times*, Britain was "put on probation" following the sinking of the Argentine ship *Belgrano*, and the Irish and Italians were ready to renew sanctions on 17 May only on condition that they were allowed to drop out. *The Times* reported that "the long and difficult negotiations [over the British budget contribution] showed that Britain cannot rely on a united Community front". That vexed question was again on the table in a meeting which Commission President Gaston Thorn described as "sombre dimanche". And young farmers demonstrated outside the meeting shouting "8 million European farmers are more important than 1,600 Falkland Islanders...If the English don not like the CAP, they should get out".

The Agriculture Council met on 11 May. The Press reported that Britain had threatened to bring the business of the EEC to a halt if the nine other members persisted in trying to force through a farm price increase against the wishes of the British government. The agriculture minister, Peter Walker, was quoted as saying that there would be "terrifying consequences" if the other nine countries sought to ignore a British veto. There were newspaper reports of a move by some member states, notably Italy and Germany, to persuade others that for Britain to invoke the Luxembourg Compromise on the agricultural price fixing would be unacceptable given that the real target of the British was the budget and their rebate. An unnamed British spokesman was quoted as saying that, were Britain's partners "to ride roughshod over her rights, then there would be very serious consequences indeed". A significant signal, almost certainly picked up by Britain's partners but evidently not given adequate weight by the British themselves, was the vote by Conservatives in the European Parliament, led by Sir Henry Plumb, former president of the National Farmers Union (NFU), to support the principle of majority voting on the price fixing, thus publicly distancing themselves from the policy of their own government.

On 18 May, Peter Walker was advised by British officials that if he were to invoke the Luxembourg Compromise, it would constitute a veto of the agricultural price fixing. They knew that there was a risk that the French would not allow the agricultural package to flounder. The French had, after all, accepted majority voting as the norm for agricultural and budget negotiations. It was possible that they would not stand by their own interpretation of the Luxembourg Compromise. On the morning of the Council, the Belgian Commission member, Stevie Davignon, who was at the heart of the plan to vote Britain down regardless, warned Michael Butler of what was afoot. But Butler and others, understandably given the past history of the Luxembourg Compromise, thought that the French position would turn out to be bluff and that France had too much to lose by calling into question the validity of the compromise by helping to overturn its invocation. So, when the moment came, Peter Walker invoked the Luxembourg Compromise by formally declaring that a very important national interest was at stake for Britain and that discussion should therefore continue until agreement was reached, with no vote being taken. To be strictly accurate, Sir Michael Butler invoked the compromise on Peter Walker's behalf since Walker had left the Council chamber. To the dismay of the British, votes were taken and the UK was outvoted.

In reporting back to Whitehall on this debacle, British officials noted that France and Germany had sided against the UK because they claimed that "our use of the Compromise was not appropriate in our case because our motives were procedural rather than substantive and related to issues in a context other than that in which the Council was reaching decisions. The Benelux and the Commission . . . reaffirmed that they had never accepted the Anglo/French interpretation of the Compromise".

The British reaction was angry. Use of the veto in the agriculture nego-tiations, as a means of getting what Britain wanted on the budget rebate, had long been factored into British negotiating tactics. The UK Permanent Representative to the European Communities, Sir Michael Butler, had written to the Foreign Secretary at the start of the year: "With the leverage given us by the annual price fixing exercise, we shall secure a reasonably satisfactory budget settlement before the end of the Belgian presidency or, if there is a serious shouting match, very soon afterwards." Moreover, the fact that the agricultural price-fixing package would have produced a massive increase in Britain's net contribution to the EC budget meant that there was a very direct British national interest at stake.

Despite the warning noises from France, British officials had believed that the French government attached too much importance to the Luxembourg Compromise to set it aside. But, at a stroke, the French had redefined the compromise and soon set out in writing their view that the compromise could only be invoked in respect of issues to which it was directly related. Ironically, a few years later, the British government was to take to its bosom this flexible interpretation when faced with the prospect of Spanish invocation of the Luxembourg Compromise to prevent EC legislation from applying to Gibraltar. On the advice of officials, ministers decided in the mid-1980s that, were Spain to invoke the compromise so as to exclude Gibraltar from such legislation, Britain would not agree to suspend voting—on the grounds that the compromise could not be used to deny Gibraltar rights that were laid down in the EC treaties.

Calm reflection was not the order of the day in May 1982. *The Times* described the crisis as by far the most serious since Britain had joined the EC. Writing in the paper, Geoffrey Rippon, who had been the Conservative minis-ter in charge of the successful accession negotiations, said that what France and others had done undermined the agreement that Ted Heath had reached with President Pompidou. Heath, said Rippon, had told the House of Commons in May 1971 that he and Pompidou had agreed that the fabric of cooperation in the Community required that decisions should be taken by unanimous agreement when vital national interests of one or more members were at stake. "The Community", Rippon concluded, "will become a fallen oak if it fails to understand that respect for the Luxembourg Compromise is a necessary part of the way in which the Community works and essential to its survival".

The Times saw the whole incident as "a gesture of exasperation at what our partners perceive as impossibly selfish and obstructive behaviour on Britain's part" and wondered whether Britain might respond by withholding her con-tributions from the EC budget. The paper concluded that such a step would be logical but mistaken: Britain should get away from the unduly negative approach to Europe she had adopted in the past. "We are not bad Europeans", the paper concluded, "unless we choose to present ourselves that way."

The Government took what Douglas Hurd called, in reply to a question in the House, "an extremely serious view of the way in which the Luxembourg Compromise was set aside". Francis Pym addressed the House of Commons on the subject of Europe for the first time as Foreign Secretary when he opened a debate, dominated by the issue of the Luxembourg Compromise, on 26 May. Pym said that he had "always been convinced that the decision we took to enter the Community was the right one and in Britain's best interests . . . It is a question of balance, not of absolutes. The balance is one that I calculate to be very much in favour of our playing a full and active part in the Community".

Pym went on to describe the Government's "deep concern and dismay" at the decision to overturn Britain's invocation of the compromise. He set out the history, concluding

The Luxembourg Compromise is thus not a legally binding instrument. But the French view was tacitly accepted and it has been the consistent practice of the Community, without any exception until 18 May that, if a member state makes clear that its important national interests are involved, discussion is continued and no vote is taken . . . The Government's objective now is to ensure that nothing like this happens again.

A Foreign Office draft of a speech prepared for Europe Minister Douglas Hurd, but not used by him in the form drafted, shows the extent of the anger, describing it as extraordinary that the French had not seen fit to inform the British of their intentions, when both the French President and the Prime Minister had visited Britain in the days before the vote, and defending the government for not foreseeing that the French, having argued so strongly at the time of our accession that Britain should accept their interpretation of the Luxembourg Compromise, should now show so little respect for it. In the end, it was left to Roy Jenkins, the SDP leader and former President of the European Commission, to point out that, in invoking the Luxembourg Compromise, the government had been "resting on an untried hinge". And Edward Heath was in no doubt that the compromise had always been a political understanding and that no quasi legal weight could be placed upon it.

The anger and dismay were in proportion to the amount of French egg on British faces. But within a few weeks, officials were taking a more sanguine view, advising ministers that the idea that a member state would henceforth have to state in writing its reasons for invoking the Luxembourg Compromise (one of the innovations being discussed in the negotiations on the Genscher–Colombo plan) should, if anything, now appeal more to Members of Parliament (MPs) because it would show that the Luxembourg Compromise was alive and well. Ministers were not persuaded. Douglas Hurd told the Foreign

Secretary that he thought it more likely that MPs would see the proposal as part of a federalist plot. Pym agreed: "I see nothing but danger and trouble here", he wrote.

The Government continued to take a tough line in the House of Commons. Pym told the House that overturning the Luxembourg Compromise had been a "serious breach" and, at the forthcoming meeting of EC Foreign Ministers, he would fight to restore the right of veto that the compromise represented. The Prime Minister remained especially concerned. Ahead of a Cabinet Committee meeting to discuss the issue, she commented:

As I understand it, a term of our entry to the Community was that voting would have to be unanimous on any issue on which a member state declared that it had a vital national interest at stake. The member state was its own judge of what was a vital interest. What is before us now suggests a considerable erosion of that basic term of entry and therefore a further diminution of the sovereign power of Parliament. Let us be clear what our partners seek. They want to ensure that we cannot get a fair deal on the budget by holding up agreement on CAP prices. They argue, falsely, that how the prices are financed is not a vital interest to the country that is responsible for finding a considerable part of the money. If we agree to "tightening up" the conditions on the Compromise as suggested we shall be changing the terms of entry and weakening our powers. I fear that would raise again the whole European question, which is precisely what the events of 17/18 May have done.

As a result, the Government remained resolute in resisting the idea of a written justification of any invocation of the Luxembourg Compromise. But it was obliged to accept that the French and others, by voting Britain down on 18 May, had de facto changed the rules of the game. The Cabinet Office advised ministers that the British interpretation of the Luxembourg Compromise (set out cogently in the Prime Minister's minute) was sustainable only if endorsed by enough member states to create a blocking minority once a vote was taken against the wishes of the member state concerned. Mr Heath and M. Pompidou had shared a common interpretation, which was that the member state was the sole judge of whether a national interest was at risk or not. The Cabinet Office concluded that that interpretation was now shared only by the UK, Denmark, and Greece. Pym put these points to the Prime Minister. "We are", he wrote, "most unlikely to get a unanimously agreed text. What we need is to get agreement by a sufficient number of member states to constitute a blocking minority so that, acting together, they can prevent decisions being taken by majority voting when one or more member states say that their important national interests are involved." On 17 June, the Overseas and Defence Committee of the Cabinet, chaired by the Prime Minister, endorsed this approach.

This difficult decision may have been eased by the fact that, two days earlier, the Falkland War had ended. On 20 June, with somewhat indecent haste from the British perspective, EC Foreign Ministers voted to lift sanctions against Argentina. On the same day, EC Foreign Ministers reached a low-key conclusion on the Luxembourg Compromise. *The Times* reported that "only the Benelux countries believed a majority vote should always be used if necessary. All the other countries were sure a veto right was sometimes essential".

So, a defeat for Britain which had seemed cataclysmic only a month before was resolved by an agreement to disagree, which is what, in practice, the Luxembourg Compromise had always been. It is in that form that the Compromise survives today. The Germans, who said they did not believe in it, used it regularly in the 1980s to support their position in agricultural price-fixing negotiations and were backed by the French, who refused to vote them down. Other countries have invoked the compromise. But Britain has never again done so. There have been occasions when ministers have made clear that the question under discussion was a "very important national interest" for Britain and, more often than not, our partners have taken the hint and avoided precipitating a vote. But the events of 1982 are so seared on the memory, and ingrained in the folklore, of Whitehall that Britain has never again actually invoked the compromise and formally asked for a vote not to be taken. Any minister who wished to do so would have to get the authority of the Foreign Secretary and it is likely that, in practice, the Prime Minister of the day would have to be consulted as well.

The main short-term effect of the brief drama was to reinforce the determination of British ministers to secure a lasting solution to Britain's underlying budget problem and a growing realisation that reasoned argument would have to be accompanied by bloody-minded resolution. In Geoffrey Howe (Chancellor of the Exchequer in Thatcher's first term and Foreign Secretary in her second) and Margaret Thatcher those two qualities were to be admirably combined. The two of them, in partnership and with the support of some of the ablest officials the Foreign Office has had, embarked on one of the most complex and controversial negotiations in the history of the EU. Long-term attitudes on both sides of the Channel were set by that negotiation. "I want my money back" is a rallying cry remembered with admiration in Britain and dismay in much of the rest of Europe. The conduct of the negotiation said a lot not only about the personalities of those involved but also about the underlying stresses in the relationship between Britain and her partners. The negotiation split the EC as never before, soured Margaret Thatcher's relationship with her fellow Heads of Government, and led some of them to conclude that Britain was a "bad European". This was the drama that was to grip Europe for the next twelve months.

2

The Dynamics of a Deal

Britain passed the ten-year mark of EC membership in January 1983. Margaret Thatcher, contributing a foreword to the programme for a celebratory dinner organised by the Conservative Group for Europe, wrote:

It is a matter of profound regret to me that much political energy in our country is still devoted to the hoary question of whether we should be in or out. That question was settled by Parliament in 1972 and ratified by an overwhelming majority in the 1975 referendum. We Conservatives must not allow ourselves to be deflected into an arid debate about the past and away from our purpose, which is to build a strong and enduring Community and to improve Britain's position within it. The unity of Europe as a force for peace, freedom and democracy is a goal for which I pledge my Government to work.

In reality, the next year and a half were to be the roughest ever in Britain's often tetchy relationship with her partners. One issue dominated the Community's agenda: the British budget rebate. Early in the year, the European Commission, under its President Gaston Thorn, published a Green Paper on EC financing. Thorn, who has largely been airbrushed out of recent EU history, was described by Margaret Thatcher in her autobiography as a man with whom she often saw eye to eye, someone who did not have "the grandiose ambitions and bureaucratic leanings" of his successor, Jacques Delors. Thorn started out being referred to by her as "Dear Little Gaston". When, inevitably, he blotted his copybook, he was downgraded to "Poor Little Gaston". He suffered an irredeemable fall from grace when Peter Carrington, usually genial and always sharp, christened him "Bloody Little Gaston".

The Green Paper was a mixed blessing for Britain. It proposed an increase in the Community's Own Resources to allow for industrial and research policies and regional and social funds. In principle, this should have been attractive to the UK, since it could expect to be a beneficiary of some of those funds by comparison with the predominantly agricultural spending from which Britain drew scant benefit. But any increase in the overall EC budget risked exacerbating Britain's position as the second largest net contributor and there was an instinctive British mistrust of the value for money of any spending at EC level on issues such as research. Indeed, Margaret Thatcher, as an ex-scientist in a private sector company, was opposed to any public spending on research and development on the ground that it was inevitably wasteful. More helpful to Britain was the Green Paper's explicit recognition of the need to correct budgetary imbalances.

Following a meeting with the Prime Minister in February to consider the government's response to the Green Paper, the Chancellor of the Exchequer, Sir Geoffrey Howe, advised her that, despite the risks and dangers for the UK, it was right to participate constructively in discussions. He proposed two possible solutions to the British problem: (i) VAT liabilities of the countries, which contributed more than they received from the EC budget, might be related to the difference between their share of CAP receipts and their contributions to CAP expenditure—the relief being phased out for more prosperous countries or (ii) VAT liabilities of member states, which bore excessive budget burdens, might be reduced so as to place an upper limit on those burdens. What was really needed, Howe noted in a subsequent minute to the Prime Minister, was a permanent safety net arrangement which would limit the net contribution of *any* member state to some percentage of its gross domestic product (GDP) defined in relation to relative prosperity. This would have the advantage of being of general application and not just a scheme devised for the Untied Kingdom. Howe was particularly attracted to this approach, that is, defining any limit on Britain's net liability in relation to GDP and not in relation to her net contributions before refunds because anything which refunded a specified percentage of Britain's contribution would leave us "acutely vulnerable" to increases in our net contribution.

For all of 1983, the British approach was based on what became a safety net scheme in which a member state's maximum net contribution would be expressed as a percentage of GDP linked to relative prosperity. So, a member state whose relative prosperity in a Community of twelve was 85–90% of the average would pay zero in net terms, while net contributions would rise to a maximum of 0.3% of GDP for member states of 140% of average prosperity. The conceptual cleverness of the scheme was that it would only come into play to the extent that the problem of imbalances was not solved by changes on the expenditure side of the EC budget. In other words, the more a country got back by way of expenditure from the EC budget, the less it would need the safety net. The fact that the scheme would return to Britain over 70% of our net contribution was another huge advantage. It was an ingenious scheme, conceptually fair and applicable to any member state, but in practice, in 1983, delivering maximum benefit to Britain.

The extent to which the budget question had risen up the agenda was plain from the Conservative Party manifesto for the General Election which Margaret Thatcher called in the spring of 1983. "Our first priority in 1979 was

to cut our financial contribution to the Community Budget to a fairer level",
said the manifesto. It claimed that the Conservatives had tenaciously sought
a permanent alternative to the annual wrangles about refunds and then gave
a hint of a threat: "Until we secure a lasting solution, we shall make sure of
proper interim safeguards for this country." At one level, that clearly meant
that the government did not absolutely rule out further ad hoc deals on the
way to a lasting settlement. At another level, it was a hint that Britain might
go further to protect her position. The Labour Party were campaigning on a
platform of withdrawal from the EC and the Tory manifesto adopted the policy of "triangulation", which was to become a speciality of New Labour nearly
fifteen years later: Labour wanted to withdraw while the Liberals and SDP
wanted to stay in but "never to upset our partners by speaking up forcefully".
The Conservatives rejected both "extreme views".

Britain's partners soon had to come to terms with a newly re-elected Margaret Thatcher, with a significantly larger majority, combined with the fact
that the EC's finances would run out within months. Deficit financing is ruled
out in the EU and the ceiling on revenue could only be raised by unanimous
agreement of the member states. So, time was on Britain's side. She could, and
would, hold the EC to ransom in order to get her way.

Against this background, the budget negotiations marked time during the
German presidency in the first half of the year. Helmut Kohl had come to
power as the new Chancellor of Germany in October the previous year.
Margaret Thatcher liked and admired Kohl's predecessor, Helmut Schmidt,
though, for Schmidt himself, the rapture was not unalloyed. In mid-1982,
he told the British ambassador to Bonn "his well known story" of how, having grown up wholly anglophile, the history of Britain's membership of the
Community and the various negotiations had driven him into the arms of the
French.

The story of Margaret Thatcher's unhappy relationship with Helmut Kohl
is well documented. They had met when Kohl was in opposition. So, when he
came into office, Francis Pym had been able to write to the Prime Minister:
"You have met Kohl. He is a nice man. He was never impressive in opposition,
but I see no reason why he should not develop into a very good Chancellor of
the Committee Chairman rather than the national leader type. In any case, I
see every reason to build him up rather than write him down." After their first
meeting as leaders of their respective countries, the Foreign Office warned our
ambassador in Bonn that the Prime Minister had been cautious in her reaction
to a suggestion by Kohl that they should meet again soon to discuss the EC in
detail. The Prime Minister was reported as "probably not particularly keen
to be exposed again in the near future to Herr Kohl's somewhat long winded
dissertations". Margaret Thatcher was, in particular, unsympathetic to what
was, for Kohl, the imperative of European union.

An exchange between the two of them in Downing Street in February 1984 is characteristic. Kohl told Mrs Thatcher that he had said to President Mitterrand that it was of the greatest importance that France, Germany, and the UK should stick together. The other members of the Community would have to be handled carefully. He would like to visit Chequers in the autumn and spend a day discussing the question: "where do we go from here?" That for him was the decisive question. German policy, he said, had two bases which were unchangeable: its links with the Alliance and its links with the EC. Germany had special need of both. In no circumstances could it afford to find itself in a no-man's land. Much of the misery of this century had been caused by a lack of clarity in Germany's position. It would be fatal to pose a choice between the United States and Europe. Neutralism was spreading through Europe. Soviet expansionism was increasingly described as harmless. There was confusion in people's minds. What was portrayed as peace was no more than neutralism—and for Germany that meant leaving the Western camp. The EC, Kohl feared, was politically stagnant. The concept of a bridge across the Atlantic was flawed. For a bridge needed a pylon at both ends and the European pylon was not strong enough. The Treaty of Rome was not just about a common market but also about political integration, of which security policy was the most important aspect. Europe should speak with one voice on security. In the United States, an important change had taken place. The centre of intellectual and economic power had moved from the Atlantic to the Pacific. If, by the 1990s, the United States felt secure against missile attacks, there was a danger of the mentality of fortress America regaining ground. So it was vital that America and Europe should be close. All these things, Kohl concluded, were more important to him than the current matters under discussion in the EC. Mitterrand too was beginning to realise that the United States was turning towards the Pacific. Britain, France, and Germany should work together to make progress on the future of the EC.

Mrs Thatcher responded that, in strengthening the European pillar, we must be careful not to undermine the arch over the Atlantic. Because of the trend in the United States to which Kohl had referred, she believed that Europe needed to move closer to the United States and to be seen to do so. She preferred to work through NATO. The best step would be for France to accept full military integration into NATO. Her worry was that in trying to intensify the unity of Europe we might be seen by the United States as attempting to act independently of them. If European countries were now to discuss defence together, we should keep the United States in touch at every stage.

Commenting in her memoirs on her good relationship with Helmut Schmidt, Margaret Thatcher wrote: "I never developed quite the same relationship with Chancellor Kohl, though it was some time before the implications of this became important." In 1983, it was clear to her that Germany was crucial to a settlement of the British budget issue. She was content to accept one further ad hoc payment to relieve Britain's anomalous budgetary position and ready to make a significant statement at the European Council in Stuttgart in June under Kohl's chairmanship on the future of the budget negotiations. The Foreign Office sent the text to all its EC embassies, describing it as "the crucial text" and "Holy Writ". The Prime Minister told her fellow Heads of Government:

These matters must be taken forward together. There is no way in which it would be sensible to prejudge one in advance of the others. In the context of a long term settlement of all these problems, I would be prepared to consider an increase in own resources provided that we reached agreement on an effective control of the rate of increase of agricultural and other expenditure and provided that it is accompanied by an arrangement to ensure a fair sharing of the financial burden so that no country has to pay a share disproportionate to its relative national wealth.

Signalling concessions was not Margaret Thatcher's habit. On this occasion, the text to which she spoke was run up on the spur of the moment in Stuttgart after what one of the participants describes as a pincer movement on her by Howe, Butler, Robert Armstrong (the Cabinet Secretary), and Hannay. It was no doubt in part because of the circumstances of its birth that the Foreign Office promulgated the text so swiftly and widely. The Prime Minister was not above stepping back from positions into which she felt she had been manoeuvred.

In her intervention, the parameters of the end-game negotiation were set: the budget ceiling of the Community could be increased, but only if Britain got her way on the issue of her budget rebate and on control of CAP spending. Foreign ministers were given the task of negotiating the details with a view to agreement at Athens, under the Greek presidency, in December.

Margaret Thatcher made one other concession. She agreed to the Solemn Declaration on European union, the final product of the Genscher–Colombo initiative launched two and a half years earlier. "I took the view", Margaret Thatcher said in her autobiography, "that I could not quarrel with everything, and the document had no legal force. So I went along with it."

At one level, the document was a success for British diplomacy and a disappointment to many of Britain's partners. Britain had successfully resisted anything which would require treaty change or ratification by national parliaments. She had prevented the document from being called an "Act" thereby showing acute sensitivity to the impact of words on British parliamentary and public opinion.

A particular British success was the Declaration's definition of EU as a process rather than a goal. The Declaration said: "European Union is being achieved by deepening and broadening the scope of European activities so that they coherently cover, albeit on a variety of legal bases, a growing proportion of Member States' mutual relations and of their external relations." It was because of this definition of European union as a process that Margaret Thatcher was later prepared to accept references to European union in the Single European Act (SEA).

In other respects, the Solemn Declaration was more significant than it appeared at the time. It is true, as the Foreign Office wrote in a memorandum on European union for the House of Lords in 1985, that the Declaration "consisted for the most part either of statements of current practice or the expressions of hope for the future", but those expressions of hope were not idly chosen and were to provide a checklist of action points for the ensuing years. The Solemn Declaration reaffirmed all the previous undertakings of EC Heads of Government, including the far reaching one to which Edward Heath had agreed in 1972, concerning "the progressive construction of European Union" as well as the will of the EC's governments "to transform the whole complex of relations between their states into a European Union". It confirmed the commitment to progress towards an "ever closer union among the peoples and Member States of the European Union" and the desire of the Heads to "consolidate the progress already made towards European Union in both the economic and political fields". Ever closer union among the peoples of Europe (the language of the original Treaty of Rome) implied a popular process, going only as far as the people of Europe themselves desired. Ever closer union of the Member States implied greater impetus towards Union on the part of EC governments.

The Declaration was significant in institutional terms as well. It affirmed that the European Council could take decisions on matters of EC law, acting as the Council for that purpose. The Heads of Government undertook to report to the EP after each meeting of the European Council and to make an annual report to the Parliament, to be presented by the President of the Council, on progress towards European union. The Presidency country was henceforth obliged to present its work programme to the EP at the beginning and end of each six-month period. The EP was accorded the right to give an opinion on the choice made by EC Heads of the Commission President and to vote on the programme of the new Commission. Its opinion was to be sought on significant international agreements entered into by the EC and on the accession of new states to the EC. All these provisions were to be stepping stones in the subsequent growth in the power of the EP.

The Solemn Declaration contained policy undertakings as well. The document called for Europe to speak with one voice in foreign policy, including political aspects of security. It introduced the notion of solidarity in foreign policy and included an undertaking that each Member State "will take full account of the positions of its partners and give due weight to the adoption and implementation of common European positions when working out national positions and taking national action". It called for the development of a European social policy and agreed to action against unemployment at the Community level as well as at the national level, including through the "improved harmonisation of social security systems". It outlined action to be taken on the road towards EMU. The Community was authorised to complement the efforts of industry and governments in the areas of energy and research. In a precursor of subsequent developments in the field of Justice and Home Affairs, the document commended the introduction of "legal instruments which can strengthen cooperation among the judicial authorities of the Member States". Twenty years later, a German colleague told me that he still bore the bruises of negotiating the document with the British and he remained resentful of the extent to which Britain had watered down the institutional commitments, especially to European union. As with most negotiations in Europe, all member states had both to agree and to come away with something. Britain secured a text that was political, not legal, and which did not commit her to a binding form of European union. Her partners, France, Germany, Italy, and the Benelux in particular, as well as the European Commission, secured a text which gave them a political and policy quarry. There were in the document areas of activity, for example, in the social and employment fields, where Britain was not keen on Community action. But while Britain could argue about the specifics, she could not claim, in the light of the Stuttgart document, that the Community had no *locus* to propose action. Stuttgart was a classic example of the way the EC/Union has evolved over the years, each provision in a European text being not just a statement of desire but a building block of future policy. For British governments, it was usually easier politically to defend the limited nature of the individual parts of any text to which they had just set their name than to acknowledge, even privately to themselves, the longer-term significance of what had been agreed.

Stuttgart was a brief, relatively peaceful, interlude on the way to the last, fraught, stages of the argument over the EC budget and Britain's contribution to it. The various occasions since then, on which the British rebate has come into question, including the one during Britain's presidency of the EU in 2005, give a glimpse of the heat which the subject generates. But that is as nothing to the bad blood on both sides of the Channel in 1983 and 1984. The scene seemed to be set fair in the immediate aftermath of the Stuttgart summit. The conclusions of the European Council established a clear linkage: there would be no increase in the EC's Own Resources without a settlement of the issues of budget imbalances (which meant, in practice, the British budget issue) and overall budget discipline. The EC leaders had agreed that the negotiations leading up to their next summit in Athens in December would cover "the financing of the Community, the development of Community policies, the issues relating to enlargement [i.e. Spain and Portugal], particular problems of certain member states in the budget field [i.e. the United Kingdom] and in other fields and the need for greater budgetary discipline. Decisions will be taken in common on all these issues at the end".

Stuttgart had also agreed to "re launch" the EC and the British government made an early contribution by submitting a paper in September on the Future Development of the Community, focussing on the Single Market. The paper noted that, twenty-five years after the signature of the Treaty of Rome, which set the completion of a Single Market as one of the new Community's priorities, the Community had in fact got little further than the abolition of tariffs. "This", said the paper, "falls well short of our business community's expectations", and it went on to call for liberalisation in transport, a common market in services, more European common standards, and for harmonisation of professional qualifications. Jacques Delors, as President of the Commission from 1985, and Lord (Arthur) Cockfield, as the member of the European Commission responsible for Single Market matters, are rightly credited with the legislative drive to complete the Single Market. But, it became a Community priority only because Margaret Thatcher put it there. However, for the next year, the budget was to dominate.

At twenty years' distance, when the notion of a country's net contribution to or receipts from the EU budget has become common currency, it is hard to remember the furore this notion created at the time. In a minute to the Prime Minister in October 1983, David Williamson, the head of the European Secretariat in the Cabinet Office, noted the "strong objections" from most member states to use of net balances and net contributions on the grounds that it was inconsistent with a system in which the money collected from customs levies and duties on imports into the Community and on the notional 1% of VAT raised from individual member states were considered the Community's "Own Resources".

From this arose the accusation against Mrs Thatcher that she wanted back from the Community budget exactly what she had put in (the so-called "juste retour") and that she was undermining the principle of solidarity. It was an argument that suited almost all member states except Germany since the overwhelming majority of them, including at that time France and Italy, were net beneficiaries from the budget. Any improvement in Britain's budget position would spell a deterioration in their own. As the argument raged, those of us dealing with these issues (I had become the Assistant Head of the

EC Department in September 1983) were receiving regular reports from our embassies in EC capitals from which it was clear that member states who were vocal in their denunciation of the whole notion of net balances were busy calculating what their net balances would look like if a concession was made to Britain. This hypocrisy was one of the aspects of the Community which was increasingly to alienate Margaret Thatcher.

In all this, Britain was paying the price for her late entry into the Community and, in particular, for having no say in the initial shape of the Community's principal common policy: the CAP which, in the 1980s, accounted for two-thirds of Community spending. Helmut Schmidt had told Mrs Thatcher in 1982 that the British could not carry the day by saying that the burden represented by the CAP was ridiculous and should be got rid of: the CAP was the price that had to be paid, however monstrous it was, in order to obtain the adherence of some of the Community's members. The French and Italians, for example, would always say that they had joined the Community knowing that the CAP was there to help them. Mrs Thatcher acknowledged that, given that the structure of the budget of the CAP had been wrong from the start, it would now be very difficult to make fundamental changes.

Despite the pressures, the Prime Minister was determined not to agree to a solution which did not correspond to the proper measurement of the budget inequity. She did not rule out contributing a small part of our net contribution above what she saw as the fair limit even though it would increase pressure on us to increase the contribution still further. She was clear that our reaction must depend on the figures that would result. For her, it was a condition of even considering an increase in the Community's Own Resources, that we should achieve the correction of our budget inequity as well as effective control of the rate of increase in agricultural and other spending. We had, she told a meeting attended by Foreign Secretary Geoffrey Howe and Chancellor Nigel Lawson, to be satisfied on both parts. She also wanted clarity on what Britain's response would be if the negotiations broke down at the Athens summit.

In the aftermath of the failed invocation of the Luxembourg Compromise in 1982, the Labour Opposition had called on the government to withhold its contributions to the EC budget, contributions which were paid automatically from the Treasury each month, as required by UK domestic and by EC law.

The pros and cons of withholding began to be debated within government from early in 1983. Within the Foreign Office there were serious fears on the part of officials about the political impact of such a course. It would, it was feared, cause revulsion and anger in the Community—and a great determination that a tactic which would be seen as destructive for the future of Europe should be seen not to succeed. Officials feared that, not only would withholding cause a serious rift, but also it would probably turn out less well than anticipated. Ministers were advised that other member states might, initially at least, refuse to negotiate under duress. Nor could the possibility be ruled out that some would suggest that the UK should leave the Community.

These arguments held sway with Sir Geoffrey Howe and he advised the Prime Minister to avoid using the term openly. She and other members of the government agreed and decided that the UK should make clear its resolve to fight for British interests but should not make an explicit threat to withhold at that stage.

The government was also advised that, to withhold our budget contribution would be subject to challenge in the British courts as well as in the European Court of Justice. The conundrum for the government was that it would have to take an action (withholding) that was illegal and then legislate to regularise actions that were known to be illegal at the time they were taken. This would have been unprecedented.

The Prime Minister was advised that the government would have to withhold from January 1984 if it was to protect itself from the effects of having to pay in 1984 a net contribution to the budget of some 2,000 million European currency units (ECUs). Faced with the actual prospect of a decision, the Prime Minister reacted with the circumspection which the officials had undoubtedly sought to provoke, commenting that any such decision would require the agreement of Cabinet. The issue was to come to a head at the end of 1983.

"The Greek Presidency, throughout the second half of 1983, was a period of immensely unrewarding work on the crucial Community agenda to which the Stuttgart meeting had committed us." That was Geoffrey Howe's conclusion in his autobiography, *Conflict of Loyalty*. Sir Michael Butler, the UK Permanent Representative to the EC at the time, gives the Greek presidency a bit more credit. Margaret Thatcher has described the Greek Prime Minister, Mr Papandreou, as "remarkably effective" in gaining Community subsidies for Greece but less skilful in his role as President of the European Council.

Papandreou faced the same problem that was to haunt Italian Prime Minister Silvio Berlusconi twenty years later. In December 2003, President Chirac and Chancellor Schroeder were simply not prepared to allow Berlusconi, whom they loathed, to have the satisfaction of doing a deal on the European Constitution. Papandreou was, in the words of American journalist John Newhouse, "methodical and businesslike". But, apart from the number of issues to be settled, Papandreou carried baggage. Newhouse was one of the most informed and astute observers of European politics. He was the author of the seminal book *De Gaulle and the Anglo-Saxons* and someone European officials would talk to privately in confidence. Writing in the *New Yorker* in October 1984, Newhouse commented that, over most of Papandreou's six-month term Greece's partners got "about what they expected—shrill critiques of Western policies". Newhouse quoted a British diplomat as saying that Papandreou had had to be "bludgeoned" into deploring the shooting down of a Korean passenger airliner by the Soviet Union. So, unsurprisingly, he was not the man who could readily generate that mixture of crisis and compromise which is essential to settling fraught European negotiations—negotiations which required the French, in particular, to make concessions on both the budget and agriculture.

The Greek Presidency can have been in no doubt about the strength of British feeling. In a speech at Chatham House in early November, the Foreign Secretary Geoffrey Howe said:

The European Community is a natural scapegoat for national failures and for the impact of world recession. These are perceptions which can be changed over time. The Government has a duty to provide information and explanation. We work at it. But there are deeper, and genuine, concerns. The Community often seems imprisoned in an elaborate and inflexible structure of national trade offs. The result can resemble apathy; not the radicalism of the founders but resistance to necessary change. There is a real danger that people are coming to see the Community as at best irrelevant and at worst obstructive to Europe's fundamental challenge to halt decline in its international competitiveness, to restore sustainable growth and to generate new employment.

Later in the month, Sir Michael Butler had breakfast with "the unfortunate Mr Varfis", the Greek deputy minister charged with trying to make progress in the negotiations. Butler reported back to London that he had advised Varfis to tell his Prime Minister that Margaret Thatcher would not accept anything but a very good solution to the budget:

We had suffered a very great deal from the budget inequity and the unwillingness of other member states over the last four years to agree to a reasonable long term solution. Nevertheless the PM had secured very substantial refunds without having any strong negotiating levers. She now did have a strong lever [the need for unanimous agreement if the EC budget ceiling was to be raised] and she was not going to settle for anything but a genuinely equitable and completely safe long term agreement.

This was classic Butler, "lean and cerebral" as Nigel Lawson called him, a man "whose understanding of the nuts and bolts of Community law and practice was as impressive as his unflagging zeal".

On this occasion, understanding and unflagging zeal were not enough. Commission President Gaston Thorn visited London shortly before the summit and Sir Michael Butler warned that Thorn feared that the summit "will either produce a bad agreement which does not tackle the real issues or break up in disorder, making inevitable a major financial crisis".

Thorn was prescient. In her opening statement at the European Council, Margaret Thatcher said:

When we in the United Kingdom look at the problem, we ask ourselves what would be a fair net contribution for a country in the position of the UK, still below average in relative prosperity now and only just above it in a Community of twelve. I have the impression that many of your governments are briefing you to look at it in terms of what it will allegedly cost you to reduce the burden on us; that is to say, in seven cases, how much your net benefits will fall. Since we are trying to devise a fair system for the longer term, we have to look at the likely outcome for all member states, ensuring that the least prosperous receive appropriate benefits and that those who will bear the burden of net contributions do so in relation to their ability to pay...I made it clear at Stuttgart that I could only concede an increase in the Community's own resources if arrangements were agreed for a fair sharing of the budgetary burden and for effective control of agricultural and other expenditure.

This rather conciliatory introduction was not matched by the rest of the debate. In particular, it was clear that Mitterrand was not prepared to settle in Athens. As Michael Butler put it in *Europe—More than a Continent*, "The French took a line which went back on the progress already made. Most observers thought that they wished to make sure that the post Stuttgart negotiation ended, not in Athens, but at one of the European Councils in the French Presidency which was about to begin."

The UK Permanent Representation (UKRep, as it is known in Whitehall) in Brussels reported after Athens that the European Council had failed to agree on any issue in the post-Stuttgart negotiation—or indeed anything else. Agriculture had taken one and a half sessions with no disposition to face up to the need to stem the production of surpluses. There had been a relatively positive discussion of budgetary discipline. However, the chances of real overall progress, already receding, were sharply set back when Mitterrand proposed that the UK should receive compensation on a year-to-year basis on the lines of the arrangements granted to the UK in 1982. According to the UKRep report, no one rose to the suggestion by the Prime Minister that the UK and France should have broadly similar net contributions, a suggestion that was to be repeated by Tony Blair nearly twenty years later. And then Mitterrand "changed the whole tone of the discussion with a long diatribe", which finished with the statement that he could accept none of the ideas on the table. The EC, Mitterrand said, had come together by virtue of a contract signed by six countries in Rome. Others had joined the same contract with transitional measures. That could not be ignored. Otherwise it would be necessary to produce a new treaty. The Treaty of Rome excluded the *juste retour*. But that was at the heart of the UK position. Adding his own comment to the UKRep report, Michael Butler concluded that there was never a moment when the outline of an acceptable compromise on the CAP, budgetary discipline and imbalances, seemed likely to emerge. Papandreou tried to pin the blame for the breakdown on the Prime Minister. Kohl, Lubbers, and Thorn resisted this unfair attribution of blame.

At her post-summit press conference, the Prime Minister could afford to be relatively sanguine about the breakdown. "The long term solution", she said, "is often much more difficult than the short term expedient. Next March, we shall be that much nearer to the money running out. That means that things cannot go on as they are. Once they cannot go on as they are you are more in a psychological mood to consider the fundamental change." This sense that time was on her side is reflected in Margaret Thatcher's autobiography despite the fact that the Athens summit was, as she put it, "widely and accurately described as a fiasco". Her own relationship with Mitterrand did not suffer, partly because, when they met for breakfast at the summit, Mitterrand seemed unaware that, in opposing a long-term deal for the British, he was going against the proposals which his own finance minister, Jacques Delors, had been advancing; partly because, not for the last time, he and Mrs Thatcher saw eye to eye on the dangers of German neutralism; and partly because it crossed the Prime Minister's mind that Mitterrand wanted to delay a settlement in order to take credit for a success in his own forthcoming presidency.

Media reactions were not so philosophical. "Mitterrand–Thatcher: Iron Lady vs. Man of Marble" was the *Le Monde* headline. Mitterrand's *éminence grise*, Jacques Attali, was quoted as saying: "Britain twists the Treaties and gets round them: she has one foot outside the Community but will not put both feet out, alas." The Dutch paper *NRC Handelsblad* said that the malaise in the EC had set in "with the pitiless immorality with which Mrs Thatcher reduces Europe to a union of money lenders who begrudge each other every last penny". But support from the Prime Minister came from an unlikely source. When she reported to the House of Commons, Roy Jenkins, former President of the European Commission, told the House that: "there was nothing on which she should have settled at Athens. There was no serious resolve to get hold of agricultural expenditure and she was right in the circumstances to play for time."

The climate was not, however, helped by the decision of the EP to take the ad hoc refund that had been agreed at Stuttgart for payment to Britain in 1983 "off the line". This meant that instead of being paid automatically under the approved EC budget for 1983, the money would have to be specifically approved by the EP. In other words, the EP was securing its own leverage. This in turn immediately raised again the whole issue of withholding. Geoffrey Howe was briefed by the FCO to tell Cabinet at the end of 1983 that the bulk of the refund should be paid by the end of March 1984 and that refusal to make that refund would oblige the government then to decide what action would best safeguard the British position.

In setting out a March deadline, Geoffrey Howe was agreeing with advice from the Europe Minister, Malcolm Rifkind, that we must give the negotiations a chance to succeed at the March European Council. Howe himself feared that the Prime Minister had already gone a long way towards making withholding at the end of March inevitable, almost whatever happened at the March summit, and was worried that no attempt had been made by others in Cabinet restrain her, especially given the risk of damaging retaliation by other member states if Britain did withhold.

In December 1983, Mitterrand appointed his old friend Roland Dumas as Minister for European affairs in the French government. This was to turn out to be a key, helpful move in the search for a solution. Dumas is a man with a chequered and colourful history. But he was a real negotiator. I saw him at fairly close quarters after he had become Foreign Minister in the late 1980s and was negotiating in the four-power group (Britain, France, Germany, and the United States) on the arrangements associated with the reunification of Germany. The four foreign ministers (James Baker, Roland Dumas, Hans Dietrich Genscher, and Douglas Hurd) met, I recall, on the day, or very close to it, that unification became an accomplished fact. Genscher was, unsurprisingly, in buoyant mood. He and Kohl had pulled off a historic achievement peacefully and remarkably smoothly. "This is a great day" said Genscher, or words to that effect. "Yes it is", said Dumas, "and one that for many of us gives rise to profound feelings." His own father had been shot by the Germans in World War II.

It was Dumas and Geoffrey Howe and their officials (David Hannay and later Robin Renwick from London) and Guy Legras (later Director General for Agriculture in the Commission) who, over a series of private meetings, gradually worked their way towards a solution. It was not clear whether, politically, Mitterrand could afford to clinch an agreement as early as March, given that Jacques Chirac and other opposition leaders would latch onto any concession to the British and anything which weakened the position of French farmers. But it looked as if he would go for the deal if he could get it on sellable terms.

There was something of a breakthrough at a meeting between Howe and Dumas in February 1984. Howe spelled out that Britain must have a solution to her budget problem which lasted for as long as the problem which it was designed to correct. Dumas went so far as to say that France could accept the principle of a systematic approach (one of the things Mitterrand had rejected at Athens). He did, however, express particular concern that the British proposal for a so-called "safety net" mechanism took no account of the costs of enlargement, all of which would fall on member states other than Britain.

As the two sides circled each other (and this was largely a private fight; other member states were not invited to join in), it gradually came to be accepted by the British that the measurement of the gap between what Britain contributed to the Community budget and what she got back in receipts from that budget would need to be expressed in a different way. Most other member states would not accept that the money which we collected on behalf of the Community in the form of levies and duties on imports from third countries was revenue forgone by the British Exchequer. So it was necessary to find a different formula. It was Michael Butler who privately, and at some risk to his own career, sold to the Germans the idea of using the VAT share/expenditure share gap as the measure. The Germans bought the idea and put it forward as their own. From the British perspective, it moved the goal posts, but not in a way that changed the parameters within which a deal would need to be struck. From the point of view of the Germans, it was a help because it did understate the level of the British net contribution by a relatively small amount, which meant that the Germans would have to contribute less to solving the British problem.

By the March summit, the shape of a deal was clear, with only the crucial question of the amounts to be filled in. But the dynamics of a European Council are hard to predict. Margaret Thatcher used to say that it was harder to reach agreement in Brussels than in other Community capitals because the Charlemagne building, which was then the venue, was so grim. Heads of Government arrive in varying states of preparedness, political well being, and temper. For most, arriving in Brussels in March 1984, the notion of the VAT share/expenditure share gap was not one they personally had had to wrap their minds round. More than twenty years later, as I write about these issues, I am reminded of how difficult I had found them when I returned from the embassy in Washington in the autumn of 1983 and had to immerse myself in the minutiae for the first time.

So, while British and French officials edged towards an agreement in the backrooms, Heads of Government had a set-to over the dinner table at Val Duchesse just outside Brussels. Margaret Thatcher was prepared to make a concession over the budget gap that was to be measured in determining the solution for Britain. But she was not prepared to concede the principle that levies and duties were not a proper measure of the extent of the British burden. So the dinner ended in confusion and bad blood. According to John Newhouse's subsequent account in the *New Yorker*, Mrs Thatcher was "domineering and finger-pointing". Lord Hannay recalls her, when the dinner was over, sweeping down the hall towards Michael Butler and himself crying out, "They say it's their money and I say it's mine."

When the Council met the next morning, the Irish Prime Minister, Garret Fitzgerald, invoked the Luxembourg Compromise (incorrectly and needlessly because the European Council was not about to take a vote on the issue) and walked out in protest. But, even at this stage, British and French officials were working behind the scenes, and thought that a deal could yet be done. But Helmut Kohl, who was not privy to these discussions, proposed another series of flat rate refunds of 1,000 million ECUs and others, including the French Presidency, rallied to the German proposal. The British government had set their face against another series of ad hoc refunds and, in any case, the sum proposed represented only about 50% of the gap for which the British were seeking redress. So the meeting broke up in disagreement.

Given the progress already made, the path to the next summit in June 1984 should have been reasonably smooth. But in the tetchy aftermath the foreign ministers of France and Italy, at a meeting of the General Affairs Council, refused to approve the rebate for Britain for 1983 that had been agreed at Stuttgart nine months earlier.

It was at this point that Britain came closer to withholding than at any other time. Geoffrey Howe made a formal statement in the General Affairs Council in which he said: "the action by the Council . . . constitutes a serious step. I shall want to consult my colleagues in the British government about the steps now open to the United Kingdom in order to safeguard its position."

In her autobiography, Margaret Thatcher acknowledges that the government "had always been advised that if we withheld contributions we would almost certainly lose any subsequent case before the European Court", but she argued that the failure of our partners to make payments to which we were entitled put us on stronger legal ground. She blames the lack of "united backing" of Conservative backbenchers for the inability to go ahead: "Unfortunately, there was a hard core of Euro-enthusiasts on the Tory back-benches who instinctively supported the Community in any dispute with Britain. Though a clear minority, they robbed us of the advantages of unity."

It was not quite as simple as that. Members of Parliament knew that withholding would be illegal in UK law. The government could well have had on its hands a much wider crisis of support because, to cover itself, it would have had to attempt to legislate to render legal actions which were known at the time they were taken to be illegal. This would have been unprecedented and of huge constitutional significance. It was that, as much as the particular European sentiment, that led the Whips to advise the Prime Minister that she could not count on having a majority in the House of Commons for the action she had in mind. So Britain drew back from the brink. So did her partners. The refund was released. Foreign ministers drew stumps on any attempt to split the difference between the 1,000 million ECUs they were prepared to offer and the larger sum demanded by Britain. Pressure for a settlement during the French presidency came from the fact that it represented the last opportunity to settle the issue before the EC's money ran out and because no one thought that the issue could be settled under the Irish presidency. This was a time when Anglo-Irish relations were still governed by suspicion and even occasional hostility. Margaret Thatcher and the Irish Prime Minister, Garret Fitzgerald, would never be soul mates. One of the measures of the improvement in Anglo-Irish relations, for which John Major and Tony Blair and their Irish colleagues are owed much credit, was the fact that, by the time (more than ten years later) preparations were under way for the Amsterdam Treaty, it was the Irish presidency, who led the discussions in the initial phase, in whom the British had the greatest confidence. The same was true in the final phases of the negotiation on the Constitutional Treaty in 2004, where the excellent relationship between Tony Blair and Bertie Ahern, and between officials on both sides, played a large part in achieving agreement. But that was not how things looked in 1984 and larger member states then, even more than now, were (quite wrongly) convinced that smaller member states were not up to managing complex negotiations such as that on the budget.

Through April and May 1984, the French presidency went in for very little public diplomacy, partly because, in the run up to the mid-June elections to the EP, Mitterrand did not want to be seen to be making concessions to the British. But there were productive meetings between Dumas and Howe, Renwick, and Legras. When the two men met on 4 May, Dumas told Howe that he had had a conversation with the Prime Minister in which Mrs Thatcher had told him that she had been surprised to hear that people were saying that she did not want to settle the dispute over budget imbalances as soon as possible. This, she said, was quite wrong. Despite that assurance, it was still not clear which way things would go. A week later, the Foreign Office gave its EC embassies an account of meetings the Prime Minister had had with Kohl and Mitterrand and of those that the Foreign Secretary had held with Genscher and Dumas. "The French", the Foreign Office reported, "appear to hope for agreement at Fontainebleau and recognise that work will now be needed behind the scenes to get it." But the Foreign Office added a caution: "They [the French] continue to refer to Kohl's proposal for five more ad hoc years and to delaying the implementation of the system until the costs of enlargement have become clearer."

Following Mrs Thatcher's clear indication to Dumas that she was in the market for a settlement, the Foreign Office sought clearance from Number 10 for Britain's ambassador in Bonn to pass a message to Chancellor Kohl, but not to Genscher who was thought to be too close to the French. The message said that the British government would be prepared to make a final move in order to clinch an agreement on budget imbalances and, therefore, to open the way for new own resources, but only in order to clinch an agreement. This would require movement from all the other member states if agreement was to be achieved. Britain, said the message, had the impression that the French presidency did not wish to bring matters to a conclusion before Fontainebleau and that was all right. But it was very important to reach agreement no later than Fontainebleau if the EC was not to be left in disarray.

One significant change was happening in British, or at least Foreign Office, thinking. The Prime Minister was already perceived to have given some ground in accepting that the measurement of the British budget burden should be based on the VAT share/expenditure share gap, though this was more presentation than substance. Inside the Foreign Office and the UK Representation in Brussels, it was realised that the eventual negotiation would be about what proportion of the gap would be compensated. It was Robin Renwick, the Foreign Office Under Secretary, who had recently taken over from David Hannay, who did most of the negotiating with the French at official level in the latter stages. Renwick was one of the most brilliant officials of his generation. He was the last man to sell Britain short. But he also had a rigorously accurate view of the realities of the negotiation. Among Britain's partners, even to talk in terms of "net contributions" was heresy, which was one reason why the Treasury's clever scheme had made no progress. Coming fresh to the negotiations, Renwick quickly saw that the British scheme was so fiendishly complicated that no more than a handful of people in the whole of Europe understood it, and most of those were British. Meanwhile, in the Council of Ministers and the Committee of EU Permanent Representatives in Brussels (COREPER), Britain was taking the fight to partners who did not want to engage on our terms.

The Treasury, in particular, remained very attached to the integrity of the system they had devised, not least because of its clever linkage between net contributions and relative prosperity. They were reluctant to accept that the negotiation would focus on percentages and were insistent on a percentage that compensated Britain for at least two-thirds of what they saw as the "real" gap, that is, the net contribution on which their own calculations had been based. Accordingly, the Foreign Office warned Geoffrey Howe early in June that if Dumas mentioned two-thirds of the VAT share/expenditure share gap as the compromise figure, then Howe would need to point out that that would be two-thirds of the wrong gap, and that a 75% return on the VAT share/expenditure share gap would be required to produce a two-thirds return on the whole gap.

Robin Renwick also worked with Geoffrey Howe to introduce a decisive change in the British negotiating stance. The relationship with the French had always been very adversarial, not least in Brussels. From the moment when de Gaulle first vetoed the British application for EC membership in 1963, the British response had been to try to enlist the support of the other member states against the France. That tactic had not worked for Harold Wilson. Ted Heath had realised that the French were indeed the key to our success or failure and that we could achieve success only by working with them to gain entry to the EEC. Renwick, who was married to a French woman and had served in the British Embassy in Paris, saw things in similar terms. He and David Williamson spent hours working with their French counterparts in search of a solution.

It was the French Foreign Minister, Claude Cheysson, who had told the BBC in 1982 that a permanent budget mechanism for Britain would be a "complete deviation of the Community" and had gone on, in so many words, to invite the British to like it, lump it, or leave. So, it is perhaps not surprising, when the European Council convened in Fontainebleau on 25 June 1984, that Cheysson led one last-minute, and potentially derailing, attempt not only to persuade Britain to accept a system involving a simple percentage rebate, but also to set the percentage somewhere between 50% and 60%. Margaret Thatcher argued for 70%. Mitterrand offered her 65%. She held out for, and secured, two-thirds: 66%, the figure that has held good ever since.

In her autobiography, Margaret Thatcher refers to the criticism she faced in the House of Commons for not getting more for the UK: "In every negotiation there comes the best possible time to settle: this was it." Her Treasury advisers did not want her to settle. In the end, in Fontainebleau, she took herself off with Geoffrey Howe, Michael Butler, and Robin Renwick to reflect on the stage the negotiations had reached. She decided, without any prompting from Howe or the officials, that the moment had come to do a deal. The Treasury subsequently blamed the Foreign Office and insisted that the negotiations that had been set in train at Fontainebleau on a system to control the growth of agricultural spending (the so-called agricultural guideline) should be handled by them rather than the FCO. That the Treasury went on to secure a modestly successful outcome, rather than a triumph, was a salutary lesson, which all British government departments have had to learn over the years, that the business of negotiation (as opposed to shouting the odds from the touchline) requires not only the toughness that British negotiators have in large measure, but also fast footwork, alliances, and judicious compromise.

The outcome of the negotiation was a success for Britain. The arrangement would last as long as the new ceiling on the Community's Own Resources lasted and could only be changed by unanimity. Because of that, the rebate has proved very robust ever since. John Major was able to preserve it intact. Tony Blair did make a concession in 2005 to exclude from the calculation of the rebate the EU's expenditure in the new accession states. But not to have done so would have done more than preserve the rebate intact; it would have generated an increase in the return to the UK, which would have been disproportionate and politically untenable.

Margaret Thatcher wanted to get the argument behind her so that the EC could "now press ahead both with the enlargement [to include Spain and Portugal] and with the Single Market measures which I wanted to see". She had said as much in her foreword to the Conservative Party's manifesto for the mid-June elections to the EP:

Britain joined the European Community with a vision. We saw opportunities for trade and greater prosperity. But we also saw in the Community the promise of peace and security, an alliance in which endeavour, enterprise and invention could flourish ... We have been right to fight for improvements in the CAP and for a fairer system of finance. We want these things so that we can put behind us the endless haggling over money and begin to develop the full potential of the Community.

But how far had the atmosphere been irretrievably soured by the length, and acrimony, of the dispute over Britain's budget contribution?

The British were pleased with the outcome. Sir Michael Butler, one of its principal authors and negotiators, concluded:

We conceded enough—in March the VAT share/expenditure share gap, and in June the basis of the threshold at 66%, rather than 70% or a bit more. The long argument, beginning with the Heath/Pompidou discussions of 1971 and the "unacceptable situation" declaration, continuing in the so-called renegotiation of 1974/75, beginning in earnest with the return of the present government in 1978 which led to the 30 May agreement ... was a major victory for the UK. In February 1980, when we tabled a proposal for a percentage of our net contribution, the French led the way in declaring that it was absolutely out of the question.

There was some recognition of this at the time. *Le Quotidien de Paris* noted that: "Mrs Thatcher, by her obstinacy, has obliged her EEC partners, and foremost among them France, to recognise the aberrant working of the Community ... Britain wants no more of the Europe which spends 75% of its budget in support of agricultural production." *Liberation* commented: "Mrs Thatcher was right [and] obliged her EC partners, not least France, to realise just how appallingly badly the Community works." On the other side of the coin, the British embassy in Bonn advised London that Britain's image in Germany was better as a result of Mrs Thatcher's strong leadership but had also suffered because we were perceived to have been too strident over the rebate. As a result, Mitterrand had gained ground with Kohl at Britain's expense, not least by responding to Kohl's views on a federal Europe.

As a backroom boy in the negotiations, I felt at the time, and still do, that without obstinacy, Mrs Thatcher would not have secured an outcome. Sometimes in the EU, the "Community" interest is, in reality, the sum total of national interests where these happen to coincide. That was so in this case. As *The Times* had put it in an editorial: "Britain's strongest argument is that every step we take to meet the other nine has to be paid for exclusively by Britain, whereas every step the others take to meet us is shared between nine." That shared pain was nonetheless real pain in terms of income foregone by all those other member states that would have to contribute financially to Britain's rebate. So, it is perhaps not surprising that they resisted for as long as they did. That this national self-interest was often wrapped in a flag of European idealism was a negotiating tactic but it was also hypocritical.

I think that Margaret Thatcher drew from it the lesson that, on the whole, our partners were not people to be trusted. That was anyway the direction in which her instincts took her. She was not someone for whom the sharing of sovereignty in an organisation with supranational characteristics was politically compelling. She was, above all, a believer in the nation state. She judged by the here-and-now of practical politics. Concepts such as European union were alien to her not only because they threatened her view of the primacy of the nation state, but also because they struck her as self-indulgently impractical. She did not see the political importance these ideas had for others or, if she did, she was not prepared to make much accommodation towards them, real or rhetorical.

There is no doubt that Margaret Thatcher's negotiating style grated. Not only was she tough, she was seen to be tough. She was almost certainly the only Head of Government of the time to have opened the pages of the Treaty of Rome, and she took with relish to waving it at her colleagues and to reading from it at meetings of the European Council. She would have attributed their less than enthusiastic response to self-interest and to the cliquey masculinity of the European Council, and correctly so. But she could, had it been in her, have wooed as well as won. On the whole, that was not her way. I recall going to a meeting of Commonwealth Heads of Government with John Major in the year after he had took over from Margaret Thatcher. The relief was palpable. It was not just that Britain's policy on South Africa had changed, or that, in a laddish way, the Heads could talk about, and even play, cricket. There was no longer the sense, when the British Prime Minister walked into the room, of a measurable rise in the tension and the temperature.

Robin Renwick, who worked closely with Mrs Thatcher to achieve the Fontainebleau deal, was standing with her one day at a window at Chequers, the Prime Minister's official country residence. She was gazing at a landscape of yellow oil-seed rape, planted with subsidies from the European

Commission. "This used", she hissed, "to be a green and pleasant land." Michael Butler had a similar experience, sitting with her in the British Embassy residence in Rome where, fuelled by ambassadorial whisky, she let rip about the iniquities of Europe.

Robin Renwick's conclusion from the Fontainebleau negotiation was that the successful outcome could never have been achieved without the ferocious energy and intransigence with which Margaret Thatcher had pursued her goal. But the success for British diplomacy had been achieved at a heavy cost, especially in terms of Mrs Thatcher's personal relations with the other European leaders. There was plenty of grudging admiration, but she did not have a single friend among them.

Renwick also believed that, apart from her style, the other leaders felt that, almost wilfully, she did not understand what the EC meant to them. Their countries had been occupied and/or devastated by war. The horrors of the CAP were as nothing to them compared with the horrors Europe had inflicted upon itself before the Community was invented. The French and Danes apart, the others all positively favoured a further pooling of sovereignty. The European Commission and others knew that they simply could not proceed without France and Germany. Without them "Europe" did not exist. But we had ourselves shown that it could exist, and develop, without us.

I am not sure that Margaret Thatcher simply calculated that the EC was unreasonable enough in its behaviour *to* us to justify just as unreasonable behaviour *by* us in return. Or whether she did in fact calculate all that was at risk. There is certainly no evidence that she ever thought of the EC as a relatively fragile creation that could be irrevocably damaged. That fear of irrevocable damage was undoubtedly part of the case made against Britain by her partners, though they undermined it by a huge dose of complete self-interest, that is, preserving the budget gains which they made at Britain's expense.

Sir Michael Butler, Britain's Permanent Representative in Brussels and one of the main authors of Mrs Thatcher's eventual success in the negotiations, saw the risks clearly. He had written in his Annual Review for 1983 (a report sent by all the Foreign Office's overseas posts summarising the achievements and failures of the past year and drawing lessons for the next):

There will be even more difficult times in 1984. It now seems to me that there is a risk...that a sufficient number of other Member Governments will simply not be up to taking the decisions required to make agreement possible. If this were to happen, the money would run out sooner, the farmers would riot and block intra Community trade and other urgent decisions would fail to get taken. The Community would simply start to rot away and there would be a grave danger that, in consequence, the trade barriers would begin to go up again and the quarrels become far deeper. The crisis could become unmanageable and damaging to our broad political and security objectives at a time when East–West and other tensions make a solid base of Western European unity essential. On balance, I still believe it is probable that when the other governments get close to this abyss ... they will scurry back to the relative security of the Community negotiating table and make a settlement.

This was quite a stark warning that the cost of brinkmanship could be very high. We do not know what attention Margaret Thatcher paid to those words. When at Fontainebleau, she decided that the moment had come to settle; did she take that decision simply because she calculated that she would get a worse deal six months later or did she reflect that there were bigger issues at stake as well? If she did, she was unlikely to have admitted it then and has certainly not done so since.

In 1984, the stakes were high, the battle bloody, and the wounds raw. Yet, we were still a long way from the hostility to the EC, which, for most Continental commentators, was embodied in Margaret Thatcher's Bruges speech of 1988. The tension in the relationship was still constructive. Britain, and Margaret Thatcher in particular, felt they had a lot to contribute. And so it was to prove.

3

European Union or European Unity? The Campaign for the Single Market

Among my papers, and I found a copy too on the Foreign Office files, is a small pamphlet. It is called *Europe—the Future*, and on its blue cover is written: "The attached paper was given to European Community Heads of Government by the Prime Minister as a contribution to discussion by the European Council held at Fontainebleau on 25/26 June 1984."

At the time, the document was given no publicity. A copy would have been placed in the libraries of both Houses of Parliament. I recall no Press interest in it. Yet, it is probably the most complete and coherent statement of European policy made by any British government. For anyone brought up on the perception of Margaret Thatcher's view of Europe that became commonplace after the 1988 Bruges speech, it will also make surprising reading. The same is true for anyone looking for significant differences of policy between then and now: they will have to look quite hard.

Europe—the Future was not written by Margaret Thatcher. Its principal author was Robin Renwick, and there would have been considerable input from Michael Butler in Brussels and David Williamson in the Cabinet Office. The editor of the pamphlet was Julian Bullard, then the Political Director in the Foreign Office and later Britain's ambassador in Bonn. But Margaret Thatcher read it and approved it, and it was not her habit to skim. If she agreed *to* it that means she agreed *with* it.

The main purpose of the pamphlet was to show that Britain was not just in the EC for what she could get, but that she had a real vision for the future, especially about the Single Market, one of the primary, and then unfulfilled, objectives of the original Treaty of Rome. The paper said:

We must create the genuine common market in goods and services which is envisaged in the Treaty of Rome and will be crucial to our ability to meet the US and Japanese technological challenge. Only by a sustained effort to remove remaining obstacles to intra-Community trade can we enable the citizens of Europe to benefit from the dynamic effects of a fully integrated common market with immense purchasing power. The success of the United States in job creation shows what can be achieved when internal barriers to business and trade come down. We must create the conditions in which European businessmen too can build on their strengths and create prosperity and jobs. This means action to harmonise standards and prevent their deliberate use as barriers to intra-Community trade; more rapid and better coordinated customs procedures; a major effort to improve mutual recognition of professional qualifications; and liberalising trade in services, including banking, insurance and transportation of goods and people.

The pamphlet was more than a rallying call for the Single Market. It called for

- Actions to make the Community relevant to the lives of its people
- Preservation of the best aspects of the CAP, combined with correction of the policy's distortions including a sustained effort to achieve a better balance between production and demand
- Better cooperation in research and development, including cooperation in telecommunications and technology
- Environmental responsibility alongside the quest for economic growth
- A flexible Europe in which some would go ahead faster than others but where "it should be open to others to join in as and when they are able to do so"
- The progressive achievement of a common external policy
- Improved European defence cooperation with Europe taking on "a larger share of the responsibility for our defence"
- Reform of some of Europe's institutions

The one area where the document, not surprisingly, now looks dated is in its failure to foresee the demise of the Soviet Union and the emancipation of the countries of Eastern and Central Europe. But its conclusion is interesting in the light of subsequent developments and perceptions of British policy:

We cannot rest on the achievements of the post-war generation. Over the next decade Europe will face new economic and social challenges, and a continuing threat to her security. Periodic expressions of pessimism about the future of the Community have never turned out to be justified. Europe needs to advance its internal development. The progress that has been made towards "an ever closer union of the peoples of Europe" of which the Treaty of Rome speaks in its first paragraph is unlikely to be reversed.

It is paradoxical that, twenty years later, Valéry Giscard d'Estaing, presiding over the Convention that drafted the Constitutional Treaty, felt it necessary to delete that definition of EU as a sop to the British government, and that no one in the British government seemed to think it a bad idea.

While in many ways *Europe—the Future* was prescient and radical, it was light on the issue that always was difficult for British governments: institutional change. The issue had not, however, gone away. Disappointed by the lack of ambition which it detected in the Stuttgart Declaration, the EP adopted its own proposed draft treaty on European union in February 1984. Often referred as the Spinelli Treaty, after the Italian Member of the EP (MEP) who was its principal inspiration and author, it was a truly radical document. The British government, in the words of a Foreign Office memorandum submitted to the House of Lords, approved "of some aspects of the Draft Treaty" but had "made clear their major objections" as well. As this description implies, the Foreign Office thoroughly disliked the document, felt, like Punch's proverbial curate, that while it was rotten through and through, it was politic to describe it as not bad in parts and, in the last analysis, did not take its prospects too seriously.

Spinelli's draft would have given to both the Council of Ministers and the EP the right to propose draft laws, removing from the Commission their sole right of initiative. The Parliament would have voted first on any draft legislation and the Council of Ministers would have been obliged to vote unanimously against a draft to kill it. The Luxembourg Compromise would have been phased out over ten years. Full monetary union would be achieved over time with participation obligatory for all member states. Political cooperation (POCO), the embryonic formation of a common foreign policy approach, would have been absorbed into the union. The union would have distinct legal personality, would enter into force with less than the unanimous ratification of the member states, and would be superimposed on the existing treaties. As the Foreign Office pointed out, this last provision would have caused huge legal confusion.

In a paper on the Spinelli Treaty in October 1984, the Edinburgh-based Centre of European Governmental Studies—whose members included Professor David Edward, later an influential member of the European Court of Justice (ECJ)—gave a perceptive analysis of the British approach to EC institutional development. Their analysis drew attention to the government's own hostility to the Spinelli Treaty, spelled out by the Europe Minister, Malcolm Rifkind, in the House of Commons; to the fact that the Labour Manifesto for the 1984 European elections had kept open the option of leaving the Community; and to the fact that the new leader of the SDP, Dr David Owen, was less enthusiastic about the draft treaty than either the Liberal Party or his own predecessor as leader, Roy Jenkins.

The Centre pointed out that membership of the EC had been sold to the British public as an economic benefit and the political aspects had been underplayed. British accession had been followed by severe economic depression.

The problems of adapting to a completely new type of political and judicial system were acute. Moreover, greater political integration was not seen in Britain as the natural development of the existing EC to which Britain had signed up. The paper saw the fact that Britain did not have a written constitution as indicative of an important feature of the British temperament and outlook. There was in Britain little awareness of the State and an innate preference for allowing institutions to develop "as the failure of all attempts radically to reform the House of Lords shows". Finally, the paper noted that the British approach to legislation involved looking carefully at the small print and leaving as little to chance as possible. In many respects, said the paper, the most significant step towards integration in the United States was neither the Declaration of Independence nor the framing of the Constitution, but the decision in the Steamship Monopoly Case when the Supreme Court first applied the Commerce Clause. In the Community, we had, as it were, started with the Commerce clause. Perhaps the time had come to embark on drafting the constitution.

If the substance of the Spinelli Treaty was controversial for a number of member states, its underlying tactics were clever. It created political pressure, which, in turn, led the EC Heads of Government, at Fontainebleau, to set up a special committee, chaired by Senator Dooge of Ireland, to study the Community's future development, including institutional development. The members of the committee were the personal representatives of the Heads of Government and all but the British appointed people who were not members of their governments. Whereas Britain's partners were content to let a thousand flowers bloom in the committee, confident that their Heads of Government would not be too dismayed by the outcome or would be perfectly happy to distance themselves from it if they were, in Britain we would take no such chance. In the British case, Margaret Thatcher's representative was the Europe Minister at the Foreign Office, Malcolm Rifkind.

After the first three meetings of the Dooge Committee, it was clear to the Foreign Office that there was a division between those (Germany and France included) who envisaged the committee recommending that an intergovernmental conference (IGC) be called to negotiate a Treaty on European union and the minority, like Britain, who believed that the way forward was to build on the potential of the existing treaties and to make the existing institutions work better. There was plenty of evidence, the Foreign Office noted, that, in the event of a disappointing outcome in the Dooge Committee, the Germans were ready to consider striking out with like-minded states towards a Treaty on European union to be superimposed on the existing treaty. The Foreign Office wrote to warn the Prime Minister that Helmut Kohl was hankering after a new treaty, possibly consisting of an umbrella treaty covering the existing treaties and POCO, and stating that the goal of European union had in some way been attained. This rather Mikado-like position, in which saying a thing was done was as good as it being done, was to manifest itself even more bizarrely in 1985.

Officials were preoccupied about how to manage the Franco-German drive towards something called Union which Britain would find unpalatable. The Cabinet Office advised Mrs Thatcher that we would have to package our ideas cleverly to avoid being left behind and the Foreign Office speculated about whether it might be in Britain's interest to see more use of qualified majority voting (QMV) in order to prevent filibusters by the smaller member states. (It is striking that we never seemed to think that large member states might filibuster as well.) The Foreign Office argued that, provided there was no interference with the Luxembourg Compromise, we would have nothing to lose by agreeing to look practically on a case-by-case basis at where majority voting, subject to unanimity on any vital issue, might best help us to achieve our objectives on the internal argument.

The Germans were seen as the main drivers towards European union, the Cabinet Office telling the Prime Minister that, while Kohl's policy towards Eastern Europe was forced to mark time, he clearly felt himself impelled to look for actions which would publicly link the Federal Republic more closely to Western Europe. This approach coincided with a widespread feeling in Western Europe that the Community had become bogged down in internal difficulties and was not pulling its full weight, which in turn explained the interest in other member states in moves towards EU. Nor were the Germans to be outflanked. Julian Bullard, by then Britain's ambassador in Bonn, asked Kohl's closest adviser, Horst Teltschik, whether there was anything in the British approach which the Germans found unacceptable or inadequate. After all, through *Europe—the Future* and Malcolm Rifkind's role in the work of the Dooge Committee, no other member state had made a better contribution to the European debate. Teltschik agreed that our paper had been "a very good starting point". Germany agreed on the need to fulfil the existing treaty and complete the Single Market. But the German government also believed that the time had come for a qualitative step forward in political union.

The French government, judging by the advice from the British Embassy in Paris, had a more cynical approach. France, they advised,

stands by the Pompidou 1972 definition as adopted by Heads of Government in October ("the major objective of transforming the whole complex of the relations of the Member States into a European Union"). What then is involved for the French in creating European Union? The delight for them is that one does not really have to know or say. There are several advantages they can see in a large bag of wind, labelled European Union: leadership. If more has to be done to anchor the Federal Republic [of Germany] into Europe (and French anxieties about drifts in German opinion are real and deeply felt) this is the most painless way of doing it.

British views were neither idealistic nor cynical but characteristically focused on practical cooperation, not institutional change. In October 1984, Geoffrey Howe, in a speech in Bonn, declared Britain's commitment to Europe to be "profound and irreversible", but, for him, the urgent task was to tackle trade, freedom of movement, environmental pollution, and closer cooperation in foreign policy. "The way forward does not lie", he said, "across a paper desert of institutional schemes. It is rather through the resourceful use of existing institutions, through pragmatic, flexible, political cooperation that we shall go forward together."

Margaret Thatcher was a deal more blunt in an interview, in the same month, with the *Sunday Express*. She said:

They all talk about political union and people like me say "well now, what do you mean by political union?" That's as far as we get. I believe in a Europe of separate countries, each with their distinctive character and identity, cooperating together in a common market. We haven't yet got a common market...and we're a very long way from it. I do not believe in what I would call a united states of Europe [the very objective Chancellor Kohl had called for publicly earlier in the year]. I do not believe in a federal Europe and I think to compare it to the United States is absolutely ridiculous. They talk about things like a two-speed Europe and people like me say: all right; if you mean a two speed Europe, let me tell you what I mean: those who pay more are in the top group and those who pay less are not. It is absolutely ridiculous to expect a change in the treaty...You might get one or two amendments for which there is a need. Just to sit down to create a new treaty is ridiculous.

Ridiculous or not, that is what the Dooge Committee was focusing on. There was much gamesmanship to try to ensure that Malcolm Rifkind did not have to enter more reservations on the report than other participants. Malcolm Rifkind did enter reservations on the greater use of majority voting, the powers of the EP, and selection of members of the Commission by its President designate. But Britain's main reservation was on the report's principal recommendation: that an IGC should be called to negotiate a draft treaty of EU.

Margaret Thatcher herself set out her views in a more systematic way in November 1984 in a speech at Angers at the annual meeting of the Franco-British Council. The Council had been set up during the Queen's state visit to France in 1972 to foster discussion and understanding between the two countries. The Prime Minister's speech was a classic exposition of the views of the British government, indeed of all British governments before and since:

Our cultures and national traditions both spring from Europe...The Community's founding fathers would be horrified at the labyrinth of its bureaucratic regulations which entwine us like Gulliver pinned down by the little men of Lilliput. Horrified, because the Treaty of Rome embodies the economic structure of a free society...The very first page speaks of "an internal market characterised by the abolition, as between Member States, of obstacles to the free movement of goods, persons, services and capital". The Community was formed to expand trade, not to protect home markets. It was conceived as an outward looking body, not one obsessed with the minutiae of internal procedures...Why cannot we make it as cheap for our citizens to travel by air within their own continent as they can to other continents?...Europe will only be strong and able to play its rightful part in the world when it attains the economic freedom which was the vision of the authors of the Treaty of Rome...Several distinguished Europeans suggested European Union...Those who addressed the subject did not cast much light on its meaning. I rather shocked them by replying that I would need to know what is meant by it before I could tell whether I was for or against it. I do not believe we shall ever have a United States of Europe in the same way that there is a USA. The whole history of Europe is different. I do believe that for nations of the EC freely to work together and to strengthen their cooperation is just as worthy a purpose. It is on the basis of working towards common goals, of using our strength and influence together that you will find Britain a strong advocate for a more united Europe. We want to see greater unity of Community action in world affairs, greater unity of purpose and action in tackling unemployment and the other problems of our time, and greater unity in the development and application of new technology. That is what I understand by a united Europe.

At the turn of the year, when the European Council met in Dublin, the British believed there was still everything to argue for and that it was possible to have the drive for completion of the Single Market, of which we were the prime movers and campaigners, without the new treaty dedicated to European union to which a majority of Britain's partners were turning. Just before Christmas, Margaret Thatcher wrote to Pierre Pflimlin, the (French) President of the EP:

This was a productive European Council. The good atmosphere demonstrated how important it was that the Community was able at Fontainebleau to put behind it the long dispute over the budget which had prevented proper attention being paid to the vital questions of the future of the Community...The [Dooge] committee endorsed our views on the need for completion of the internal market for goods and services, and on changes to give a more strategic role to the European Council. During the next stage, we want to see realistic proposals put forward on the future development of political cooperation, the implementation of the treaty powers in relation to the common market and the improvement of decision-making procedures.

In the early 1950s, my late father-in-law, Norman Reddaway, was a young First Secretary in the British Embassy in Rome when the Coal and Steel Community was first proposed. His ambassador received instructions from the Foreign Office to lobby the Italian Foreign Minister, Count Sforza, and to explain all the practical pitfalls of such a scheme. My father-in-law accompanied his ambassador on this mission as note taker. The ambassador set out the British government's view with the persuasive rigour on which all Britain's envoys pride themselves. When he had finished, Count Sforza smiled and said: "My dear ambassador, there are times at the opera when you should enjoy the music and not worry about the words." With their presidency starting in January 1985, the Italians were about to give us a lesson in grand opera.

Margaret Thatcher can lay a better claim than any other EC Head of Government to be the author of the Single Market project that culminated in the Single European Act (SEA). Without her pressure, the measures necessary to turn the promise of a Single Market on page one of the Treaty of Rome into hard policy might well have continued to lie dormant, as they had for the first thirty years of the Community's existence. But it was easier for Britain to will the policy ends than to articulate the institutional means, and the new President of the European Commission, Jacques Delors, was quick to see that the Single Market project was not only desirable in itself, but also a vehicle for the kind of treaty change that would be necessary to achieve the union that Germany and France wanted. He could also see that the Single Market could be made to encompass a social dimension and that the scope for increased Community competence and, therefore, for more power for the Commission, was considerable.

The British Government had been happy to agree to Delors's appointment as the new President of the Commission, though the route by which the decision had been taken left a sour taste in British mouths. The Foreign Office set out what had happened in a letter to the British embassy in Bonn in August 1984:

The Germans' behaviour over the Presidency of the Commission was certainly curious: the PM told Kohl in November 1983 that we would be ready to support a strong German candidate...At no point did the Germans give us any detailed indication of their thinking...We have naturally been concerned at the way the German government behaved over this issue i.e. not giving any information about their thinking and letting us know only in response to our repeated enquiries that they would, after all, have no candidate to offer...They were clearly in close contact with the French government and Chancellor Kohl's wish to please President Mitterrand must also have been a factor. That in itself is a pointer for us for the future.

The French President first proposed his Foreign Minister, Claude Cheysson, to be the next Commission President, no doubt because he wanted to move him on to allow his friend Roland Dumas to take over at the Quai d'Orsay. But, in Geoffrey Howe's words: "Cheysson ... did not appeal to Kohl any more than he did to us." Margaret Thatcher herself favoured Stevie Davignon, the Belgian member of the Commission responsible for Industry, and was dismayed that her colleagues among the Heads of Government were prepared to overlook what she saw as his outstanding ability. It was, she told Garret Fitzgerald (who had the job as EC President of brokering a deal), "a slap in the face for Belgium, a country which has contributed mightily to the Community". She told Fitzgerald that she thought highly of M. Delors (whose name was by now emerging at the head of the field), but objected to the way the matter was being rushed through. In the end, she and Geoffrey Howe won a significant concession in return for their agreement to Delors's appointment. The Secretary General of the Commission (its most senior and important official) had been a Frenchman since the very beginning in 1957. Emile Noel was due to retire and the Prime Minister and Foreign Secretary secured a commitment from Mitterrand and Dumas that when this happened, the President would be "personally committed" to supporting a British candidate to succeed him. David Williamson (now Lord Williamson) became Secretary General of the Commission in 1987 and served ten years in the job with a characteristic mixture of charm, decency, efficiency, skill, and ingenuity. As Margaret Thatcher's closest European adviser, he had never misled her but had often led her to solutions that her instincts might have rejected. He was often the oil on the troubled waters of Britain's relations with her partners. While Delors became President of the Commission, Cheysson was appointed the second French Commissioner, in which capacity he assiduously sustained his relationship of mutual dislike with the British.

Following Delors's appointment, the British government wasted no time in pressing for action. Howe told Delors in January 1985 that we were very frustrated by the lack of progress on the internal market. We wanted improved decision-making but saw it happening by making better use of the existing rules (which already made provision for member states to abstain on issues requiring unanimity). There were some areas of the treaty (and Howe singled out tax as the main one) where unanimity would remain essential.

At the Dublin European Council in December 1984, Margaret Thatcher had, on Foreign Office advice, proposed that member states agree to a self-denying ordinance. In other words, in order to secure rapid agreements on EC-wide standards, they would not use the unanimity requirement to block decisions. This would have required no formal change in the existing Treaties but would have involved a change of practice. But when the Foreign Office reverted to the issue in January 1985, the Prime Minister was not so keen. The Foreign Office had three ideas in mind: identifying areas where unanimity should be retained in the Treaties but not insisted on in practice; maintaining the Luxembourg Compromise but requiring greater formality in its invocation and justification; and an annual policy statement from the European Council. This would be akin, as Geoffrey Howe saw it, to the Queen's speech. At the same time, the Commission should be encouraged to weed out hopelessly blocked pieces of draft legislation. The Foreign Office advised against conceding joint decision-making between the Council of Ministers and the EP.

In response, the Prime Minister thought that the idea of an annual statement of priorities would be meaningless; the self-denying ordinance she had proposed at Dublin would mean going beyond the present treaty. Her proposal at Dublin had been a mistake, not to be repeated. If anything, she wanted to strengthen resistance to any increase in the role of what she called the European Assembly.

The Foreign Office returned to the charge. The proposal for a self-denying ordinance had gone down well with other member states. As to the idea of an annual statement of priorities that was, the FCO pointed out, one of the ideas put forward in *Europe—the Future.* The Prime Minister accepted the advice second time around, but the exchange is illustrative both of her instinctive attitude and of the relationship between Number 10 and the Foreign Office.

In Brussels, in the Dooge Committee, the argument was slipping away from Britain. The majority view (opposed only by Britain, Denmark, and Greece) was that more use should be made of majority voting. Most of Whitehall was vehemently opposed. From their point of view, the protection of unanimity was more important than the prospect of speedier decision-taking under majority voting. The argument was that it would be difficult to explain to Parliament why we were prepared to discuss amendments to the treaty when key articles on the internal market had never been implemented and without insisting on changes in the articles dealing with the CAP. The first argument overlooked the fact that one reason why the Single Market articles had not been implemented was because the unanimity requirement made it impossible to secure agreement in the Council. For this reason, the Foreign Office still hoped that it might be possible to formalise the Luxembourg Compromise, even in a judicially useable form, and then to justify treaty amendments as the only way to achieve the genuine common market.

In the run-up to the March 1985 European Council, there was a prevailing gloom. In a preface to its final report, the Dooge Committee noted that, while the original foundation of the Community had "answered the complex and deeply felt needs of all our citizens", the Community had failed to do what it had promised in 1972. The member states had got caught up in differences which had obscured the economic and financial advantages which would be obtained from the realisation of the Common Market and from EMU. After ten years of crisis, Europe, unlike the United States and Japan, had not achieved a growth rate sufficient to reduce the disturbing figure of almost fourteen million unemployed. *The Times* commented that "just about everyone" in the Community resented having agreed to give Britain a £600 million budget concession and that Britain was seen as an unconvinced European. But the difficulty in branding Britain in advance as the spoilsport was, *The Times* argued, that her reputation for being un-European was not entirely borne out by the facts. There was no more staunch supporter of the principle of opening up the internal market, of allowing free movement of insurance policies and cheap air tickets, and of harmonising new technology standards. The trouble was that Britain alone was properly geared up to profit from such moves, so that the other member states would not easily agree to them. It would be wrong, *The Times* concluded, to present Britain as a paragon of EEC virtue (despite the fact that, according to a Commission report, it was easily the most law abiding of the four large member states): "The trouble is that it has so far failed to learn the fine EEC art of persuading others it is fighting for Europe, when all it is really doing is defending its own corner."

The European Council in March 1985 approved the terms of Spanish and Portuguese membership, the price for which was a hefty subvention to the Mediterranean member states, Greece in particular, in the form of what were called Integrated Mediterranean Programmes, which in turn led Greece to lift her block on the enlargement going ahead. Margaret Thatcher pressed the case for the Single Market employing "a little ridicule to make my point about the way in which directives spewed forth from Brussels". She told the Press afterwards:

Now, needless to say, we in the UK are enthusiasts for the completion of the common market and will be working very hard for that ... We are not interested in changing the Treaty as far as majority voting is concerned and, obviously, the unanimity rule will have to remain for major things ... But there are quite a number of things that can be done with the present treaty. Europe is not a Community designed to manufacture more and more regulations, but a Community to free up markets and not, in fact, to put increasing shackles upon them.

"I made absolutely clear", she subsequently told Parliament, "that the completion of the single market does not imply tax harmonisation."

In the meantime, the debate between Whitehall departments about the case for more majority voting to complete the Single Market continued. The Foreign Office was trying to open up the argument. But the debate within Whitehall was less about whether to change the Treaties to allow majority voting where unanimity still applied than about whether to make use of the majority voting provisions that already existed, rather than insist on consensus as mostly happened in practice. In a characteristically forensic way, Malcolm Rifkind, the Minister of State for Europe in the Foreign Office, unpacked the arguments that we, as officials, were putting to ministers. Rifkind wrote in a minute on 8 March:

The crux of the Department's argument is ... that, since in a significant minority of cases a vote could be against our interests, it makes sense for the UK to argue for more use to be made of majority voting but ... to discourage the wholesale application of the majority voting provisions of the Treaties. But if we are to be able to pick and choose, blocking proposals which we do not like by means of institutional mechanisms short of formal invocation of the veto, then others will have the same ability. [The Department's] conclusion might be reversed: full application of the majority provisions of the Treaties would result in votes against our interests in a significant minority of cases but (with the ultimate safeguard of the Luxembourg Compromise) that is a price worth paying for the equally significant number of cases in which decisions would be taken which suit our interests and which would not otherwise have been achieved.

Malcolm Rifkind went on to outline a dilemma for Britain: it was possible that some votes, which might be against our interests in the short term could, in the longer term, help achieve the Single Market which we so wanted. The fundamental question we had to face was whether we wanted improved decision-taking or not. If the answer to that question was "no" then, as with Britain's position on the powers of the EP, what we would be doing was seeking "the positive presentation of a determination not to budge on the real questions at issue". Rifkind concluded that on the question of decision-taking we did want change. Without it, and especially after enlargement, decisions in the EC were going to become harder and harder to take at all.

Three European issues were preoccupying the government: what stance to take on the pressure from others to call an IGC to negotiate treaty change (and how to secure our Single Market objectives without more majority voting being introduced into the treaties); how to tackle the pressures for moves towards something called EU; and the implications of the forthcoming enlargement to include Spain and Portugal.

On the first issue, Malcolm Rifkind was clear that substance was more important than form. In other words, while we should try to avoid an IGC, in the last analysis, we should not let ourselves be isolated on the issue. Geoffrey Howe was more circumspect. He agreed that it would be tactically unwise to exclude a conference on principle but thought that, if there were a serious proposal for one at the Milan European Council in June, the Prime Minister could counter by recording her view that any changes would have to include a formalisation of the Luxembourg Compromise, that is, there would be a price to be paid by those countries that wanted a conference. In due course, Howe thought, Britain would have to go further than her existing position which was that, where the treaty made provision for majority voting, more use should be made of voting, as opposed to consensus, than was now the case. We should continue to argue that treaty amendment was not a practical proposition, given the need for ratification in all member states, but be ready to contemplate a change of procedure whereby the European Council would decide on the need to achieve a specific result by a specific date, together with an undertaking by the member states not to invoke the unanimity rule to prevent it.

On political union, the British ambassador in Bonn, Julian Bullard, advised the government that there was an opportunity for Britain to "leap in before France and Germany do". The driving force behind Kohl's policy had been a determination to strengthen trans-Atlantic and West European solidarity. His commitment to the progressive integration of the Federal Republic in the West was without reserve. Therein lay the full significance of Kohl's identification with the European ideal. He saw the EC as an oasis of freedom, peace, and democratic values in a world where those achievements could not be taken for granted. It followed that those who professed the same beliefs must stand together. For that reason, the Germans had consistently favoured the enlargement of the Community even at the expense of weakening the primacy of the original Six founder members within it. While Kohl himself liked the idea of a United States of Europe, he accepted that it was an unrealistic ambition. But he was convinced—and his friendship with Mitterrand had encouraged him in that belief—that the time was ripe for strengthening Western Europe as a political entity. Hence his interest in some kind of Treaty on European union. Hence the desirability of Britain putting her ideas in first.

Howe agreed with this approach and sought, and secured, Margaret Thatcher's support for it, arguing that no one was now seriously suggesting that a federalist structure was appropriate for a Community of Twelve. But we should, Howe argued, respond to the importance Kohl attached to formalising POCO (political cooperation; the term of art for foreign policy coordination) in a new agreement. Such an agreement must not of course tie our own hands if we needed to take action ourselves. The best way to achieve this was for Britain to put forward our own draft of an agreement on POCO: whoever put forward their own ideas would be able to oblige the others to work on that basis.

It is clear, from Malcolm Rifkind's advice that Britain should not avoid an IGC at all costs and from Geoffrey Howe's decision to go ahead with a formal British proposal on POCO, that Foreign Office ministers were acutely aware of the risk of Britain being on the back foot and of the need to counter that. Against that background, the French and German treatment of the British proposals on POCO was one of the more bizarre aspects of the run-up to the Milan European Council in June. The British paper proposed the formalisation of POCO with a small secretariat and a binding commitment from Heads of Government to consult before launching foreign policy initiatives. POCO would also cover more security issues. This new draft agreement had the Prime Minister's backing and she gave the British paper which set it all out to Kohl at a meeting in Chequers in May. She sent it subsequently to Mitterrand. In case either man was in any doubt about the importance she attached to it, our ambassadors in Bonn and Paris were sent in to enquire as to

German and French reactions. Answer came there none until, shortly before the Milan European Council, the French and German governments produced their own draft treaty on political union which was, topped and tailed, the British draft agreement on POCO. As one Foreign Office official put it: "The Franco German draft is based 85% on our draft on POCO. In other words, the Germans have come up with a Treaty on 'European Union' which involves no treaty amendment and consists exclusively of political cooperation."

This piece of Franco-German theatre was rightly seen as absurd by most of the EC. But it was also an inexplicable slight to Margaret Thatcher and she commented in her memoirs that "the ill-feeling this created was, in its way, an extraordinary achievement". Geoffrey Howe, writing his own autobiography nearly a decade later, said: "She [Margaret Thatcher] was furious. So was I. We have never received a word of regret or explanation from Helmut Kohl or anyone on his behalf."

Much of the indifferent relationship between Chancellor Kohl and Margaret Thatcher can be put down to chemistry. She had that chemistry with Mitterrand, as is clear from his celebrated remark about her having the eyes of Caligula and the mouth of Marilyn Monroe and from her own comment to officials after a meeting with the French President: "He likes women, you know." She did not have it with Kohl. Moreover, she was quite out of sympathy with his view that Germany needed European union to embed her in the Western democratic system. Nonetheless, it has to be said that, as slights go between partners and allies, Kohl's behaviour in June 1985 cannot easily be glossed over. If he had simply failed to appreciate the importance of the document, that would have been careless both on his part and that of his advisers. But he clearly did appreciate its significance and, without saying anything to the paper's authors, plagiarised it to turn it into a document tabled by Mitterrand and himself, thereby showing how much importance he attached to the relationship with France and how little to that with Britain. Robin Renwick recalls that, at the time, Margaret Thatcher observed that the behaviour of Mitterrand and Kohl was the kind of thing that would have got them thrown out of any London club. Renwick also saw the behaviour of the French and Germans as a clear warning that, having been forced to give way to Mrs Thatcher at Fontainebleau, the other member states were not going to do so again.

Writing at the beginning of July 1985, when the Milan European Council had, against British wishes, launched an IGC, Howe said in a minute to the Prime Minister:

In the period before the European Council we put forward positive proposals which offered a practical alternative to the fundamentally impractical course of large scale Treaty amendment. The Germans and French made a ludicrous attempt to take over our proposals on political cooperation. By entitling their document "European Union" they brought out the worst in the Benelux who were made the more determined to press for Treaty amendment.

There was more to it than that. Ahead of a meeting between the Prime Minister and Foreign Secretary and the President of the Commission, Jacques Delors, in May 1985, Foreign Office officials noted that we would face pressure at Milan from the Italian presidency, and probably others, to agree to an IGC. At their meeting, Delors spelled out that there were two main problems to be dealt with: whether to enlarge the scope of the EC to bring in new areas of cooperation and whether it was necessary to change the treaty to improve decision-making. The Prime Minister said straightaway that there was no need to change the treaty. Much of it had still not been implemented, and decision-making could be improved by applying its existing provisions more fully. If the Community consumed its energies in trying to amend the treaty, no practical work would get done. Delors responded that thirty-two articles of the treaty required unanimity. The PM said there were good reasons for this. Delors suggested that it would be easier to complete the internal market if majority voting were introduced for two or three of the articles concerned but he admitted there would be a problem in getting the necessary treaty amendments through national parliaments. Geoffrey Howe commented that the Italians seemed wedded to the idea of an IGC. Margaret Thatcher observed that some member states seemed to take the view that they must always be pressing for something new, even when they did not know what it was they wanted. Their attitude seemed to be: have a meeting and something will come up. This was not an efficient way to conduct business and would be against the recent trend in the Community. She thought more practical work had been accomplished in the last eighteen months than in the preceding few years. The one point on which the Prime Minister and Commission President did come close was on the EP, though even here there was a difference. Delors said he had no enthusiasm for giving the EP the power of co-decision with the Council of Ministers. Mrs Thatcher made clear she was not in favour of *any* additional powers for the Parliament.

At a subsequent meeting between Delors and Howe, the latter returned to the charge on treaty change. The Treaty of Rome was, he said, the constitution of the EC. It was extremely difficult to change since that required the assent of twelve governments and twelve parliaments. The Community could advance without taking on that "difficult and unnecessary task".

Britain went to the European Council in Milan at the end of June believing that it could still fend off the idea of treaty change. There is no formal, agreed record of European Councils, other than the Conclusions. The European Council consists, by treaty provision, of the Heads of Government and foreign ministers, though finance ministers also participate on occasion. The only officials in the room are those of the Commission (usually the Secretary General and one or two others), the Head of the Council Secretariat and his legal adviser, and one or two national officials of the Presidency country. Officials of the member states (the Antici group) sit in another room and, from time to time, receive an oral briefing on what has transpired based on notes taken in the Council by a member of the Council Secretariat. The members of the Antici group in turn write down what they are told and transmit it (these days electronically) to the office of their national delegation. This quaint system is designed to guarantee the privacy of the Heads of Government. It is also designed to include a time lag which is long enough to ensure that, by the time senior officials from national delegations wake up to the fact that something they do not like is about to be slipped past their inadvertent Head of Government, it is already too late. The European Council is like a boxing match: the seconds are out of the ring and the combatants slug it out, being cooled down, fired up, congratulated, or cajoled by the men and women who hold the proverbial towel and sponge in between rounds.

The boxing metaphor is not absolutely precise because national officials are, on a limited basis linked to a restricted system of red badges, allowed access to their leaders but they are not permitted to remain in the room for more than a few minutes. But Britain had one advantage over other delegations, at least in terms of a complete account of what had taken place: in the days of Geoffrey Howe, the British delegation also had its own record since Howe, the trained lawyer, took detailed notes, a habit only subsequently matched in thoroughness by one of his successors, Jack Straw, also a lawyer.

Geoffrey Howe's record of the initial discussion at Milan shows that the argument was conducted on by then familiar lines. Delors argued that it was difficult to make progress without treaty amendment: the Council failed to vote by majority even when this was foreseen. Out of 100 decisions gathering dust on the Commission's shelves, only 45 required unanimity. Fifty-five were held up because of the "invidious effect" of the Luxembourg Compromise.

Helmut Kohl indicated that he favoured using majority voting as provided for in the treaty. He would also be prepared to amend the treaty in specific ways for specific objectives. Mitterrand spoke in similar terms. Mrs Thatcher argued that the Council "should now take the decisions which could be taken. There was no point in remitting to an IGC issues which could not be settled by the Council".

Prime Minister Bettino Craxi summed up that, although different views had been expressed, they were not irreconcilable. Everyone wanted more majority voting but without overriding vital national interests. Everyone agreed that the

Council should have the final say (i.e. no co-decision with the EP). He believed the treaty had to be revised: no treaty could be changeless.

When foreign ministers met later in the day to look at the draft Conclusions, they found that the Italian presidency had proposed postponing all institutional decisions until December, but that they did envisage an IGC to be called under Article 236 of the EC Treaty. The Italian Foreign Minister, Andreotti, floated the idea of calling an IGC by majority vote but does not seem to have done it in a way that led the British delegation to think that the threat of being outvoted was imminent.

In the event, Craxi did use Article 236 to secure support for an IGC by a simple majority of the Heads of Government. In so doing, he was within his rights under the terms of the treaty. But it was the first time a vote had ever been taken in the European Council. British officials had not foreseen the ambush. It came as a slap in the face for Britain. Margaret Thatcher had learned to perfection the art of getting her way by deft use of the unanimity provisions of the treaty. Those provisions were still on her side in that any actual changes to the treaty could only be made by unanimous agreement. But the Italians had blindsided us.

In her autobiography, Margaret Thatcher wrote:

Geoffrey Howe would have agreed to it [the IGC]. His willingness to compromise reflected partly his temperament, partly the Foreign Office's *deformation professionelle*. But it may also have reflected the fact that Britain's membership of the European Community gave the Foreign Office a voice in every aspect of policy that came under the Community. And the more the Community moved in a centralized direction the more influential the Foreign Office became in Whitehall. Inevitably, perhaps, Geoffrey had a slightly more accommodating view of federalism than I did.

Even allowing for my own *déformation professionelle* as a lifelong member of the Diplomatic Service, I believe this is a misjudgement. Firstly, by voting against the IGC (along with only Denmark and Greece), we demonstrated our isolation and our impotence. We had lain down in the path of the advancing train and it had simply sliced through us. The smart thing to have done in the circumstances would have been to reiterate our view that treaty change was unnecessary, but to rally to the consensus on the basis that the impetus towards the Single Market, for which the IGC had been called, owed everything to British lobbying and leadership, and that our interests were protected by the need for unanimity on any proposed treaty change.

In my later time as British Permanent Representative to the EU in Brussels, I was struck by the occasions when British ministers of both main parties thought it better to go down to defeat in a majority vote in order to demonstrate political toughness, rather than rally to the majority when it was clear that, otherwise, defeat was inevitable. I never felt there was any such thing as glorious defeat, merely defeat. And if you were not part of the majority in favour of a piece of legislation, it was difficult to influence the subsequent negotiations with the EP because the Presidency would take account of the view of only those who had comprised the adopting majority in the Council.

Foreign Office views and motives are less easy to characterise than Margaret Thatcher's comment suggests. David Owen, with first-hand experience of the Foreign Office as Europe Minister and then as Secretary of State, believed that a generation of officials had been scarred, first by the misjudgement of the 1950s that had held Britain aloof from the formation of the EC and secondly by de Gaulle's two rebuffs and the difficult years leading to our eventual accession. He concluded that British officials were too inclined to feel the need to ingratiate themselves with their opposite numbers and not confident enough in our own credentials as "good Europeans" with nothing to prove.

It is true that officials were scarred by the experiences of the 1950s and 1960s. It is also true that, if you are a diplomat, you play on a different pitch from that of your political masters. For them, the domestic political environment must be paramount. If they are thought by colleagues, or the Press and public, to be failing to protect British interests, they are vulnerable. There is not always an obvious, immediate price to be paid at home for fighting with foreigners, seeing negotiation in terms of defeat or victory, and playing the patriotic card. Our own winner-takes-all electoral system and adversarial Party system reinforce this tendency, by comparison with the majority of our Continental partners who have coalition systems of government and with whom the habit of compromise is therefore ingrained.

Most diplomats spend at least half of their careers overseas living in countries where a large part of their task is to understand the politics and culture, to report on them accurately and perceptively to their ministers back home, and to help secure British policy objectives. That could not be achieved if diplomats regularly used with their foreign colleagues the kind of language used by politicians and the media at home. Doors would quickly become closed. I can think of one distinguished and experienced British ambassador to the United States, who, on one occasion, very robustly represented the views of his Prime Minister to the US Secretary of State and was never again received by that Secretary of State. The most effective diplomats are those who empathise with the country in which they are posted and are liked and trusted by a large enough group of influential people in that country to enable them to send back to their governments insights not available to an assiduous internet surfer and to make judgements about the way the government of their host country will behave which usually turn out to be right. A diplomat's first priority has to be to represent his or her country and government to the country and government where he or she is posted. It is possible to get so immersed in a country that you start to understand it better than you do your own. This risk of "going native" is why the British Diplomatic Service has rarely left its staff in post for more than five years. But diplomats cannot be effective unless their advice and judgement enable their own government to frame their policy and approach in ways that are likely to be receivable in the country to which they are addressed. For any diplomat, finding the balance between getting close to your host country without becoming remote from your own is a crucial part of the job.

So, it is true that members of the British Diplomatic Service do not generally relish confrontation. But, none of the senior Foreign Officials involved in European policy under Margaret Thatcher (Michael Butler, David Hannay, Robin Renwick, and John Kerr) was other than strong-minded and robust. All of us who were involved in the campaign to secure a fair budget deal for Britain, in however minor a capacity, were 100% behind her. The same is true of David Williamson who ran the European Secretariat and who came from the Ministry of Agriculture.

As time went on, a gap opened up between Number 10 and the Foreign Office; it was because of reservations about Margaret Thatcher's tactics (e.g. her handling of the Milan summit) and, ultimately, about whether her perception of our European partners and her judgement of Britain's interests in Europe were accurate. Geoffrey Howe, in particular, was ultraloyal throughout his time at the Foreign Office, seeking to persuade by reasoned argument even when those arguments were given short shrift. But, at the end of the day, he reached a different view of where Britain's interest lay and certainly took a different view of strategy and tactics. John Major, whom Margaret Thatcher saw as her most loyal lieutenant, handled his relationship with her in a different way. But, on the issue which precipitated Geoffrey Howe's removal from the Foreign Office, British membership of the exchange rate mechanism (ERM), Major's view was the same as that of Howe and Lawson: it was in Britain's economic interest to join. It was Chancellor of the Exchequer John Major, acting on rigorous economic analysis, who persuaded her to take that decision, not Foreign Secretary John Major under the influence of what she saw as an overaccommodating Foreign Office. But he was one and the same person and the analysis of both Departments was a shared one.

Margaret Thatcher also suggests that the Foreign Office was motivated by a wish to maintain its determinant position in Whitehall and that the more there was centralised decision-making in Brussels, the more influential the Foreign Office thought it would be. It is true that the Foreign Secretary has, ever since Britain joined the EC, been the senior minister responsible for coordinating government policy on EC issues. As such, the Foreign Secretary chairs the

Cabinet subcommittee responsible for ministerial discussion of EU matters. No Foreign Secretary would lightly surrender that role. But Geoffrey Howe's early years as Foreign Secretary, from 1983 to the completion of the SEA negotiations in 1985, probably represent the last period in which the General Affairs Council (foreign ministers) could claim to be the true coordinators of EC business. Already, the European Council was indisputably the principal strategy-making body as well as the court of appeal on issues that could not be settled at lower levels. Direct contact between capitals was at an embryonic stage and British embassies in EC capitals played a bigger part than now in the conduct of EU diplomacy, but the Head of the European Secretariat in the Cabinet Office at the time, David Williamson, was the de facto senior partner in a triumvirate of officials, also comprising the Permanent Representative to the European Communities and the Foreign Office Assistant Under Secretary, who sought to orchestrate the management of EC business in Whitehall. And Williamson, like all his predecessors, was a home civil servant. If the Foreign Office had clout in the Whitehall coordinating meetings that happened week in, week out in the Cabinet Office, it was primarily because of the resource the Foreign Office devoted to Europe and the acquired expertise of its officials. There was no automatic acceptance of the Foreign Office view. On the contrary, at a time when unanimity still prevailed in the majority of EU decisions, the capacity of Whitehall departments to determine a British position of "no compromise" was much greater than it is now and was frequently and forcefully exercised. Throughout the negotiations leading up to the Fontainebleau agreement on the British budget rebate, it was the Treasury that originated the ideas and the policy and called most of the shots. That only changed in the end game. By the time Margaret Thatcher left office, the General Affairs Council (the foreign ministers) was less and less involved in EC-wide coordination and was increasingly focused on the specialist business of foreign affairs. That weakening of the role of EU foreign ministers as coordinators of EU business has increased ever since.

The vote at Milan was a jolt to the British. It showed that our partners were learning ways to get round Margaret Thatcher, that we were in a minority on an issue where we had sought to show a lead, and that we faced a risk that other member states might seek ways to go ahead without us. Before she gave her press conference at the end of the Milan summit, Mrs Thatcher was urged by her officials not to tell the journalists that we would refuse to agree to any treaty change. It was, after all, just possible that we could negotiate changes that would be acceptable to us. The Prime Minister swept off with no reply. But in her press conference, under intense pressure from the journalists, she did not say that she would never agree to treaty change, only that she was not convinced of the need for it. When she was asked by a correspondent from

The Times if she had read an article in his newspaper criticising her dictatorial style, she replied: "If you think I have time to read editorials in *The Times*, you are sadly mistaken."

On their return to London, senior officials sought from the Prime Minister, and were granted, a licence to explore with other member states whether we could agree treaty changes acceptable to us. "Yes", they were told, "and please bear in mind that, when you come back, I may disavow you."

The search for minimal, acceptable treaty change, avoiding risky isolation for Britain and the possibility of our partners seeking to make progress without us, was to be the work of the next six months.

4

The Single European Act and Economic and Monetary Union

Two months before what Mrs Thatcher saw as the Milan ambush, the Foreign Office had sent her a paper about the implications of Spanish and Portuguese accession to the EC. The dramatic economic impact of enlargement was only partly foreseen. The paper noted that the reasons which had led the existing member states to support the accession of Portugal and Spain were almost entirely political. Both new member states were convinced that membership would make a contribution to political stability in their countries. On the back of enlargement, the border between Spain and Gibraltar had been reopened and enlargement was likely to have a beneficial effect when Spaniards voted in a referendum on whether to join NATO (and so it proved). But French and Italian agricultural interests were directly affected by Spain joining the Community; hence the opposition to Spain's accession from Jacques Chirac and part of the Opposition in France. France would find it hard to reconcile her interest in expenditure under the CAP with the need to contain her increasing budget burden. These factors had already started bringing France's view of her interests in the Community closer to those of the UK. At the same time, the growing difficulties of running the enlarged Community, combined with a sense of injustice over the distribution of burdens, could cause the Germans to become more truculent. Tying the Germans into the West European system would be a continuing French preoccupation. Nor was it in Britain's interest to see the development of more nationalistic attitudes in Germany.

Given these factors, and the fact that the Netherlands would be disadvantaged by longer-term changes in the Community's financial system, the Community was likely to develop its own "north/south" divide. The first shared interest and task for Britain, France, and Germany would be to ensure that the Community did not become intolerably costly. Convergence between rich and poor would be brought about not by transfer payments, but by modernisation of national economies. The costs of the CAP would not be contained without greater differentiation between small and large farmers and some element of national financing. Some measure of variable geometry would also be necessary, and indeed desirable, in the enlarged Community. It must not disrupt the unity of the market or discriminate against certain member states.

The Foreign Office paper went on to argue that, in all this, while France and Germany would try to establish a position of leadership, they would have their work cut out adjusting their policies to the new situation and were both well aware that they needed the active involvement of the UK, given our central role in Europe's defence and security. It would be more than ever difficult to get things done in the enlarged Community and our ability to do so would depend on the effectiveness of Britain's cooperation with the French and Germans. This cooperation would have to be organised bilaterally if it was not to cause trouble with the Italians and others.

The Foreign Office foresaw the emergence of core groupings—more probably as a series of concentric circles than as a single cohesive group. The danger for a Community of twelve was that it would break up, rather than break down, because the application of Community rules throughout the Community would be even more difficult than at present. This was the context in which the views of Kohl and Mitterrand on European union needed to be judged. Neither man, the Foreign Office argued, had in mind a federal or even a confederal system. But for political reasons, which were as much domestic as European, they wanted to give some new impetus to the Community before enlargement took place. The paper concluded with this advice:

Membership of the enlarged Community could have limited value unless we form part of the inner groupings that are likely to develop in areas of key interest to us. The French and Germans are finding their relationship by no means easy. Both, for their own reasons, want our participation . . . The French continue to attach the very greatest importance to measures intended to keep tying the Germans ever more firmly into the West European system . . . Despite the inevitable conflicts of interest on some subjects, permanent French egocentricity and the no less permanent and damaging confusion in German policy, a determined effort must be made, by means of intensive bilateral consultations, to attempt to formulate a shared strategy for the encouragement and development of the enlarged Community.

Twenty years on, there is much that remains compelling about this analysis. The argument about part national financing of the CAP is still with us. Because of pressures from the British farm lobby on the Ministry of Agriculture (now Department for Environment, Food and Rural Affairs [DEFRA]), modern British governments find it as hard as did Mrs Thatcher to bite the bullet and agree to skew farm payments away from large farmers and towards smaller ones. The paper made a prediction about Spain's economic advancement that has come true. The picture of Portugal was more pessimistic than justified by events. The paper underplayed the importance of economic transfers in providing a stimulus to the modernisation of economies for which it also called.

But the most striking aspect of the paper was its invitation to the Prime Minister to recognise that some fundamental changes would be brought about by enlargement and to embrace a new strategic partnership with France and Germany in which Britain could have a leading role as one of the governments which was at the centre of European policy development. This was exactly the role that Tony Blair sought when he came into office in 1997.

Margaret Thatcher's response was also significant. She found the paper "interesting and to the point", a rare compliment to the Foreign Office. It was said that her view of the Foreign Office was the mirror image of her view of the Church of England: she liked the Church of England as an institution but had little time for a number of the people in it, whereas she had little time for the Foreign Office as an organisation but respected a number of the individual officials in it. But more important was her reaction on substance. She said:

- We must intensify our efforts to bring the CAP under control.
- We must steer Community R&D firmly towards cooperation between companies and away from Community-funded programmes.
- While decision-making might well become more difficult in the enlarged Community, the importance of being able to insist on unanimity on matters of vital national interest would increase because there was a greater likelihood of costly initiatives we should have to oppose.
- Nothing must be done to weaken the Luxembourg Compromise.
- We should exploit divisions between France and Germany but be ready to work with each of them as suited the issue.
- We should de-dramatise the concept of variable geometry within the Community because it would probably suit our interests in the enlarged Community for there to be smaller groupings. There were several reasons for this: we should probably not want to participate in everything; smaller groupings might sometimes be the most effective way to get things done; and variable geometry would counter moves towards "union".
- We must avoid the appearance of a two-tier Community with Britain in the second division. The concentric circles analogy was a good one.

The Foreign Office had suggested that Britain had an opportunity to build a strategic relationship with France and Germany, which would enable us to manage the future development of the EC. The Prime Minister's response concentrated more on the threats to British national interests, focusing on preventing decisions we might not like rather than promoting decisions which would be in our interest. She saw the relationship with France and Germany more in the tactical terms of "divide and rule" than as a strategic partnership.

After Milan, officials saw even more clearly the need to get alongside France and Germany. David Williamson, Head of the Cabinet Office's European Secretariat, sent a minute to Geoffrey Howe in early July telling him that, ever since the deal at Fontainebleau, Britain had been working hard in day-to-day contacts with the Community, while protecting our essential interests, to build up a position in which leadership on important issues would increasingly be based on UK understandings with France or Germany or both. Those achievements, Williamson argued, were heavily overshadowed by what had happened at Milan, but had not been lost. We were not yet at a parting of the ways but, at the end of the IGC, we should be. The risk for Britain was that the original Six might conclude a separate treaty on new areas of cooperation, including POCO. Williamson therefore proposed that, in the IGC, we should moderate the proposals and language of others wherever possible, but that we should not commit ourselves to oppose specific treaty amendments unless it was absolutely imperative to do so.

This tactic was agreed by ministers on the basis that not opposing the ideas of others did not imply that the Prime Minister would ultimately have to accept them. We would simply keep our powder dry. For Whitehall, sitting on its hands was supremely difficult. Inactivity, even with malice aforethought, comes hard to British officials of all departments. But the Foreign Office was able to note in the autumn that, in Whitehall, senior officials in the Treasury, the Department of Trade and Industry, and the Ministry of Agriculture appeared to accept that we might need to contemplate some limited treaty amendment, for instance, of a kind which might express in juridical form the proposals on easier decision-taking that Britain had put forward before Milan, in order to avoid a split with the French and Germans that could be damaging to British interests.

Sitting on our hands was especially difficult when the European Commission came forward with their own proposals for treaty amendment to allow for majority voting covering the internal market, technology, and the environment. Officials advised ministers that these proposals were both far too sweeping and not specific enough. The Common Market was defined by the Commission, not just in terms of goods, workers, services, and capital, but the complete abolition of all frontier controls. On the other hand, there was nothing in the Commission's text which could actually bind member states to adopt the kind of directives Britain wanted, covering free movement of goods and services, freedom of establishment, and freedom of capital movements.

Moreover, the Commission had acknowledged that their text as drafted would involve majority voting on tax harmonisation.

But the tactic of (relative) silence worked. Other member states came out of the woodwork. A month later, officials noted that the French and Germans had obliged the Commission to amend their document to maintain unanimity for directives which did not promote the removal of direct impediments to the free movement of goods, persons, services, and capital and for all directives harmonising national powers concerning taxation. The Commission had also been obliged to recognise that, if a directive would involve a reduction in the standards of safety in any member state, that state must vote in favour before the measure could be adopted. The French and Germans also appeared to accept the British view that freedom of movement of people should be limited to those defined by the treaty, that is workers, and that harmonisation of indirect taxation should remain subject to unanimity.

Sir Michael Butler, the UK Permanent Representative, who had been one of the authors of the Fontainebleau settlement, retired in the autumn of 1985 halfway through the negotiation on the SEA, to be replaced by David Hannay who, apart from a brief interlude as number two in the British Embassy in Washington, had spent his recent career as the senior official responsible for EC matters in the Foreign Office, had been one of those involved in the original accession negotiations, and had subsequently been Chef de Cabinet to one of Britain's first European Commissioners, Christopher Soames. David Hannay was clever, quick, tough-minded, and supremely self-confident. He led from the front and, for the best part of a generation, was one of the central figures in the evolution and execution of Britain's European policies. Like David Williamson, he was adept at delivering what Mrs Thatcher knew she needed, which was not invariably the same as what she said she wanted. Hannay and Williamson (hard cop and soft cop) were the principal British negotiators of the SEA.

On his retirement, Butler had a final meeting with the Prime Minister. In his valedictory despatch (despatches were the means by which ambassadors communicated formally with the Foreign Secretary on major, long-term issues, by contrast with Foreign Office telegrams which were the daily means of communication), Butler set out his views on British policy. Despatches were printed by the Foreign Office and given a wide circulation round Whitehall and to the Queen. So Butler would have chosen his words advisedly. He wrote:

The democratic countries of Western Europe need unity if they are to protect and promote their interests in the modern world, to organise Western Europe so that it can bargain on less unequal terms with a United States which seems to be drifting slowly away from us. So the Community has to be made to work. For it is the only means we have to achieve these ends ... There is a widespread feeling that the European ideal has lost impetus ... The most deep rooted and worrying cause is that so few people in any of our countries have a clear picture of what the Community is now about ... How then to convince people that Europe is already uniting fast and must unite faster? How to convince them that the constant clash of views and interests is not a sign of fundamental disunity but the breadth of the front on which European integration is moving and the vitality of the process? Only a static Europe would be calm and united. We can all only slog away at it, as you [Geoffrey Howe] do tirelessly ... It is in our interests to convince the other member governments that the British government and people are with them on the voyage. We shall get our way more often if we are prepared to be more in favour of the aim of European Union. For in the eyes of our partners, the Community is not just a permanent negotiation about important but boring detailed issues. It is a common enterprise to unite a continent and those who proclaim this are forgiven minor sins and granted considerable favours.

At her meeting with Butler, the Prime Minister was as interested in the tactics of the negotiation as in long-term strategy. She was turning over in her mind what the possible impact of more majority voting would be on British interests. She was sceptical about the need for new treaty articles on the environment and technology but acknowledged that, in some circumstances, such articles could actually work to British advantage. Her conclusion from the meeting was that, for the time being, we should continue to play our cards close to our chest and go on grinding down the unrealistic aims of other member states and the Commission. Nearer the time of the European Council, officials might need to become more closely involved in drafting elements of a package which might be acceptable. But we should be clear, if we entered into such an exercise, that it was without commitment. Officials should explain that they did not know what the Prime Minister would or would not be able to accept when it came to the European Council itself. The Prime Minister was, however, in no doubt that, if we could get an acceptable deal, it was in our interest to reach agreement at the Luxembourg European Council in December, since the longer the IGC dragged on, the greater the risk of others trying to do more.

As the Luxembourg meeting approached, the main preoccupation of British ministers and officials was to constrain the wish of the Commission to extend majority voting into areas such as taxation and workers' rights, to avoid extensions in the power of the EP at the expense of national parliaments and the Council of Ministers (which must retain the last word on legislation), to avoid extending the definition of what was meant by freedom of movement, and to ensure that majority voting did not allow any weakening of Britain's phytosanitary controls on imports of agricultural products such as plants and seeds. Britain was also terrified that majority voting might compel her to give up her controls over rabies which, until their abolition was painlessly and successfully achieved over a decade later, were regarded as our only defence against a potentially deadly disease.

Jacques Chirac, as French Prime Minister, would attend the December Summit in Luxembourg, along with President Mitterrand, under the cohabitation arrangement resulting from the French Assembly elections. Chirac's political personality was summed up by the British Embassy in Paris:

He is an instinctive political fighter rather than a profound strategist and he is capable of sharp twists and turns. He condemns what he claims have been French sell-outs over the British budget contribution and Portuguese and Spanish entry and promises to wage a battle in Brussels on behalf of French farmers. Whatever problems this may cause with France's partners, he expects a calculated display of French chauvinism to be popular at home.

Anyone who has had dealings with President Chirac would recognise that description. He had some famous battles with Margaret Thatcher and could be a hectoring bully. But she recognised in him a political fighter, as well as a fellow conservative, and she liked him. Twenty years on, Tony Blair would probably have said much the same.

The success of the Luxembourg summit owed much to the skilful chairmanship of the Luxembourg Prime Minister, Jacques Santer. Recent history has not been kind to Santer. He was a quiet and unforceful President of the Commission after the whirlwind Delors years. His inability to exercise control over his fellow Commissioners, especially Edith Cresson, contributed to the crisis which eventually forced his Commission to resign. But one reason why he could not bring Cresson to book was that President Chirac would not cooperate to allow him to do so. And, on the other side of the coin, it was his Commission that set the course for, and successfully managed, the biggest enlargement of the EU in its history. It was also Santer who, when the British government got themselves into a blind alley of confrontation with their partners over bovine spongiform encephalopathy (BSE: "mad cow disease"), helped to construct the ladder which John Major was then able to climb down.

At Luxembourg in December 1985, Santer's low-key, patient approach, looking for a deal not a grandstand for himself, helped defuse the tensions. One of the most intractable issues for Britain proved to be that of the regime of phytosanitary controls on agricultural products. The Heads of Government spent three hours debating the issue and had reached deadlock. British officials came up with a new formula. They passed it into the conference chamber to Geoffrey Howe who, much relieved, read it out to the meeting. Santer, hoping to sum up in favour of the suggestion put forward by the British Foreign Secretary, asked: "Does anyone disagree?" "Yes; I do", said one Head of Government. That Head of Government was Margaret Thatcher. In the end she came round.

Britain secured her objectives. A new cooperation procedure for EC legislation gave a greater role to the EP, but left the last word with the Council of Ministers. It was, inevitably, only a step towards the greater powers that the EP would successfully seek in later treaty negotiations. The changes had one minor consequence which gave disproportionate satisfaction to officials like me. Paragraph 2 of Article 7 of the SEA read: "In Article 7, second paragraph of the EEC Treaty the terms 'after consulting the Assembly' shall be replaced by 'in cooperation with the European Parliament'." Margaret Thatcher had always insisted on referring to the EP as "the Assembly" because she was at pains to maintain that it was not a proper parliament like our own. The Treaty of Rome had given her a basis for doing so, though her insistence irritated MEPs who were just as directly and legitimately elected as national MPs. Once the SEA had been incorporated into UK law as part of our ratification procedure, we were able to point out to an irritated Charles Powell, Mrs Thatcher's Private Secretary, that in UK law, the correct title was now "European Parliament". In fairness to her, Mrs Thatcher accepted the change and used it thereafter.

Both Margaret Thatcher and Geoffrey Howe were concerned at the reference in the SEA to EMU, but the Prime Minister felt obliged to accept it. "Whereas at their conference in Paris from 19 to 21 October 1972 the Heads of State or of Government approved the objective of the progressive realisation of Economic and Monetary Union", read the preamble to the Single Act. The Prime Minister felt she could not object to this historical reference, even though she did not share the objective to which Ted Heath had signed up. But she felt she had circumscribed the meaning of the reference by securing, in the substantive part of the Single Act, a heading: "Co-operation in Economic and Monetary Policy (Economic and Monetary Union)". In other words, in her mind, EMU meant no more than policy cooperation. The key moment was a meeting between Thatcher and Kohl in the UK Delegation office in Luxembourg. Present on the British side were the Prime Minister and Foreign Secretary and an adviser from the British Treasury. Kohl was accompanied by his advisers. Neither the UK Permanent Representative, David Hannay, nor the Foreign Office Under Secretary, Robin Renwick, was allowed in. Kohl said he was firmly opposed to EMU, but the text was harmless and meaningless. Indeed, by saying that further treaty change would be needed, it was a barrier against "creeping EMU". Mrs Thatcher accepted this, and she and Kohl returned to the conference room and approved the text. If, as she did, Mrs Thatcher subsequently felt that she had been double-crossed by Kohl, she was not double-crossed on the basis of official Foreign Office advice.

Just as significant in the short term were the implications of two articles of the SEA over which there had been much agonising in Whitehall. Subsequent interpretation of these articles is one reason for Mrs Thatcher's own later disenchantment with the SEA.

According to Article 8A of the SEA, the internal market was to comprise "an area without internal frontiers in which the free movement of goods, persons, services and capital is ensured in accordance with the provisions of this Treaty".

Foreign Office legal advisers were confident that this definition did not provide freedom of movement for all Community citizens, whether seeking work or not, let alone for third country nationals living within Community borders. In order to bolster the position, Britain secured a General Declaration which was appended to the SEA and which read: "Nothing in these provisions shall affect the right of member states to take such measures as they consider necessary for the purpose of controlling immigration from third countries, and to combat terrorism, crime, the traffic in drugs and illicit trading in works of art and antiques." It was recognised that the Declaration had political force only and was not legally binding, but British officials believed it made explicit what was already implicit in the specific treaty article.

As I recall, the Law Officers believed that our interpretation was a reasonable one though it could not be guaranteed. The European Commission never shared our interpretation, even at the time. And, over time, the findings of the ECJ favoured the view in a majority of member states, which was that the EC was committed to a genuinely frontier-free travel zone with no passport controls on EU citizens or on the citizens of third countries once they had satisfied the entry requirements at the first Community border they crossed. This was not acceptable to the Thatcher or Major governments or, in 1997, to the incoming Labour government. The Home Office attached importance to frontier controls for three reasons: illegal immigration, cross-border crime, and drug trafficking. They argued that the ability to check an individual passport was an important deterrent and the means by which people who wanted to transgress were actually caught.

The one weakness in our argument was that we had an open frontier between the UK and the Republic of Ireland, and did not seem too preoccupied by that despite the fact that, at the time, the one source of terrorist danger in the UK came from terrorists some of whom were based in the Republic.

Over time, the role of intelligence in combating terrorism and drug trafficking grew in importance, but the role of the passport check in combating illegal immigration was thought to be of continuing significance. So, as our partners moved to a frontier-free Europe, we maintained our controls, albeit with a special channel for EC citizens and a relatively light regime. At one time, we even considered what was known as the "Bangemann wave", after the European Commissioner who was at its origin. The idea was that EC citizens would not have to have their passports inspected but would simply wave them as they passed through immigration so that the immigration officer could see (from the red cover that became standard when the European common format passport was introduced) that the holder was allowed free access. Not surprisingly, this idea did not ultimately find favour since it constituted neither free movement on the one hand nor an adequate control on the other.

For several years, the British government lived with the fear that it might be prosecuted for being in breach of EC law, either by the Commission or by a citizen aggrieved at being held up at Dover or elsewhere. Under John Major, one junior Home Office Minister, John Wardle, resigned because he believed that the public was being given a false sense of security about the legal safety of Britain's frontier controls.

In the end, the issue was resolved amicably in the Amsterdam Treaty. Two things changed to make that possible. First, our partners had made an inter-governmental agreement (the Schengen agreement) to abolish frontier con-trols between the participating countries. That agreement was made outside the framework of the EC treaties but was fully consistent with their interpre-tation of them. Not surprisingly, they wanted to incorporate the Schengen arrangements on a frontier-free Europe into EU law. They needed Britain's agreement to do that. Secondly, the growing problems of illegal immigration, drug trafficking, and terrorism meant that other member states were less insistent on the magic of open frontiers, especially for island nations such as Britain and Ireland. And the truth is that the British controls were, certainly before 9/11, operated in a light way which did not cause too much aggravation. And so, an opt-out was secured at Amsterdam, authorising the continued existence of frontier controls in Britain and Ireland. The Irish would probably have signed up to the agreement among the Schengen countries, had it not been for the fact that their common frontier with the UK meant that they could do so only if Britain was prepared to do the same.

The second issue where the evolution of the SEA did not go as predicted was in respect of Article 21 (Social Policy). As with all such negotiations, the end product was a compromise and therein lay the seeds of future problems. "Member States", said the Article, "shall pay particular attention to encour-aging improvements in the working environment, as regards the health and safety of workers, and shall set as their objective the harmonisation of con-ditions in this area, while maintaining the improvements made." QMV was to be introduced for directives in this area. Those directives would establish "minimum requirements for gradual implementation, having regard to the conditions and technical rules obtaining in each of the Member States". At

British insistence, the Article also stipulated that: "Such directives shall avoid imposing administrative, financial and legal constraints in a way which would hold back the creation and development of small and medium-sized undertakings."

Margaret Thatcher took a lot of persuading that this Article was watertight from a British perspective. In fact, her doubts were justified. British officials believed that the Article was limited to measures related to health and safety. The Commission, backed by a sufficient number of other member states, used it in practice as the basis of social legislation going beyond health and safety. This was to be, and remains, a preoccupation of British ministers and officials.

In the immediate aftermath of the Luxembourg European Council, Commission President Jacques Delors was despondent. The final product of the negotiations on the draft treaty was a SEA sharply cut down to size, consisting principally of provisions for the single market and POCO, with many Commission trimmings jettisoned. Delors's despondency was explained in David Hannay's first annual review from Brussels at the end of 1985:

One qualitative change, much bemoaned by the Euro-federalists, a weakening of the Commission, vis a vis the Council, is not very apparent to me. The reality is not that its role is much diminished; it is that it is much the same...There are not many important Community decisions being taken now about the customs union in which we live but there is an awful lot of business being done on the decisions taken in 1958...What at the time [the Milan European Council] looked like the possible beginning of a dangerous split in the Community, with the UK becoming isolated from the mainstream of Community policy making, has not turned out like that, not least because we ourselves set about preventing it from doing so. The maximalists (Italy, Belgium and Commission) in the event had little support and, above all, not that of France and Germany.

Set against this analysis, Delors's dissatisfaction was understandable. He should, like Brer Rabbit, have proclaimed at this juncture that he had been born and bred in a briar patch. Instead, he bemoaned the failure of the EC governments to respond to the temper of the times and make bolder moves towards EU. But he swiftly recovered. British officials soon saw, privately, the text of a document which Delors had circulated within the Commission instructing its officials to make the maximum use of the flexibility created by the majority voting provisions of the new treaty and to use those articles wherever possible. This the Commission did, sometimes making dubious use of majority voting articles to get round the unanimity rule.

It was during this period that the image of a power-hungry Commission, bent on ever greater harmonisation, grew up in the UK. Delors was a man who believed in a federal Europe in the sense of a Europe with a powerful executive (the Commission) answerable to the EP and with the Council of Ministers as a revising chamber. He set out that view explicitly in a speech in 1990 in which he said: "The Commission should be turned into a proper executive answerable for its actions. The executive would, of course, have to be answerable to the democratic institutions of the future federation." Under Delors, the sense of a Commission keen to extend EC competence at every opportunity was strong. The imposition of burdens on smaller enterprises seemed of secondary concern, despite sustained British efforts to secure rigorous assessment of the regulatory impact of new measures, efforts that are only coming to fruition now in a changed political climate.

From a British perspective, it would have been much easier if the drive to complete the single market had focused exclusively on market-opening measures and less on the social and environmental at a time when Britain's environmental track record was one of the worst in Europe and when the Thatcher government were implementing radical domestic reforms in industrial relations. But, although the Commission were undoubtedly power hungry, and subsidiarity not a notion that was recognised in the Berlaymont building, it cannot be said that Delors was out of tune with the wishes of the majority among the member states. Nor, even from a cautious British perspective, was a raft of harmonising single market measures wholly undesirable. Had it been easy to open up the single market, it would have happened during the first thirty years of the Community's existence. But it was not and it had not. Teddy Taylor, one of the leading euro-sceptic Conservative MPs, used to make play with the lawn mower noise directive as an example of needlessly interventionist, pettifogging legislation. But the noise level of lawnmowers was used in some member states as a barrier to trade, so the acceptable level of lawn mower noise had to be spelled out in legislation to ensure that exporters had a free market in which to operate. Harmonising legislation was necessary for the Single Market. That was why, in *Europe—the Future*, Margaret Thatcher had said: "We must create the conditions in which European businessmen too can build on their strengths and create prosperity and jobs. That means action to harmonise standards."

But it was not just particular British problems with the interpretation of the SEA, or the extent of EC legislation, which dominated much of 1986 and 1987. In 1986, Lynda Chalker, who had succeeded Malcolm Rifkind as Europe Minister at the Foreign Office, steered the SEA through the House of Commons against the opposition of the Labour Party. There was also slight opposition from a very few Conservative backbenchers, but that opposition was limited because the Prime Minister herself, rather than just the Foreign Secretary, had sponsored the legislation in Parliament. This ensured that Conservative backbenchers thought twice before voting against the bill. Defying Geoffrey Howe was one thing; defying Margaret Thatcher quite another. The passage of the bill was straightforward, if lengthy. On the government benches, revolt was confined to seventeen Euro-sceptic MPs. The Labour Opposition voted solidly against.

Pressure for reform of the CAP, untouched by the SEA, remained a big British preoccupation. Once again, the European budget was bumping up against the ceiling, so Britain had leverage to secure CAP reform. In March 1987, the Prime Minister told President Mitterrand that she accepted the importance of a strong rural society, but the Community could not go on fixing prices at levels calculated to ensure the survival of the least efficient farmers. If necessary, subsidies should be found from national social budgets. Mitterrand agreed that the present system could not go on. But France's partners had to understand that food was France's basic industry and French society was dominated by the rural approach. He himself was relatively moderate on these issues. He supported reform of the CAP.

A rather different tune was sung by Prime Minister Jacques Chirac in the summer when the Prime Minister was fiercely resisting a proposed oils and fats tax, a thinly disguised protectionist measure against overseas agricultural exports to the Community. Chirac claimed that Mrs Thatcher's position was in direct contravention to the treaty. CAP spending, Chirac argued, was obligatory spending [this was true in the technical sense that the Council, not the EP had the last word but it did not mean that the Council was not allowed to determine the level of expenditure; that was what the annual CAP price fixing was all about]. Perhaps, said Chirac, it would be necessary to eliminate all non-obligatory spending [i.e. all non agricultural spending]. Or renegotiate the British Accession Treaty. The UK was seeking to undermine the basic mechanisms of the CAP. France would never accept this. The Prime Minister concluded that she and M. Chirac could argue all day, but she would not accept an oils and fats tax. Nor did she.

At the Brussels European Council in June 1987, Margaret Thatcher was intransigent. In his autobiography, Geoffrey Howe lays some of the blame at the door of the Belgian Chairman, Prime Minister Wilfred Martens. But he argues that the differences over the control of agricultural expenditure could have been ironed out with "a calmer approach from the British corner". Eleven member states could have found agreement. Geoffrey Howe clearly felt that the twelfth should have been able to do as well and that, by our not doing so, "a dangerous, and unnecessary, precedent had been set".

In the autumn of that year, a German paper, *Der Spiegel*, put it to Mrs Thatcher that she had been accused by Chirac of acting "like a housewife". She replied:

It's a shame that more politicians don't act like housewives...Anyone who wants to win votes should have a good opinion of housewives. Housewives of the world unite...I am such a passionate believer in the Community that I accept all the accusations of being a troublemaker. No, I am not awkward; I just want the EC to work. I am also passionately committed to the building of the Channel Tunnel. That is something that our generation can do for the next generation.

The Copenhagen European Council in December 1987, still centred on agricultural reform, was a failure. The Foreign Office explained afterwards to its overseas posts that six different issues would have had to be settled for an agreement to be reached: overall levels of agricultural spending, control of spending on individual crops, the rate of growth of the structural funds, continuation of the UK abatement, the Own Resources system, and the overall level of Own Resources. There was disagreement on structural funds, with southern member states wanting a 100% increase in structural funds and northerners wanting much lower growth, concentrated on the four poor member states (Greece, Portugal, Spain, and Ireland). But the breakdown came on agricultural stabilisers, that is, automatic price cuts when excess production threatened ceilings for individual commodities. The Germans, with French support, had refused to accept Commission proposals on cereals.

In January 1988, the Germans took over the EC presidency and the Prime Minister had another robust meeting with Chirac: If M. Chirac thought that ganging up with the Germans to isolate "Mrs T" would lead her to give way, he was, she told him, sadly mistaken...M. Chirac seemed to be suggesting that the Community should not accept any imports but aim for self-sufficiency. That was a ludicrous position...She had no fear at all of being isolated in demanding that surpluses be brought under control. Chirac responded that if there was to be a bust-up on agriculture there would be a bust-up on the UK's abatement. The Prime Minister advised Chirac not to threaten her. The UK remained the second largest net contributor to the Community's budget and our contribution had gone up faster than anyone else's since Fontainebleau. Without a satisfactory solution on agricultural spending and on our abatement, there would be no increase in the Community's own resources.

The stage was set for a showdown in Brussels in February. It is vividly described in Mrs Thatcher's autobiography. Margaret Thatcher and Dutch Prime Minister Ruud Lubbers were subjected to two days of French and German bullying, Kohl thumping the table, Chirac shouting and throwing papers around and greeting one of Mrs Thatcher's interventions with the word "couilles". Mrs Thatcher says in her autobiography that she eventually concluded that the text on budgetary discipline for agriculture was more binding than she had thought and that she was right to settle. She was also running out of rope. One close observer reports her as shedding tears of rage when Ruud Lubbers decided that he could no longer hold out against French and German bullying. Even more significant was the preparation by the Council Secretariat, behind the scenes, of a text which, at Kohl's instigation, might have formed the basis of an agreement at eleven, leaving Britain to one side. It was not used because, in the end, and as usually happens at the thirteenth hour, a compromise was reached. But the whole negotiation had brought Britain's partners close to calling her bluff. The lesson of that episode was drawn to Margaret Thatcher's attention but not heeded, with consequences for Britain two years later when Britain's partners found themselves up against her opposition to progress on EMU.

It was hard not to cheer Margaret Thatcher at her rumbustious best, let alone disagree that she was right to press for radical reform of the CAP. But the fault line through European policy as seen by the Foreign Office was evidenced in a letter sent by Britain's ambassador in Bonn in the autumn of 1987. Julian Bullard was a brilliant official, clever and subtle, and a determined advocate of Britain's interests. But in October 1987, he wrote to the Foreign Office:

Here we have a Prime Minister in her ninth year in office, with vast international experience, including more than twenty five European summits, presiding over a country whose economy, thanks largely to her, is turning out enviable statistics . . . You would think, wouldn't you, that in these circumstances Britain would be giving the lead in Europe and the Continentals would be following it. But is this happening? I think not. Why not? Because we don't seem to be interested in any particular objective except the Internal Market in which Smarties can be sold in the same packet everywhere from Copenhagen to Constancia . . . What I think is missing: Vision . . . I see two results . . . The first is that we reduce our ability to trade points in the negotiating market place . . . Second, and much more important, is the danger which the Secretary of State [Howe] has identified and termed "self marginalisation" in those subjects where we cannot block but will not cooperate.

Bullard went on to analyse the relationship between France and Germany.

The pattern of this [Franco/German] relationship has been for the two Heads of Government to plant flags far ahead of their respective front line, towards which the troops then gallantly struggle. Meanwhile, in the ground already occupied, fraternisation continues apace and gaps in Franco-German joint activity are steadily filled in, to the point where others find it difficult even to get a place in the diaries of the two privileged partners. I would plead that at least more thought be given to the style of British policy in Europe. The plain speaking of the House of Commons does not translate well into Continental languages, especially in countries that live by coalition and compromise. Chancellor Kohl said to me once that in any political argument one should bear in mind not only the current battle but the next. And not everything unquantifiable is unimportant.

Bullard had set out a view that would have been widely shared in the Foreign Office. But not universally. Writing two months later, after the Copenhagen European Council, the UK Permanent Representative David Hannay said:

Copenhagen provided a good chance to test Julian's theses and I am led to draw some rather different conclusions. It has long suited other member states to caricature our insularity and our narrowness of vision since our main message—budgetary rigour and a fairer budget burden—were respectively electorally unpopular and financially onerous to them. It has been politically convenient for them to explain to their public opinion that HMG were to blame for the medicine they knew we would all have to swallow sooner or later…Copenhagen showed the reality that all member states will if necessary defend their national interest at the expense of the Community interest. The other three large member states, in particular, were just as ready to forget their rhetoric—their Genscher/Colombo declarations and the like—when sectoral and Community interests conflicted…That said, I do endorse Julian's view that we should be able to extract more influence and a better image out of the fact that we now have a stronger economy, the best contacts with the two super powers and the most experienced and effective Head of Government in the Community. Viewed from the continental angle, our problem is that we are more effective in blocking other peoples' ideas than in putting forward ideas of our own…There is a market for ideas…the more we can generate positive suggestions the less we will find ourselves reacting defensively to other peoples'.

Hannay was to comment in somewhat similar vein at the end of the German presidency in July 1988. Before then, in February, when agreement was reached at the special summit in Brussels on agricultural reform, the German paper *General Anzeiger* had commented: "The Council cleared the way for the gradual transformation of the Community from a league of independent states to a genuine federation. The necessary checking of agricultural spending, which had so long eluded the Community, was achieved only thanks to the strong will of the British Prime Minister and her Dutch allies." And thanks to the fact that the Germans, in the Presidency, were keen to broker a deal and the responsibilities of the Presidency made German public opinion more tolerant of them doing so. Hannay wrote:

The key lesson for us to learn from the German Presidency was what it showed about the Federal Republic's attitude towards the Community and its future development. That the Community remains for them an absolutely vital focus of their national policy cannot really be in doubt. That they are willing to pay a price for its success in terms of money spent and national positions forgone is also not in doubt. When the largest member state takes that attitude, things move in Brussels. And we need to be aware of it.

The reunification of Germany, less than two years later, was gradually to change German perspectives on Europe. In the short term, it was to prove a divisive issue between Germany and the UK, since Mrs Thatcher's fear of German resurgence, and her desire to prevent reunification, influenced her judgement of the inevitability of events.

But the most divisive issues for the British government vis-a-vis her partners, and internally, were the ERM and EMU. To which must be added Margaret Thatcher's own growing, and related, hostility to the ambitions of the European Commission and some of the member states.

At the June European Council in Hanover in 1988, a committee had been set up, chaired by Commission President Jacques Delors, to report on the next steps to EMU. Coming on the back of Margaret Thatcher's agreement to the references to EMU in the SEA, Chancellor Nigel Lawson felt that she had made a huge and damaging concession. The ERM was an agreement between sovereign governments. EMU was a step towards a federal Europe.

The Foreign Office had been keen for some time that the Prime Minister should make a major speech on European policy. An invitation to speak at the College of Europe in Bruges in September provided the occasion. Before moving from the European Communities Department of the Foreign Office to be Geoffrey Howe's Private Secretary that summer, I had written the first draft of the speech. As eventually delivered, I could recognise a few "and"s and "the"s from my original version.

It was in response to a combination of developments (the drive to EMU, the proactive approach of the Commission to acquiring new competences via the single market agenda, and the Prime Minister's fury at Delors's address to the Trades Union Congress (TUC) in September 1988) that the Bruges speech acquired its now renowned characteristics. The paradox of Delors's address to the TUC is that, while the Prime Minister saw it as intolerable political interference, it played a large part in converting the British trade union movement to a more positive view of the EC.

Drafts of the Bruges speech, rewritten by Charles Powell, were batted backwards and forwards across Downing Street in early September with John Kerr, the FCO Undersecretary responsible for the EC, being the principal broker of the changes he and Geoffrey Howe wanted to see. John Kerr had been on secondment from the Foreign Office to the Treasury, where he had been chosen, against competition from the Treasury's finest, to be Principal Private Secretary to the Chancellor, Geoffrey Howe. Kerr subsequently returned to the Foreign Office and, in 1987, after a posting in the British Embassy in

Washington, had taken over from Robin Renwick. John Kerr was subsequently Permanent Representative to the EU, British Ambassador to Washington, and Permanent Undersecretary at the Foreign Office. He was to play a crucial role in the decision to join the ERM and in the negotiation of the Maastricht Treaty. In 1988, he was my boss, as Hannay and Renwick had been before him. David Hannay always signalled his punch, which did not mean that his opponent had time to get out of its way. John Kerr favoured the stiletto. He was one of the subtlest and most successful negotiators the Foreign Office has had.

Commenting on an early Number 10 version of the draft speech, Geoffrey Howe, who always strove for accuracy of fact and judgement, wrote that while he agreed that a stronger Europe did not mean the creation of a new European superstate, it had and would require the sacrifice of political independence and the rights of national parliaments. That was inherent in the treaties.

Two weeks later, Kerr felt able to report to Howe that the latest edition of the Bruges speech had bought some 80% of the suggestions which the FCO had put forward and which had been "strongly supported" by Nigel Lawson, the Chancellor, and Lord Young, the Secretary of State for Trade and Industry. "It thus looks", Kerr commented, "as if our damage limitation exercise is heading for success. While it isn't going to pick up many ticks across the Channel, I do not think the Bruges speech is now likely to cause trouble with Community partners." Sending a copy of the revised draft to the FCO Permanent Undersecretary, Patrick Wright, Kerr wrote: "To be aware that Number 10 have (largely) come to heel on this." I recall Geoffrey Howe saying of the final draft that it was 95% all right. But the text circulated by Number 10 around Whitehall as the final version was subsequently amended inside Number 10 before it was delivered.

The shocked reaction to the speech in much of Europe at the time, as well as the iconic status it has achieved among Euro-sceptics, owed much to the way it was briefed to the Press by Mrs Thatcher's spokesman, Bernard Ingham. For in many respects, it is a classic exposition of British views. Indeed, Mrs Thatcher's first guiding principle, as set out in the Bruges speech ("willing and active cooperation between independent sovereign states is the best way to build a successful European Community"), was taken, almost word for word, by Tony Blair as his defining vision when he spoke in Oxford in February 2006. Mrs Thatcher's other guiding principles were:

- Community policies must tackle present problems in a practical way, however difficult that may be.
- Community policies which encourage enterprise were needed.
- Europe should not be protectionist.

- "The European countries' role in defence" must be achieved through NATO albeit with the Europeans taking on a greater role.

Margaret Thatcher's statement that "the European Community is a practical means by which Europe can ensure the future prosperity and security of its people in a world in which there are many other powerful nations and groups of nations" was wholly unexceptional. Even on EMU, she was relatively emollient, avoiding saying that there should be no European Central Bank (ECB) and suggesting only that there should be a series of practical steps and that "when those have been achieved and sustained over a period of time, we shall be in a better position to judge the next move".

The speech *is* remarkable for two passages. In the first, the Prime Minister said that: "the European Community belongs to *all* its members." Europe, she said, was more than the EC: "The European Community is *one* manifestation of that European identity, but it is not the only one. We must never forget that east of the Iron Curtain, people who once enjoyed a full share of European culture, freedom and identity have been cut off from their roots. We shall always look on Warsaw, Prague and Budapest as great European cities." Today, that statement would be a commonplace. Then, it was almost radical. It was seen, not so much as a call for a Europe whole and free, as an invitation to a Europe that would be wider, not deeper. I do not believe that a diluted Europe was the primary motivation of Margaret Thatcher's or, subsequently of John Major's, championing of enlargement. She was a passionate believer in democratic freedoms and, in that respect, had a clearer and more prescient vision than many of her partners in the EC at the time.

The second remarkable passage in the speech was the one which owed something to the extreme irritation provoked by Delors's decision to address the TUC two weeks earlier:

working more closely together does not require power to be centralised in Brussels or decisions to be taken by an appointed bureaucracy. Indeed, it is ironic that just when those countries such as the Soviet Union, which have tried to run everything from the centre, are learning that success depends on dispersing power and decisions away from the centre, there are some in the Community who seem to want to move in the opposite direction.

That was followed by the sentence which was spun to the British press and which was perceived by Britain's partners as the most hostile: "We have not successfully rolled back the frontiers of the state in Britain, only to see them re-imposed at a European level with a European super-state exercising a new dominance from Brussels."

This was dynamite. Explosive shockwaves resonated around the EC. Even Margaret Thatcher had not previously made such a frontal assault on the EC's institutions, the Commission in particular. Part of it was a correct perception that Delors was ambitious to put more power in the hands of the Commission, making it the executive of the EC, answerable to the EP. Part of it was the realisation that something was moving on the issues of economic and political union that went beyond the ambitions of the Commission, which resonated with most other member states but with which she had no sympathy, indeed the reverse.

EMU and the European superstate were to become increasingly associated in people's minds. In some respects, the scene was set by the argument over membership of the ERM. At this stage at least, the Prime Minister was much more concerned about the ERM than about EMU.

It was an ingenious suggestion from Sir Michael Butler that had persuaded Jim Callaghan, Denis Healey, and David Owen that Britain should, in 1978, join the European Monetary System, but not its ERM. When the Conservatives came back to power in 1979, their policy was that Britain would join the ERM when the time was right.

The case for the ERM was put by Nigel Lawson to the House of Commons in the single sentence: "It would reduce exchange rate fluctuations and we would be able to use it to assist us in our anti-inflationary policy." Mrs Thatcher, advised by her economic guru, Alan Walters, was convinced that the scheme was damagingly unworkable. I am not economically qualified to judge, though I still doubt whether the cycle of "stop–go" economic policies that bedevilled the British economy from the 1950s to the late 1980s could have been broken without the discipline that the ERM imposed. Certainly, Britain's economic performance compared with France, Germany, and even Italy had suffered because, unlike them, we were unable to pursue a consistent economic course for more than a year or two at a time.

The arguments that led to the eventual decision to join the ERM, and the near resignations of Nigel Lawson and Geoffrey Howe in the summer of 1989, are fully rehearsed, from their different perspectives, in the auto-biographies of all three protagonists. I was the person who, reclining on a sunny bank at my son's prep school sports day, made the phone call to the Prime Minister's private secretary, Charles Powell, that set up what became a fateful meeting between Howe and Lawson, on the one hand, and the Prime Minister on the other, the following day, the morning of Sunday, 25 June. On that day, Thatcher and Howe were due to leave for the European Council in Madrid. At that Sunday morning meeting, Lawson and Howe threatened their resignations if the Prime Minister did not set a date for Britain to join the ERM.

The atmosphere in the British delegation throughout the Madrid European Council was electrically awful. On the Royal Air Force (RAF) plane to Madrid, the Prime Minister sat conspicuously in a compartment curtained off from the one in which Howe and his team were seated. Whenever the curtain threatened to open with the movement of the plane, one of Mrs Thatcher's staff would get up and conspicuously close it again. On the way in to Madrid from the airport, I shared a car with Charles Powell. My nervous efforts at normal conversation were greeted with monosyllabic responses. The whole delegation had been invited to dinner at the house of our ambassador in Madrid, Nicholas Gordon-Lennox. The Prime Minister did not show. She took supper in her room in the hotel.

I suspect it was then that she determined to get her revenge on Geoffrey Howe at the next ministerial reshuffle, despite the assurance he had from the Chief Whip that he would not be moved. But, at Madrid in the meantime, she did what she had been asked to do, not to the letter since she did not name a date, but she did set out the circumstances in which Britain would join the ERM. Howe and Lawson were satisfied.

In her autobiography, Margaret Thatcher attributes to Foreign Office political arguments Geoffrey Howe's insistence on joining the ERM. But the arguments which convinced him and Lawson, and later John Major, were economic, more than political. The principal suppliers of data and technical advice to the Foreign Secretary were the Foreign Office economists and their arguments were based on an assessment of the performance of the currencies within the ERM and the stability that membership would provide to the pound. Of course, Foreign Office officials saw political advantage in Britain not being isolated from the rest of her partners, but to argue that the Foreign Office would have made a political case not backed by economic rigour is to misunderstand both the direction given to it by Howe, the ex-Chancellor, and later Major, the ex-Chief Secretary, as well as its own instincts.

Had the Foreign Office simply wanted to be on good terms with our partners, it would not have pursued with the determination it did, first the quest for a fair budget settlement, secondly the measures necessary to achieve a single market, and thirdly the campaign for agricultural reform. It was the Foreign Office, just as much as the Treasury, which pressed the case for CAP reform and which sought to persuade a reluctant Ministry of Agriculture that the only way to secure real reform was to pursue a mechanism which would not continue to reward large farmers. Since Britain had, and has, a predominance of large farmers, the Ministry of Agriculture was always reluctant to accept this argument because of the domestic political cost. In the end, even Margaret Thatcher was not prepared to be as tough on CAP reform, for the same domestic reasons, as the Foreign Office would have liked. The argument persists to this day. The Conservative Party, Geoffrey Howe used to say, was the NFU at prayer.

The Madrid European Council also set in train the work that was to lead, eighteen months later, to the IGC on EMU and to the Maastricht Treaty. The conclusions of that Council were in turn based on the work of a committee, chaired by Jacques Delors, which had been established by EC Heads of Government at their summit in Hanover in June 1988.

As I began writing this book, my former boss, and former Foreign Secretary, David Owen told me in characteristically robust terms that I had a duty to explain why, when Lawson had warned Mrs Thatcher of the dangers of EMU, she apparently ignored his advice and allowed herself to be inveigled into it.

I do not *know* the answer to that question. I believe that the main reason is that until, from her perspective, it was too late, she did not take the threat seriously enough. She told the Press at Hanover that there had been a lot of pressure to set up a group whose task would be to study the setting up of a ECB. But that had not been agreed. Instead, there would be a group, consisting primarily of central bank governors, which would look at "further concrete steps towards the progressive realisation of Economic and Monetary Union". She added that journalists might recognise those words because they came from the preamble of the SEA, which had been approved by all national parliaments in the EC. She hoped the study would indeed focus on practicable and realisable steps.

Two days later, in the House of Commons, Opposition leader Neil Kinnock accused her of selling the pass on EMU at Hanover. She repeated what she had said to the Press and added:

We have taken part of the Single European Act, which went through the House and which said that we would make progressive steps to the realisation of monetary union. Monetary union would be the first step, but progress towards it would not necessarily involve a single currency or a European central bank. Long before monetary union could be achieved many other countries would have to come up to the level that we have reached. We have freedom of capital movement; most of them do not. We have no exchange control; most of them have. We have a variety of currencies in our bank reserves; most of them have not. We also deal in the ECU; most of them do not. So they have a long way before they go nearly as far as we have gone on these matters.

Further evidence of Mrs Thatcher's thinking is shown by comments she made at press conferences in Luxembourg in September and Italy in October 1988, following bilateral meetings with their Prime Ministers. The meeting in Luxembourg, with Jacques Santer, took place just after the Bruges speech and Mrs Thatcher was asked about the contrast between her approach of cooperation between independent countries and the desire of others for something more. She replied: "They tend to talk in generalities, you know, very frequently in European speeches. You must have heard it many times. And I think I am one of the few people who says: 'What do you mean by that? What do you mean by European Union? What do you mean by monetary union?'"

In Rome, a month later, it was put to her that her Bruges speech had provoked strong reactions in the press in Belgium and the Netherlands, and that Chancellor Kohl had accused her of excessive pragmatism and of insular individualism because of her hostility to complete European integration. She responded that the Bruges speech had needed to be made. She believed that the greatest cooperation would be obtained by free cooperation between sovereign states. She then cited the Head of the Bundesbank, Karl Otto Poehl, who had said that the creation of an ECB would require economic policy to be surrendered to that bank and she added: "I neither want nor expect ever to see such a bank in my lifetime nor, if I am twanging a harp, for quite a long time afterwards. What I suspect they will attempt to do is to call something a European Central Bank."

I think, in other words, that with memories of her experience of her text on POCO being purloined by Kohl and Mitterrand and turned into something which was no different in substance but was given the grandiose title of a Treaty on European Political Union, she thought that the threat of a genuine monetary union was not real and that what she was dealing with was a political problem that could be managed. She had, moreover, been assured by Kohl at an earlier stage that he was opposed to EMU. That certainly chimes with my own recollection of the prevailing mood in Whitehall at the time. In any case, the ERM was a more central British preoccupation; and the momentous events starting to unfold in Eastern Europe a much more compelling issue for British foreign policy overall.

One factor common to both the handling of EC issues and the collapse of the Berlin wall and German reunification was that of a Prime Minister who had been in office for ten years. She knew her own mind. She had been vindicated by experience on many issues. None of her ministers had been in their jobs as long as she had. She was less inclined to consult them, as the memoirs of Lawson and Howe testify. She had her own group around her. Foreign Office officials were rarely summoned to Number 10 to advise her or to take part in meetings, a contrast with her early days. Few such advisers went with her on overseas journeys. The Africa expert from the Foreign Office who, exceptionally, did go with her on a tour of Africa in 1988 had little contact with her throughout the trip.

Before the 1979 General Election, I had been working for two years as Assistant Private Secretary to David Owen, the youngest British Foreign Secretary since Anthony Eden. I dealt mostly with African matters, mainly what was then Rhodesia. It was one of the best periods of my Diplomatic Service career, not least because Dr Owen was the most exciting and original-minded of the many politicians for whom I worked. I stayed on after the 1979 General Election to work for Owen's successor, Peter Carrington, and went with him, and therefore with Margaret Thatcher, to the Commonwealth Heads of Government meeting in Lusaka which took place only three months after the election. I remember her from those days as formidable but friendly and approachable. I was the most junior member of the Carrington Private Office but I was invited to join her, Carrington, and one other for supper on the plane to Lusaka. In Lusaka, she would wander into the delegation office in the evening and, glass of whisky in hand, take part in vigorous argument. I recall being rather shocked by her views about the aid programme to Africa, which were almost identical to those my mother, on a Christmas visit a few years earlier, had expressed loudly and embarrassingly from the audience, while I was giving a lecture on the subject at a university in Addis Ababa.

Ten years later, as Private Secretary to Foreign Secretary John Major, I was with Mrs Thatcher at the Commonwealth Heads of Government meeting in Kuala Lumpur. During the six days of the meeting, John Major did see Mrs Thatcher every day. The rest of the delegation had not a single meeting with her. She got herself into confrontational isolation over South Africa; Major was not permitted to meet the African National Congress (ANC) delegation, though Nelson Mandela was to be released from jail three months later, and she quibbled over Major's attempts to deal tactfully with the issue of South African sanctions. She returned to Britain, made a combative statement about the Commonwealth meeting to the House of Commons and, by that evening, had appointed John Major as Chancellor of the Exchequer following Nigel Lawson's resignation.

The contrast between 1979 and 1989 was striking. From being combative and opinionated, but fresh, open, and approachable, she had gone to being tired, closed, and cut-off from outside advice. She made a number of mistakes in her last months in office, of which the Poll Tax at home and her misreading of German reunification were the most prominent. But she also misread, admittedly not alone, the seriousness of intent of our partners over EMU and their determination to turn what she saw as airy declarations into hard policy.

Europe was the proximate cause of Margaret Thatcher's enforced resignation in that her attitude towards Europe precipitated Geoffrey Howe's resignation from the government in 1990. But her policy on Europe was just one symptom of behaviour that alienated a section of the Conservative Party and made MPs start to fear for the safety of their parliamentary seats. As with quite a lot of other issues, her attitude to EMU was a mixture of the pragmatic, ideological, and emotional. The judgements she came to make about EMU and Britain's national interest were not very different from those made subsequently by John Major or Tony Blair. But, perhaps because she woke up late to the impending reality of EMU, she was inclined to see it as a more cataclysmic event than did her advisers, from John Major downwards, and to see Britain's role as being to prevent it rather than to find a way around it. Even so, despite everything that she has said since she left office, the evidence does not point compellingly to her rejection of the pragmatic course that John Major was to advocate and eventually, as her successor, to follow.

Pragmatism was not the hallmark of Margaret Thatcher's last months in office. In retrospect, her downfall seems to have the doom-laden inevitability of Greek tragedy. But even a few weeks, let alone months, before it happened, most people in Westminster and Whitehall thought that she would, as she had promised, go on and on. For those engaged in European policy, the task of persuading her, first to accept British membership of the ERM and then to find a way of protecting British interests in the face of an impending monetary union, were the pressing, frustrating causes of dissent between both the Treasury and Foreign Office on one side and Number 10 Downing Street on the other.

5

The Euro and Union: Thatcher, Major, and *Fin de Régime*

Nigel Lawson viewed Margaret Thatcher's agreement, at the Hanover European Council in June 1988, to a committee to examine EMU as a disaster. Lawson was always in favour of Britain's membership of the ERM and against EMU. This became the received wisdom at the Treasury. Lawson hoped that something might be recouped through the Prime Minister's personal representative in the group, the Governor of the Bank of England, Robin Leigh-Pemberton. Nigel Lawson and the Prime Minister also hoped that the Chairman of the Bundesbank (Karl Otto Poehl) would somehow prevent Chancellor Kohl from going ahead with EMU. Both central bank governors failed to live up to those expectations.

Sir Michael Butler, by now working for Hambros in the City, set up a City Committee to monitor the whole issue of EMU and the work of the Delors Committee, and himself began to advocate a scheme which was the brainchild of a brilliant young economist at Midland Montagu, Paul Richards. Known as the hard ECU, the idea was to replicate the rigour of the Deutschmark (DM) in a common currency, rather than a single currency. The common currency, based on the hard ECU, would bring the benefits of a robust, shared currency without the problems of a single interest rate, or the implications of a single currency for national sovereignty. The common currency could evolve into a single currency over time, but it would not inevitably do so. The British government did not immediately warm to the scheme, with some long-term costs, as will be seen.

Michael Butler recalls that it was difficult to get Mrs Thatcher to take a close interest in the work of the Delors Committee. I think she hoped it would come to nothing and there was virtually no input from Number 10 into the contribution that Leigh-Pemberton was making to the Delors group. Nor did Leigh-Pemberton seek guidance, perhaps out of understandable apprehension of the Prime Minister's ferocity, perhaps because this was not his own area of expertise. So it was not surprising that, early in 1989, Delors came up with a fully fledged plan for EMU comprising three stages, beginning with all member states joining the ERM in the first stage, a transitional Stage Two, and a Stage Three in which exchange rates would be fixed and the ECB would be set up. This was not at all what the British government wanted.

Thanks in part to some fast footwork by Nigel Lawson, the European Council in Madrid that summer, which saw Britain commit herself more whole-heartedly and precisely to ERM membership than ever before, avoided specific endorsement of the Delors report or of anything beyond Stage One. Stage Three (a single currency) was then, and subsequently, unacceptable to the British government. The Prime Minister was very clear in her understanding of what had, and had not, been agreed. She told the Press at Madrid that further work had indeed been agreed on what might eventually follow Stage One

but we have reached no conclusion about that. We have accepted the Delors report as a good basis for further work but not the only basis. It will be possible to bring in other ideas and other approaches for the progressive realisation of EMU but let me emphasise that there is absolutely nothing automatic about going beyond Stage One. That is for future decision.

On her return to London, the Prime Minister said much the same in her statement to the House. And she went further: "Stages Two and Three of the Delors report", she said, "would involve a massive transfer of sovereignty which I do not believe would be acceptable to this House. They would also mean, in practice, the creation of a federal Europe."

In truth, the conclusions of the Madrid summit were both exactly as Mrs Thatcher described them and much more. The words safeguarded the British position, but the sense of the conclusions was that a new stage on the road to EMU, that is, a single currency, had been embarked on. Why did we not see it clearly? In part because we still did not altogether believe it would happen; in part because our own preoccupation had been with the ERM and there was a feeling, among relieved ministers and officials, of "sufficient unto the day" when the Prime Minister was persuaded to commit herself definitively to ERM membership on a measurable time scale. The world was also entering a new, dramatic, and dizzying phase with the collapse of the Soviet Union, the fall of the Berlin wall at the end of 1989, and German unification in 1990.

The collapse of the Soviet Union, the reunification of Germany, and the independence of the countries of Eastern and Central Europe were our principal preoccupations in the Foreign Office. The reunification of Germany had been predicted by a few in the Foreign Office but not by many in the years immediately before it actually happened. It was part of the received wisdom that a divided Germany was, on the whole, a good thing for Britain, because a united Germany would be too powerful for her own good, and certainly for ours. Britain was not alone in that view and Mrs Thatcher's own misreading of what was happening was in part due to the gypsy's warnings she had from President Mitterrand on the subject. When the European Council met in Strasbourg in December 1989, under French chairmanship, a central preoccupation was the (unsuccessful) desire of the British delegation to prevent a decision being taken to call an IGC on EMU in the following year. We were equally preoccupied with fending off attempts by Delors and the French government to skew action on the single market in the direction of social action that Britain saw as damaging to jobs and growth. But I vividly recall that the most memorable part of the two days was a private meeting between Mrs Thatcher and President Mitterrand in which he told her that the subject matter of the European Council was not what mattered. What mattered was the fact that Germany, a country which had never known its own borders, was on the march again.

Mrs Thatcher drew from this the belief that German reunification was not inevitable. But, if she had hopes of French support for her own subsequent public hostility to reunification, those hopes were disappointed. Mitterrand was too canny and controlled to get himself out on a limb. And he had other fish to fry, notably his strong wish to see progress towards EMU—all the more so as German reunification, and the prospect of German economic dominance, became more imminent. The Prime Minister's hostility to the idea of German reunification undermined her judgement of what was actually happening. Some of the experts who were present at her famous Chequers meeting to discuss Germany did not recognise what they had said as portrayed in the Number 10 record which found its way into the Press and which suggested that they agreed with Mrs Thatcher's view of the dangers of a reunited Germany. Although the Foreign Office had not foreseen reunification, it did accurately read the signs that it was inevitable and that Britain's good relationship with Germany depended on managing the process in a constructive way. Their advice which I, as the Private Secretary to the Foreign Secretary, regularly conveyed in writing to Number 10 was largely discounted by the Prime Minister until reunification had become a fact of life. By then, President Bush had publicly referred to Mrs Thatcher, in doorstep remarks outside 10 Downing Street, as "his anchor to windward", a comment that was correctly interpreted by the media as meaning that the United States did not regard her views on what was happening in Germany as being part of the mainstream.

In so far as the consequences of Mrs Thatcher's misjudgement could be remedied, it was Douglas Hurd, as Foreign Secretary, who did so. In his three months as Foreign Secretary from the summer of 1989, John Major had had a relationship of trust with the Prime Minister. For a start, he had the great merit in her eyes of not being Geoffrey Howe. I had been one of those who were with Geoffrey Howe in the painful few hours in which, in a state of grief and shock at his removal from the post of Foreign Secretary, he had to make the most difficult decision of his political career: whether to stay in the government or resign. Had he left at that point, it would have been relatively easy for him to have been portrayed as having gone off in a huff. The Prime Minister had, after all, offered him the job of Home Secretary, one of the top three ministerial posts in the government, and while he turned it down, he did accept the post of Leader of the House of Commons with the title of Deputy Prime Minister. His eventual resignation in the following year, and the devastating resignation speech that precipitated Mrs Thatcher's downfall, were in part provoked by the humiliatingly unforgivable way with which she treated him. Her view of him (and indeed of the Foreign Office) was poisoned by those close to her who heard her grumblings and prejudices, magnified them, and played them back. As she became more unreasonable, her irritation increased with Geoffrey Howe who, more than any other politician I worked for, believed in the power of reason and exercised it with patience, humour, and humanity. Those were not qualities which appealed to the Prime Minister in her latter period.

Mrs Thatcher felt that John Major was her political soul mate. She had, after all, plucked him from the relative obscurity of Chief Secretary to the Treasury. The job of Chief Secretary is, or was then, one of the least known but most powerful jobs in the Cabinet. The Chief Secretary was the man who negotiated the budget of each government department. The secret of success was for him to know the details of those departmental budgets better than the Secretary of State himself or herself. I had witnessed John Major, in that role, negotiating with Geoffrey Howe over the Foreign Office budget. Howe, the consummate master of detail with years of experience as a commercial barrister, deployed charm, humour, and a dead bat. John Major deployed charm, humour, and a deft stiletto. As Chief Secretary, John Major, while out of the limelight, was closer to Mrs Thatcher than most realised. When offered the job of Foreign Secretary, he demurred, arguing that Douglas Hurd was the obvious candidate. But the Prime Minister replied that it was too late: John Major's appointment was the centrepiece of the reshuffle. Prime ministers like to spring surprises. Jim Callaghan had done something similar in 1976 when he appointed David Owen, aged 38 and not even a Cabinet Minister, to the job of Foreign Secretary.

John Major felt from the outset that the Foreign Office had made a tactical error in not always exposing to the Prime Minister's forensic mind all aspects of the issues on which it needed her decision. She, he thought, had felt that the Foreign Office was attempting to pull the wool over her eyes and that we would do better to expose the downsides of a particular course of action more frankly than we had and trust her to agree with us if she could see that what we were advocating was the lesser of two evils. During his brief tenure, the tactic worked well. Equally, when the Prime Minister, via her Private Secretary Charles Powell, ticked him off for something he had said about the Falkland Islands in a speech at the UN in New York, Major stood by his words and refused to be browbeaten.

Douglas Hurd was not a natural Thatcherite by background, temperament, or persuasion. He was the last Home Secretary of recent times, apart from Jack Straw, who believed that penal policy should be about rehabilitation as well as punishment. John Major, who had been instrumental in persuading Mrs Thatcher to appoint Hurd as his successor at the Foreign Office, told her that Hurd was someone she could trust. And so it proved.

Douglas Hurd was incisive and decisive. The Foreign Office were inclined to see him as "one of us" because he had started his career in the Diplomatic Service. But he had long since left the bureaucrat behind and become a skilled politician. I wrote to a friend and colleague early on that Hurd "is not a bureaucrat made good but someone who sees himself as having changed from a caterpillar to a butterfly". In the same letter, written as we in his private office were still getting to know Hurd, I said (rather patronisingly as I look back) that we seemed to be settling down well with our new boss who was

pretty impressive ... calm, very clear minded and decisive ... He has tremendous self confidence ... There is quite a lot of humour there and, at the end, an obviously deep-felt conviction about Europe. One of the attractive things about him is that he obviously does have convictions—liberal ones. He has already shifted our disastrous Cambodia policy. He will stand up to the PM on Europe though whether he will be able to do more than "put a fig leaf over Mrs Thatcher's more virile parts", as one newspaper put it, remains to be seen. At meetings, he allows people their say but chairs briskly and authoritatively.

It was Douglas Hurd who rescued British policy on German reunification. He established a good relationship with Helmut Kohl. Kohl had pretty much given up on his relationship with Margaret Thatcher, but he was a Conservative politician and wanted a good relationship with the other leading Conservative government in Europe. Douglas Hurd became Kohl's main interlocutor in the British government, calling on him during visits to Bonn and being treated to Kohl's homespun but shrewd view of the world. He was also instrumental in establishing, and running, the so-called 2 + 4 process by which the implications of reunification for Russia's presence in, and eventual withdrawal from, East Germany were managed.

Late in 1989, Douglas Hurd visited East Germany and crossed through the broken, but still standing, wall into the West. The government of the German Democratic Republic (GDR) was clinging on by its fingertips. The ministers were driving around in battered Volvos having consigned their Mercedes Benz to the garage, for fear of provoking the public. We visited Leipzig and saw what the foreign minister of the Federal Republic, Hans Dietrich Genscher, had told us: that reunification had to happen because the East was collapsing. In Leipzig, public services were grinding to a halt as people voted with their feet and went west. The hospitals were running out of nurses. The buses were being driven by soldiers because there were not enough civilians left.

One of the paradoxes of reunification was the brief euphoria, followed by sullen indifference or even hostility, on the part of the people of West Germany. A few months after reunification, Kohl complained to Hurd about the unwillingness of Germans to sacrifice their standard of living to help their new compatriots: all they were interested in was their new swimming pool, as he put it. Several years later, when I was working for Tony Blair in Downing Street, I asked a German colleague, a man in his forties, how he felt about German reunification. His answer was that he "didn't give a ****".

Few in Europe overtly shared Mrs Thatcher's opposition to German reunification. But the implications were undoubtedly feared in France. In June 1990, Jacques Attali, who had been Mitterrand's closest adviser and was about to take up his post as President of the new European Bank for Reconstruction and Development (EBRD), told the Chancellor of the Exchequer, John Major, that the motivating force behind French pressure for EMU was fear of a united Germany which would be dominant in Europe. In particular, said Attali, the fear was that Germany would acquire nuclear weapons within five to ten years. Attali could imagine a world in which the G7 had been replaced by a G4 consisting of the United States, USSR, Japan, and Germany. The French were willing to surrender part of their sovereignty, in the form of EMU, to prevent the German nightmare which he had conjured up. One of the decisive differences between John Major's premiership and that of Margaret Thatcher was to be that, unlike her, he did not share that nightmare. It was not so much a difference of analysis as of instinct: she, whose teenage years had been marked by war; he, who had no memories of the war into whose final years he had been born.

Even those who did not fear a politically dangerous united Germany expected Germany to be economically dominant and that that would have inevitable political consequences. At a meeting with the Chairman of the US Federal Reserve, Alan Greenspan, a week before John Major's meeting with Attali, Margaret Thatcher speculated that the effect of unification would be to increase Germany's economic strength and give her a dominant position in Europe. She expected the Federal Republic to make a success of the East German economy within about seven years.

Greenspan was less certain and, as it turned out, closer to the mark. He thought it would take longer. The good news in Eastern Europe was behind us. The outlook in East Germany was more fragile than we realised. During the cold war, we had consistently overestimated East Germany's standard of living. East Germany ought to go into a major recession as a result of the merger of the two economies, with some 30% of its firms going bankrupt. Mrs Thatcher commented that Gorbachev had told her that the East German Prime Minister, De Maziere, wanted to slow down unification: no doubt East German ministers enjoyed office and wanted to hold onto it for longer. Greenspan was sceptical: once your monetary system and your fiscal system had been taken over, what sovereignty did you have left?

Greenspan and the Prime Minister went on to talk about the ERM. Mrs Thatcher said that she did not believe in fixed exchange rates. They had to be able to float in order to accommodate differences in economic conditions. She had always been suspicious of the ERM and expected it to snap. The only real argument for going in was to borrow Germany's spine in order to reinforce downward pressure on inflation. But there were some signs that the spine was no longer as strong as it was. Other member states wanted an ECB because they saw it as an opportunity to substitute political considerations for spine. If we were to have a spine, she would prefer it to be an objective standard like the gold standard or a commodity basket.

Greenspan said that he had always been in favour of the gold standard as an international spine. He had been surprised that the ERM had held together. The main reason for its success was the decision of the French and Italian governments to drive down their inflation by holding fixed rates against the DM. The effect had been to make the ERM operate like a gold standard within the European Community ... If we [the British] were prepared to use the ERM like a quasi-gold standard, as the French and Italians had done, we could probably join at an appropriate time. The Prime Minister responded that if one could find an objective standard to act as a spine, there was no need for a ECB or a single currency. It was only necessary that all ERM members should adopt sound economic and monetary policies.

It was not only EMU, in the sense of a decision on a single currency, which was at stake. There was pressure for direct progress towards political union as well. The case for political union was set out in classic terms by Jacques Delors in a speech to the EP in January 1990. It was a speech that chimed perfectly with German sentiments and not at all with British ones. Delors said:

The Twelve have no choice but to remain a focal point, a rock of stability, for the rest of the continent. This is not a role they have inherited from history but one they have earned by constant effort and resolve as the pioneers of European integration. Strengthening the Community means pressing ahead with implementing the Single Act. But this alone is no longer enough. The pace of change is gathering momentum and we must try to keep up. Only a strong, self-confident Community, a Community which is united and determined, can truly hope to control that process. We need to progress on two fronts: Economic and Monetary Union and political coopera-tion...Basically, there are three questions to be answered: what kind of executive? What form of democratic control? What powers? The Commission should be turned into a proper executive answerable for its actions...The executive would, of course, have to be answerable to the democratic institutions of the future federation...And it would be appointed democratically, the other two authorities deciding initially on a mechanism for appointing its President, who should have a genuine power to influence the choice of the other members...To deal with the democratic deficit, Parliament [i.e. the European Parliament] would have to be given more powers. However, a better arrangement for democratic control will have to be devised: there must be an acknowl-edgement that the two reflections of the popular will—the European Parliament and national parliaments—are in partnership...Subsidiarity must be the watchword underlying any scheme for allocating responsibilities between the Community, the national authorities and the regional authorities. And in the federation of the Twelve—which will be unusual in that the central authority's primary role will be to provide impetus—the principle of subsidiarity will have to act as a constant counterweight to the natural tendency of the centre to accumulate power.

In stressing the principle of subsidiarity, Delors probably thought he was making a nod in the direction of the British government. But it was the notion of the Commission as executive which most aroused the deep suspicion of British ministers and officials. This smacked of an embryo government, answerable to the EP, with the Council of Ministers relegated to a relatively minor role. In this context, subsidiarity was seen by the British, not as the EC doing only those things which the member states could not do better by themselves. Subsidiarity was seen to mean that the member states would have the power to do only those things which had been left to them by Brussels. That was a complete reversal of the traditional British concept of the EC in which member states freely decided to share some of their sovereignty and in which the primary driver of European strategy was the European Council, representing national governments.

In truth, neither view encapsulated the complicated reality of a unique set of institutional arrangements in which the Commission had the sole right of legislative initiative, the EP competed for the available democratic space with national parliaments, and Community legal competence was bound to increase because, as laws were adopted at European level, the subject matter they covered became a matter of Community competence. The logic of this process was impeccable, but it meant that a minister taking a decision on a piece of legislation governing the slaughter of seals, for example, had to realise that the decision was not just about protecting seals from the cruelty of an inhumane cull. By adopting the legislation, an EC competence was being acknowledged in the field of animal welfare. This in turn meant that all governments were faced with the difficult choice between inaction on a matter they cared deeply about, and action which achieved what they wanted but at a price: the future limitation of their own freedom to make national policy and to legislate in the area concerned.

This was particularly tough for Britain because the sharing of sovereignty was an especially neuralgic issue. The difficulty was compounded by the enthusiasm with which Delors and his officials inside the Commission sought to increase the areas of EC competence and, with it, their own powers. When Douglas Hurd, a lifelong European, made his celebrated speech in which, picking up the words of the famous law lord, Lord Denning, he called for an end to European regulation which seeped into "the nooks and crannies of daily life", he was giving mild vent to a huge British frustration.

In institutional terms, this argument was to be played out, through the Maastricht and Amsterdam treaties and the Constitutional Treaty, in the efforts of successive British governments to have subsidiarity defined in the sense they wanted. In practice, the issue has not been resolved, though it is less of an irritant than it was. Delors was responding, not only to his own ambitious agenda, but also to the mood of the majority in the Community at the time. His present-day successor, like Jacques Santer and Romano Prodi before him, has his foot off the institutional and legislative accelerator, reflecting the very different political atmosphere of the early twenty-first century.

But in 1990, political union, as well as economic union, was firmly on the cards. It was something for which member states such as Italy, Belgium, and the Netherlands had long pressed, as had the Commission. It had always appealed to Germany. The French were prepared to go along with it as the price that had to be paid for keeping a firm hold on Germany. If EMU was in part the price Germany had to pay for France's acquiescence in German reunification, then political union was in turn the price extracted by Germany for the loss of the DM. In German eyes, the politics had to follow the economics: there had to be some means whereby what Mrs Thatcher termed the spine provided by the DM was replicated in a single currency. In part, that spine was to be the rules of the system itself; in part, political arrangements which would enable the disciplined member states such as Germany to exercise authority over those (meaning Italy, though that was rarely said out loud) who would otherwise finance their profligacy at the expense of others' thrift.

It had been agreed in Strasbourg in December 1989 that an IGC on EMU would be held, starting late in 1990. As the European Council to be held in Dublin in April 1990 approached, Kohl and Mitterrand made it clear they wanted a second IGC to cover political union and that the Council should set work in train. This was unwelcome to the British government, though not wholly unexpected. In February, the Prime Minister had told the Foreign Secretary that we should start work right away on formulating some proposals of our own for institutional reform. It was not necessarily the case, in her view, that institutions which had been appropriate for the Community in its earlier years were right for a larger and more mature Community. We also had to consider the possibility that developments in Eastern Europe would lead to further significant enlargement of the Community over the next ten years. Our broad objective should be a looser Community, or at least to prevent any further centralisation. It was probably not feasible to curtail the powers of the EP, but we should have no truck with any extension of them. There was a strong case for reforming the role and powers of the Commission. Its main function should be to service and respond to the needs of the Council of Ministers rather than act as a body with an independent power of initiative. This was no longer necessary. The Foreign Secretary responded that it would be difficult to secure broad support for such ideas, although some of our misgivings about the Commission were more widely shared. But he agreed they were at least a good negotiating ploy.

A few weeks later, the Prime Minister tried out some of her ideas on Michel Rocard, the French Prime Minister. She had had a bit of a dress rehearsal two weeks beforehand at a dinner with French industrialists at the French embassy in London where, according to the record, she "did not spare" the assembled company on the shift which had taken place in the relative power of France and Germany as a result of reunification. She expressed her "fierce preoccupation" with Germany's future economic strength and the implications of it for the rest of Europe. The industrialists "parroted the French government's refrain" that the best way to cope with reunification was to bind Germany into the EC, above all by pressing ahead with EMU. Mrs Thatcher was "pretty blunt" in putting the opposite point of view. Her Private Secretary recorded that the Prime Minister "drew the cheerful conclusion at the end of the discussion that there was not a free trader among them".

The discussion with Rocard was more measured but equally robust. The Prime Minister told Rocard that Germany would come to dominate Europe unless Britain and France made certain that she did not. The smaller countries would rapidly be brought to heel unless they could see that Britain and France were ready to stand up to Germany. She did not accept that the right way to prevent Germany's dominance was to integrate Germany more closely. That would just give Germany Europe on a plate.

Rocard disagreed. One had, he argued, to find a framework in Europe which would allow unification to take place without causing instability. France did not share Britain's pessimism that increasing Europe's unity would make the Community into a German preserve.

Picking up on the thoughts she had expressed to Douglas Hurd in February, the Prime Minister said that Europe would need to rethink its strategy in just the same way as NATO. At the time of the Community's founding, there had been a need for strong central direction, and that was why the Commission had been given powers of initiative. But now the trend everywhere was away from centralism and bureaucracy and she could not accept that the Community should choose this moment to move in the opposite direction. The Community would be stronger by not merging the sovereignty of its individual members. A federal Europe went right against the grain. Moreover, we needed to remain open to the countries of Eastern Europe.

As the European Council approached at the end of April, the Prime Minister told Leon Brittan, one of the two British members of the European Commission, that she was not very pleased that Mitterrand and Kohl had chosen this moment to propose a second IGC to discuss political union. The Community had more than enough on its plate and this was not the time to be fiddling once again with institutional reform. But we would, she said, have some ideas of our own to propose.

A week later, the Prime Minister had a meeting with David Hannay, the UK Permanent Representative to the EC. She told him that she had been giving some thought to the line she would take at the European Council on the subject of political union. She would start by saying that the phrase political union caused far more difficulty than good, at least in the UK. The first task of the European Council should be therefore to try to relieve anxieties and suspicion about it. We should define what political union did not mean: giving up separate national heads of state; abolishing or substantially reducing the powers of national parliaments. They would continue in existence and retain the right to pronounce on all major decisions in the Community. Nor did political union mean altering the Council of Ministers' role as the main decision-making body in the Community, or any attempt to accrue more powers to the central institutions at the expense of national governments and parliaments. The principle of subsidiarity should be embedded in the Treaty of Rome to secure this. Union must not mean weakening in any way the role of NATO in assuring our defence. Within these broad parameters, we would be happy to see closer cooperation, particularly on issues which stretched across national borders, both within the Community and beyond it. Once we were all clear on what we were not considering, it would be much easier to make progress.

In her autobiography, Margaret Thatcher described how she set out the views which she had outlined to Hannay at the Dublin European Council a few days later. "I hoped", she wrote, "that I had at least put down a marker against the sort of proposals which were likely to come before us at some future stage." She also gave top marks for the political ambiguity of the Italian Prime Minister, Signor Andreotti, "who suggested that although we must set up an IGC on political union, it would be dangerous to try to reach a clear-cut definition of what political union was". In that sense, not much had changed since the Franco-German sleight of hand of 1985 in taking Britain's text on POCO and issuing it, under their own moniker, as a treaty of political union.

In her autobiography, Margaret Thatcher says that she made her statement at the European Council tongue in cheek, knowing that it was the very antithesis of what those in favour of European union had in mind. But it did not seem like that at the time. Britain's experience over the SEA had been that, when challenged on what treaty changes they actually wanted, most member states had a very short wish list. I believe the Prime Minister's statement was partly designed for domestic consumption, and it was heavily briefed by her spokesman, Bernard Ingham. But it was also intended to try to constrain the terms of future debate and to set the parameters of what would and would not be acceptable to Britain. So what was undoubtedly a bit of a rearguard action vis-a-vis our partners was also a way of putting the British people on notice that some steps towards something called European union were inevitable.

Nor did Britain think the game was up on EMU. Jacques Chirac, former French Prime Minister and leader of the Gaullist right in France, had given an interview to *Les Echos* early in April in which he came down in favour of a common currency and against a single currency. A single currency, said Chirac, would lead to transfers of sovereignty which would be completely excessive—at the very moment when France must keep in her hands the essential instruments which allowed her to control her destiny.

It was at this point that Sir Michael Butler returned to the charge, writing to the Prime Minister at the end of April 1990 to say that he fully understood why she had political difficulties with the idea of a single currency. He saw no reason why Mrs Thatcher should not continue to say that the British people would wish to retain the pound. But he did not believe that she would be able to win acceptance for an evolutionary Stage Two (the intermediate stage between the ERM and fixed exchange rates) without agreeing that, in the last stage of EMU, there would either be permanently fixed parities or a single currency. Butler went on to advocate his idea of the hard ECU as something that would preserve the "spine" which the DM had hitherto provided and which would be evolutionary in approach. In other words, there would be no inevitability about the common currency provided by the hard ECU becoming a single currency, or of Britain being forced to sign up to an unpalatable goal. Equally, from the point of view of other member states, it would be open to them to envisage the common currency evolving into a single currency in due course.

It took some time for Michael Butler's idea to take root. It was only in the aftermath of the decision taken in December 1989 to hold an IGC on EMU that officials were finally, and belatedly, authorised to set up an inter-departmental committee (chaired by Nigel Wicks at the Treasury) to consider our negotiating position. The Bank of England was represented, as was the Foreign Office (John Kerr) and UK Representation (David Hannay). Within the Treasury, the options were seen as being: (i) No full EMU. But if the UK blocked an EMU Treaty, the remaining eleven member states would go ahead with a separate treaty on their own. (ii) A treaty which defined full EMU but in terms which the UK did not accept. That would require the UK to insert a reservation clause. (iii) The UK might sign the treaty but ensure that no member state could move to Stage Three without the agreement of the UK. That was thought to be un-negotiable. (iv) Sign the treaty but with a specific provision that the UK would never move to full EMU. That too would not be negotiable and it would deprive the UK of the discretion to opt into full EMU should we eventually wish to do so. (v) Sign the treaty but retain discretion for Britain to opt into full EMU should we eventually wish to do so. This had the disadvantage that it would commit Britain to the definition of EMU contained in the treaty.

Right at the outset, the members of the Wicks Committee agreed that the UK could not hope to stop EMU by refusing to move to Stage Three (full monetary union). They also agreed that it would anyway be against British interests to exclude ourselves because we would then be excluded from all future decision-making on the issue. David Hannay proposed what was then called the "fire-break" approach, effectively an option whereby the other member governments would be allowed to go ahead while Britain would have the right to opt in, if it so chose, at a later stage. By this means, we could keep our own freedom of decision while also staying in the decision-making game.

By the spring of 1990, this approach had been endorsed by the Chancellor, John Major, and the Foreign Secretary, Douglas Hurd. But, when it was put to the Prime Minister on the aeroplane going to the Dublin European Council in 1990, she rejected it.

Within the British government, others realised that the game had moved on. The Chancellor of the Exchequer, John Major, told the Prime Minister at the end of April 1990 that recent discussions among finance ministers in the Economic and Financial Affairs (ECOFIN) Council had left him in no doubt that all other EC governments would be ready, at the IGC, to agree treaty amendments which would adopt the definition of EMU in Stage Three of the Delors report, that is, a single currency with fixed exchange rates and an

ECB. He warned that the goal of EMU as described by Delors was shared by all except the UK. Our evolutionary approach had been brushed aside and was regarded by others as overtaken by events. If we were not prepared to engage in discussion on the basis that the goal should be full EMU as defined by Delors, there was a significant risk that the other eleven member states would go ahead and sign a separate treaty. This would be politically damaging. We should do our utmost to preserve a Community of Twelve and our influence in it. In short, we needed to devise a policy which would maximise our influence in the negotiations and minimise our commitment to the outcome.

There was no disagreement between the Prime Minister and her Chancellor that the substance of EMU as defined by Delors (single currency, fixed exchange rates, and an ECB) was not acceptable. The House of Commons had made its opposition very plain. They agreed, therefore, that we had to find a way to delay and frustrate the ultimate objective of EMU as defined by Delors without placing ourselves outside the game. On this occasion, when the Chancellor again put forward the idea that Britain should negotiate for a mechanism to allow her to opt into a single currency if she so chose, the Prime Minister did not absolutely rule it out. But she felt that it had the disadvantage of requiring UK to sign up to the objective of full EMU. This was objectionable on practical grounds. The Prime Minister did not believe that the government could subscribe to a treaty amendment containing the full Delors definition of EMU. So, in the first instance, further work should be done to develop our idea of a European Monetary Fund which could be put forward as the most that it was necessary for the EC to agree on for now. Further thought was needed on how to finesse attempts to impose a binding commitment to full EMU in a treaty amendment.

The Prime Minister told the House of Commons on 3 May that, in the next few weeks, the government would present some ideas to make the European institutions work better on the basis of sovereign states working through national parliaments and through the Council of Ministers. Britain would also be introducing some different ideas for EMU, "bearing in mind the approach of the House, which is not to move in anything like the Delors direction, as that would rob us of our powers".

Work on the twin tracks (political and economic) continued. Early in June, Number 10 commissioned work on diversionary tactics, including the idea of a North Atlantic free-trade area. This idea is sometimes now presented by those who dislike the EU as an alternative home for Britain outside the EU. But as conceived at the time, the idea was to link the EC and North America in a free-trade zone and avoid a world divided into three protectionist blocs (the EC, Japan, and the United States). These ideas got short shrift at the time from the Treasury and from Nick Ridley, the Secretary of State for Trade and Industry. Paradoxically, a variant of the idea was put forward by Leon Brittan in the late 1990s when he was the European Commissioner responsible for trade. But the United States never paid more than polite lip service to the idea and it was anathema to the French because a transatlantic free-trade area would have required dramatic action on reform of agricultural subsidies, albeit on both sides of the Atlantic. For the French, too, the idea of giving such public primacy to a privileged relationship with the United States was politically problematic, especially coming from a British member of the Commission. A sector-by-sector, low-key approach to removing the remaining barriers to transatlantic trade has therefore been the preferred, more practicable, approach.

In June, the Prime Minister also discussed EMU with Leon Brittan. Leon Brittan was clear that agreement would be reached in the IGC on EMU which had been agreed at the EC summit in Strasbourg in December 1989 and which was due to start, under the Italian presidency, before the end of 1990. That agreement would involve a single currency and an ECB with control over monetary policy. The Prime Minister said that the government would not be able to accept that, and that refusal would be backed by Parliament. She believed that membership of the ERM would provide all that was necessary in terms of monetary policy so long as the DM continued to provide a spine. If other member states were very keen to have a new institution, we could propose a European Monetary Fund to manage a hard ECU. We were not prepared to hand over control of monetary policy to an ECB whose directors would be swayed by political considerations.

Leon Brittan repeated that there would be agreement on a central bank with control over interest rates and a common currency. If the other eleven member states went ahead without us, the implications would be very difficult for the UK. The Prime Minister reiterated that Britain could not sign up to permanently fixed exchange rates. They made no sense. The poorer member states would be able to accept EMU only if they were to receive massive subventions from the richer ones. The Germans would accept a central bank only if it was fully independent, while the French would have it only if it was subject to political control. The Prime Minister would prefer to see the adoption of an objective standard for currencies on the lines of the gold standard. If the EC went the way described by Leon Brittan, it would become too close knit, inward-looking, and shackled by bureaucracy.

Leon Brittan said that the only way by which we might be able to avoid isolation was by having an opting-in mechanism. This would allow member states to postpone a decision to join the final stage of EMU until the end of Stage Two. It would be a great pity if the UK remained outside EMU. The only way to control German hegemony in Europe would be to ally ourselves with the French and Italians. But we could do that only if we were inside EMU. It was an historic choice.

The main focus was now on the British plan for a hard ECU, to be launched in a speech by the Chancellor of the Exchequer, in July 1990. At a Foreign Office meeting, chaired by Douglas Hurd, it was agreed that the message that should be got across was that the Chancellor's plan was not a device to get round a British difficulty over the Delors proposals, but a plan which was better from the point of view of other member states than the Delors big bang approach. The hard ECU could lead to a single currency without the convulsions implicit in Delors. The Foreign Secretary told the meeting that John Major had said to him that we ourselves would use the hard ECU but that it would not supersede our own currency. In a subsequent instruction to Foreign Office officials, Hurd said that the Foreign Office and its overseas posts should present themselves as rowing in behind the Chancellor of the Exchequer and the Prime Minister in support of a solid plan, "well baked by experts, not a diplomatic soufflé".

John Major made his speech. The main features of the plan were provision for the general circulation of ECU bank notes and a European Monetary Fund and the creation of the hard ECU. The hard ECU would be a new international currency in its own right, no longer a basket of twelve national currencies. It would co-exist beside the existing currencies of the twelve member states. The new ECU would never be devalued. It would always be at least as strong as any other Community currency.

In his autobiography, John Major says that the proposal came to nothing, badly undercut by the Prime Minister telling the House of Commons that the proposal "does not mean that we approve of a single currency", whereas, of course, the one potential attraction of the scheme for Britain's partners was that it could lead to a single currency over time. It is doubtful that she thought that she would thereby undermine the proposal for the hard ECU. Her remarks were more likely a reflex drawn from private conversation with sceptical companions. She probably also saw the hard ECU as a useful political gambit, more than as an economic instrument in which she believed.

John Kerr, then the Foreign Office Undersecretary responsible for the EC, was similarly concerned at a statement made by Douglas Hurd in a television interview in July when Hurd said that he did not see "how in 1991 we could possibly accept a single currency or a single central bank". Kerr pointed out that if we moved on from denouncing Delors Stage Three to denouncing *any* Stage Three, as the Prime Minister sometimes did on grounds of monetary sovereignty, we damaged the market for the Major proposals. The final paragraph of John Major's speech had, Kerr argued, said in effect that the monetary sovereignty arguments would not matter, and a monetary union would be acceptable, if it emerged as a result of market forces, and in the very long term. "Those in other countries", Kerr concluded, "who rightly find this interesting would be the more interested if they knew that the relevant words in the speech were written by the Prime Minister herself." At this distance, it is impossible to verify whether the words were actually written by Margaret Thatcher. But she clearly approved of the speech.

The hard ECU proposal was, from its inception, a brilliant idea whose day was already past. That much was evident to all of us at the time. Had it been introduced during the discussions leading to the Delors report in 1989, which was Sir Michael Butler's original hope and intention, it might have stood a chance of at least being weighed as a viable option. But it came a year too late, in circumstances where the Delors plan was already accepted by the rest of the EC member states and where Britain's hostility, or at least that of the Prime Minister, to a single currency was all too evident.

In July, Margaret Thatcher told the German Foreign Minister, Hans Dietrich Genscher, that the economic situation in Spain and Italy (whose high inflation rates were pulling in a tremendous inflow of money attracted by their high interest rates) demonstrated the difficulties of trying to fix exchange rates while disparities between the economies of member states remained so great. In these conditions, a single currency could be maintained only by massive transfers between the better-off and the less-well-off member states. The UK, the Prime Minister said, would join the ERM in order to use the DM as a sort of gold standard which would help bear down on inflation. But the whole purpose of this would be lost if there was a single currency and an ECB whose governing board would be composed of representatives of countries who would not agree that the sole objective was to maintain the value of the currency. There was no case for going further than the existing ERM for the foreseeable future. Europe needed time to adjust to the full consequences of the single market and did not need the fresh turmoil which would be caused by the attempt to move to a single currency. Britain had agreed to go further than she herself considered strictly necessary or wise by proposing a common currency and a European Monetary Fund. But this was as far as we could agree to go. There was also, Mrs Thatcher added, the aspect of sovereignty: a national currency and national decision-making on economic and monetary policy were among the most substantial attributes of sovereignty in the modern world.

In his memoirs, Douglas Hurd recalls a Spanish minister saying of the hard ECU: "Right idea. Wrong country." John Major had said something similar privately within the Treasury even before he made his speech on the subject. In August, the UK Representation to the EC in Brussels reported that, at a meeting of the European Commission, a number of Commissioners had intervened to insist that the momentum towards EMU must be kept up at all costs. No one had objected openly to the need to give proper consideration to the British hard ECU proposals but there was a tendency to write the UK out of the negotiations.

David Hannay had by then left Brussels, to be replaced as UK Permanent Representative by John Kerr. In July, Jacques Delors gave Hannay a farewell lunch at which Hannay, making clear that he was speaking without the authority of the British government, described to Delors in some detail how a scheme to allow Britain to opt into EMU if/when she decided to do so might work. Delors, who did not want a separate treaty of eleven member states, excluding Britain, agreed that this was indeed the only way to square the circle.

Later, in August, the European Commission produced a paper on EMU which described it as "the natural complement of the full realisation of the Single European Act". To be fully effective, the paper said, EMU required a qualitative institutional jump which would bring the Community considerably nearer to a political union. This meant ensuring that the Community was not saddled with a system "which is bogged down in sterile tensions between Community institutions or in irresolvable conflicts between Community decisions and national wishes, between the European Parliament and national parliaments". Among the objectives which the Community had to achieve "only those which are fully associated with the success of EMU are mentioned here: the single market by the end of 1992, reinforced cooperation in the fields of research and technology, infrastructure networks, the social dimension and, even more directly, economic and social cohesion". The paper acknowledged that there need not be a single economic policy in the same way as for monetary policy, but it saw increasing Community involvement in "competition policy, commercial policy, research and technological development, EU-wide infrastructure, labour markets, the environment and some aspects of taxation". Unanimity, it noted, "could prove to be a major obstacle".

A decade and a half later, the paper does not seem either as radical or as ambitious as it did then. At the time, it reinforced fears in London that the EMU project was just what Mrs Thatcher had told Genscher she feared it would be: a vehicle by which the sovereignty which defined the independence of nation states would be undermined.

The Italian presidency called a special meeting of the European Council in Rome for the end of October to launch the process of treaty change on EMU and political union. Some ten days beforehand, Mrs Thatcher held a preparatory meeting with the Italian Prime Minister, Signor Andreotti. With Kuwait under occupation following Saddam Husseins's invasion in August, with an important General Agreement on Tariffs and Trade (GATT) negotiation reaching a crucial phase and with the future of the Soviet Union a critical preoccupation for Western governments, the Prime Minister told Andreotti that she wanted the European Council to focus on those issues and not on IGCs. She did not herself have much time for the term political union, she told Andreotti. In practice, we were talking about how to make the Community's institutions work much better than they did now. Britain was not prepared to accept steps towards a federal Europe. Nor did we want detailed and binding rules which would make it more difficult for the countries of Eastern Europe to join the Community eventually. It was becoming increasingly clear that it was not possible to progress much further with EMU until there was a greater convergence of economies. She believed that Britain's membership of the ERM, which had happened two weeks earlier, would contribute to that. It was ironic that, at a time when countries in Eastern Europe were moving towards greater democracy, many governments in Western Europe seemed ready to hand over powers to non-elected bodies.

Andreotti responded that the ECB would be democratically answerable: to the EP. The objective must be to fix a united Germany firmly in the EC. Mrs Thatcher disagreed. The best way to balance a united Germany was by preserving the traditional nation states of Europe. A Community on the lines sought by Signor Andreotti would be under the thumb of the dominant nation. Andreotti replied that the Community must evolve and not just be a free-trade area. He had thought we had gone beyond Gaullism.

When the European Council met on 27 October, the Prime Minister had a private lunch with President Mitterrand at the British Embassy residence in Rome at which she reverted to her central preoccupation with the GATT negotiations, taking the President to task for the failure to agree an EC stance for the negotiations. The root of the problem, she said, lay in divergent interests within the EC. Perhaps we needed to look more fundamentally at the CAP. It was after all a pretty strange system which fixed agricultural prices in order to provide a living for inefficient farmers. Perhaps we should move to a system of income support. The Prime Minister said she intended to raise the issue at the beginning of the European Council and to insist that the European Council direct the Community to table proposals for reform of the CAP in the GATT within the next few days. Failure would be a signal to the world that Europe was protectionist. President Mitterrand interjected that of course the EC was protectionist: that was the point of it.

The Prime Minister and Mitterrand went on to talk about political union. The Commission, she said, seemed to be perpetually trying to extend its powers. M. Delors's recent interview in which he had talked of the Commission as the Executive of Europe, the EP as the legislature, and the Council of Ministers as the Senate was proof positive of his ambitions.

President Mitterrand appeared to agree with her. The EP was just as bad in wanting too much power. It was not a real parliament and few people had any idea what they were doing when they elected it. On these institutional issues, he very largely saw eye-to-eye with the Prime Minister: power must rest with the Council of Ministers.

In her autobiography, Margaret Thatcher expresses some scepticism about Mitterrand's willingness to come good at meetings of the Council on what he had said in private. And so it was to prove. The Italian presidency saw her determination to raise the GATT negotiations as a ploy to distract attention from the central business of launching the next phase of EMU and political union and effectively blocked discussion. The Prime Minister found herself faced with German pressure for a start date for Stage Two of EMU and with language in the conclusions on political union which she felt she could not accept. For the first and only time in the history of the EC, the conclusions were issued with one member state, the UK, dissenting via a separate footnote.

The following week, when she reported on the Summit to the House of Commons, Margaret Thatcher told the Leader of the Opposition, Neil Kinnock: "The President of the Commission, M. Delors, said at a press conference the other day that he wanted the European Parliament to be the democratic body of the Community, he wanted the Commission to be the executive and he wanted the Council of Ministers to be the Senate. No, no, no". Later, in answer to Dr David Owen, who had described the Rome summit as "a bounce which led only one way—to a single federal United States of Europe", the Prime Minister said, "What is being proposed—EMU—is the back door to a federal Europe, which we totally and utterly reject." That "no, no no" during the exchanges in the House, and the Prime Minister's determination to rule out any possibility of a single currency, proved the last straw for Geoffrey Howe and precipitated his resignation and the challenge to Margaret Thatcher's leadership of the Conservative Party that followed.

I was present at the Commission on Security and Cooperation in Europe (CSCE) summit in Paris during which the result of the first leadership ballot was announced. Mrs Thatcher had not won by a big enough margin to avoid a second ballot. It was a sign that her support was ebbing. I recall the late-night phone conversations between Douglas Hurd, lodged in the British Embassy residence in Paris, and John Major, recovering from a wisdom tooth operation in Huntingdon, the brave way Margaret Thatcher went on with the show, putting on her glad rags and going off to a gala evening at Versailles, and the anxious huddle between her and Hurd and her immediate advisers on the RAF plane home. I cannot say that I knew then that it was all over, though the atmosphere was as tense and gloomy as it could be.

Within a few days, it *was* all over; John Major was Prime Minister, Britain was on the verge of war in the Gulf, and my forthcoming posting as number two in the embassy in Paris was cancelled. On the morning after John Major confirmed that he wanted Douglas Hurd to stay as Foreign Secretary, Hurd went across to Number 10 to discuss with the new Prime Minister who from the Foreign Office should succeed Charles Powell. Powell had served for seven years as Mrs Thatcher's Foreign Office Private Secretary. Not surprisingly, he wanted to see in the new Prime Minister and then move on. Hurd took with him a list of names. I was not on it. Hurd returned shortly afterwards saying: "It should have occurred to me. Of course, he wants you." I was less surprised. I had been John Major's Private Secretary for his three months as Foreign Secretary. We had got on well. I was at least the devil he knew.

6

At the Heart of Europe: The Road to the Maastricht Treaty

John Major, though born during World War II, was a child of post-war Britain. Unlike Margaret Thatcher, who was already a teenager when war was declared, he had no visceral fear of what a reunited Germany might do. He did not share her sense of a Britain which, almost alone, embodied the values which he held dear. His famous speech in which he quoted Orwell to evoke the charm of long shadows on village cricket pitches, old ladies cycling to church, and warm beer in the village pub was an attempt to summon up British, or at least English, values which were being lost. It was not in any sense Britain versus the Continental Europeans.

I recall discussing with John Major our respective attitudes towards the EC. We had both voted in the 1975 referendum in favour of staying in, had both felt doubts and frustrations as we had lived through the struggle over the British rebate and the undoubted power-hunger of the European Commission under Jacques Delors. But we both believed that making a success of our membership of the EC was the only sensible option open to Britain.

That was the conviction which John Major brought with him to Number 10. John Major was warm, clever, and, in private, devastatingly funny. He felt strongly about certain issues but he was cool and methodical in taking decisions. The view that he dithered over decisions is far removed from my experience. Where he hesitated, it was almost invariably because of the problems of party management, notably over Europe, which beset him after 1992. He knew he had no majority for European legislation and that his opponents were ever ready to vote down the government on European matters.

His first act as Foreign Secretary in 1989 was to recommend to Cabinet that Britain refuse to sell Hawk trainer aircraft to Saddam Hussein's Iraq. Today, it may seem inconceivable that such a sale could even be contemplated. Then, it had been the subject of intense and unresolved debate for months beforehand, not least because of the value of the order for British manufacturing.

As his Private Secretary, I watched John Major in action as Prime Minister over Iraq, the coup d'état in Russia against President Gorbachev, the end of apartheid South Africa, Bosnia, as well as during, and after, Black Wednesday when Britain withdrew from the ERM. In each case, he was calm, rational, and methodical. As Foreign Secretary, he was acutely aware of his inexperience after the wisdom and long tenure of Geoffrey Howe. But his judgement, reached after weighing systematically the pros and cons of a course of action, was good. And, by the time I joined him in Number 10 in March 1991, he had led the country successfully in a military campaign to liberate Kuwait. His knowledge and confidence were of a different order than when I had first met him.

John Major did not wish, as the new Prime Minister, to change the fundamentals of Britain's EU policy. But he was by temperament someone who believed that, as he put it, "you catch more flies with honey than with vinegar". The substance of policy would remain robust but the approach and presentation would change. This Prime Minister would want to be active in making a success of Britain's EU membership. He did not share his predecessor's view that all the problems of his lifetime had come from Continental Europe. He wanted to rebuild the relationship with Helmut Kohl which had had to be kept alive by Douglas Hurd in the last part of Margaret Thatcher's premiership.

The new Prime Minister was acutely aware that a change of tone, though not the same as a change of substance, could be interpreted as such—for good by our partners but possibly for ill by those in the Conservative Party who saw Margaret Thatcher as the defender of the true European faith. Tristan Garel-Jones, the Minister for Europe, minuted to Douglas Hurd in the first days of the new Prime Minister's tenure: "We have to handle the PM's relationship with Europe with great care, particularly in the early days. Clearly, an invitation to Delors [which Foreign Office officials had recommended] would be helpful but if it is too early it could well be taken as a signal by the party which the PM may not want to send at this early stage." This shows just how acute the sensitivity was. In any event, Douglas Hurd commented: "They do not get on."

That, in my recollection, is true. John Major had been wary of sitting down to a one-on-one meeting with Delors during his few weeks as Foreign Secretary until he was sure that he would be a match for Delors's formidable command of every European topic. That attitude changed over time. But part of the secret of Delors's success as President of the Commission was that, at a European Council, he knew more than anyone else in the room, something that was not true of his successors, Santer and Prodi. Meetings between Delors and Geoffrey Howe had been amicable, wine-lubricated dinners, at the home of the UK Permanent Representative on the eve of meetings of the General Affairs Council. That friendly tradition grew up again under Douglas Hurd. Meetings between Delors and John Major were more of a sparring match.

A good, if somewhat extreme, example was a meeting between the two men during the British presidency of the EU in 1992. We were in the middle of a GATT negotiation in which the (Irish) European Commissioner for Agriculture (Ray McSharry) had put forward some quite far-reaching proposals for agricultural reform, proposals which had British support but which were being rather disreputably undermined by Delors, who appeared to be taking more of a French national, than an independent Commission, view. Delors was in London and the Prime Minister invited Delors to call on him. John Major was not a man ever to forgo the courtesies. I have been at meetings where, not until John Major's victims noticed the blood at their feet, did they realise that the stiletto had been deftly and fatally inserted. On this occasion, Delors can have been in no doubt of the Prime Minister's meaning because Major made it plain that we, as presidency, felt that he, as Commission President, was not doing what he should to back McSharry in seeking an agreement with the United States on agricultural subsidies which then, as now, were the key to success in the entire GATT round. When he had listened to John Major's strictures, Delors said huffily and portentously: "If the President of the Council does not have confidence in the President of the European Commission, then I shall resign." Having lit this particular blue touch paper, Delors sat back. John Major smiled sweetly and said: "If that is how you feel, then so be it." At which point, Delors rather rapidly withdrew the resignation and the meeting came to a swift conclusion. At the European Council that December, held in Holyrood House, the Queen's palace in Edinburgh, John Major was particularly pleased when he could allocate as Delors's office the room in which Mary Queen of Scots' lover, Rizzio, had been murdered—with a stiletto as I recall.

Two months after the Rome European Council that had precipitated Margaret Thatcher's departure, the new Prime Minister was back in Rome for another meeting of the European Council. In October, the Italian presidency had achieved a breakthrough in setting the agenda for, and launching, the IGC on EMU. They wanted to achieve something similar on political union at the December meeting including agreement in principle on co-decision for the EP; greater powers for the EP over the EC budget; bringing the Western EU (WEU)—whose Article 5 defence guarantee had preceded that in the NATO Treaty—into the auspices of the European Treaty; and a few other ideas not particularly palatable to the UK. Rather than take the Italians head on, Major focused instead on getting a menu for the IGC which would include British ideas for reform as well. He told the Press at the end of it: "We have a menu for the IGC. Our favourite dishes are on that menu. So are others' favourite dishes. But the Community has not yet determined what orders to place." He went on to say that, during the various bilateral discussions he had held during the Council, "I was able to say something about Britain's general approach to the Community. And that approach is that we have a very positive attitude and intend to be wholeheartedly engaged in the enterprise of building, shaping and developing Europe." Asked what he meant by his stress on a liberal Europe, he said: "Essentially, we mean two things: a Europe that is open for trade, a free market Europe and a tolerant Europe."

The substance was not essentially different from that of his predecessor, but Major had calculated that there was no point in trying to keep off the agenda of the forthcoming IGC things that others would press for but to insist instead that options, including for objectives which Britain espoused, were kept open. And the style was more conciliatory. In a letter to a Conservative backbencher a few days later, Major wrote:

I believe that Britain's destiny does lie in the European Community. But it must be a Community that remains true to the ideals of its founders: open and free. That is why we have been in the forefront of the campaign to complete the Single Market programme which will benefit all European citizens by liberalising their economies, and why we have persistently, and successfully, argued for reform of the CAP.

The impending war with Iraq to liberate Kuwait was a much greater pre-occupation than Europe. The way the war was handled by the United States President, George Bush, and by the coalition put together under UN Security Council authority, of which Britain was a prominent member, represented the high point of the hopes that gripped the Western world following the collapse of the Soviet Union and the emancipation of Central Europe. This "new world order" was not the naïve belief that henceforth the lion would lie down with the lamb but a hope and determination that the end of the cold war would create a commonality of interest between what had been contending super-powers and conflicting ideological systems. The first Gulf War was the first and most successful example of the policy in action. It succeeded not least because the coalition acted under the authority of the UN Security Council and, therefore, with complete legitimacy. It succeeded too because at no time did Bush or Major contemplate exceeding that legal authority by invading and conquering Iraq. Had they done so, the American President and British Prime Minister would have entered the war under international law and ended up breaking that law. That apart, the coalition would have broken up. Far from being a mistake, I believe that on grounds both of law and practical feasibility it was the right decision to take. Certainly, the war established John Major in the trust and esteem of the British people.

One aspect of European, and British government, policy in the context of Iraq is worth recalling. In the aftermath of the first Gulf War, at the end of March 1991, the plight of the Kurds fleeing from the wrath of Saddam Hussein became a tragedy enacted out each day on British television screens. John Major determined to do something about it and the plan for safe havens for the Kurds, under international protection, was devised. In early April, there was an EU summit in Luxembourg and John Major decided to launch the plan there and to seek EU support for it. At the time, I was in daily touch with the US National Security Adviser, Brent Scowcroft. I suggested to John Major that I should telephone him and tell him what was in the Prime Minister's mind. But John Major instructed me not to. I was to wait until the European Council had given the idea its backing and use that to help bring the Americans on board.

Before the meeting of the European Council began, Major secured the backing of Kohl and Mitterrand and, when the meeting convened, the others rowed in behind. It was on that basis that I then telephoned Scowcroft: to try to get the Americans on board for a European policy initiated by a British Prime Minister. It took some anxious days, two telephone calls from Major to President Bush, and the pressure of public opinion in America, roused by the sight of the suffering Kurds on their television screens, to get the Americans on board. But it was one of very few occasions on which a British Prime Minister has acted as a bridge *from* Europe *to* the United States.

Europe's internal preoccupations were not forgotten. When, in February 1991, the government published one of its regular six-monthly reports to Parliament on "Developments in the European Community", the document contained for the first time ever a foreword by the Prime Minister. "It is in the interests of the United Kingdom to build the future of Europe and to do so with enthusiasm", wrote John Major. But he also affirmed that: "being a good European does not mean accepting every proposal from the Community ... We shall resist protectionism. We shall discourage impractical dreams. We shall urge our partners to concentrate on practical and positive steps: completing the Single Market, reforming the CAP, making Europe's industry competitive, widening opportunity for Europe's citizens and giving Europe a stronger voice in the world."

All of that could have been taken straight from the Margaret Thatcher song book. John Major also set out the principles that would govern his approach to the impending IGC on political union:

- the need to balance a strong Community with respect for national institutions;
- building the Community on the basis of individual freedom and opportunity;
- making the EC more efficient by playing by the rules, by better monitoring of compliance by the Commission and the EP and by tougher powers for the ECJ;

- making the EC more democratic and accountable, principally through full involvement by national parliaments;
- enhancing Europe's role in the world.

These principles, too, were firmly rooted in traditional British attitudes. Indeed, many of them had been set out in *Europe—the Future* seven years previously.

Not for the first time, EMU and political union were running in tandem. Whether Margaret Thatcher, had she stayed, would have accepted the advice of the Chancellor and the lawyers that Britain could not prevent the other eleven member states from making their own treaty on EMU and that Britain should, therefore, focus on being neither excluded from, nor committed to, EMU is unanswerable. Her autobiography suggests that she thought John Major had gone too far. The evidence of the discussion between the two of them while she was Prime Minister and he was her Chancellor suggests that, while she did not like the idea of any treaty which required Britain to sign up to the Delors definition of EMU, even with a specific British opt-out, she had not said her last word on the subject. John Major found that trying to tie down Margaret Thatcher over EMU was like trying to catch butter. She knew the realities of European politics but they were painful to her and she did not wish to face them. It was easier to try to delay commitments she probably knew she would one day have to make. As it happened, she was forced from office and John Major made those commitments.

Certainly, that issue of EMU was a central preoccupation for the new government. The Chancellor of the Exchequer, Norman Lamont, minuted the Prime Minister in January 1991: "Although our partners would be reluctant to move ahead without us, I am concerned that, if we refused to countenance any move forward they would (and our legal advice is that they could) create EMU among themselves by agreeing a separate treaty of eleven." The Chancellor went on to say that the crucial issue was to secure arrangements which would provide for the possibility of the UK participating in a single monetary policy and the single currency but would also unambiguously make it a necessary condition for Britain's participation that the British government and Parliament should make such a choice. He recommended that the government should say publicly that it hoped and expected that the IGC would be able to reach an agreement acceptable both to HMG and its Community partners. Its acceptability to all participants, including Britain, could, however, "only be judged at a much later stage of the negotiations".

John Major's main preoccupation, then and later, was with the economic viability of EMU. He was particularly concerned about the lack of economic convergence and told one visitor to Downing Street that he did not see a remote prospect that there would be a sufficient economic convergence to enable a single currency to operate for several years. Britain had not completely given up on her proposal for the hard ECU. Leon Brittan, the UK's senior Commission member in Brussels, made a speech in Paris in January 1991 in which he argued that the hard ECU could be a useful stepping stone to EMU. But Brittan told a member of the British embassy staff that the politics of the idea would remain wrong so long as its proponents did not subscribe to the final objective of a single currency: advice on steering a car was more likely to be accepted if it came from someone who shared the other passengers' chosen destination.

Meeting Mitterrand in Paris in the same month, John Major told him that it would be very difficult if other governments insisted on a commitment from Britain now to move to a single currency by a fixed date. The British Parliament simply would not accept that. In his own case, his reservations were not so much about sovereignty or defence of the pound as about the credibility of trying to move to a single currency without adequate economic convergence. The difficulties which were being experienced within the ERM showed the problems which could arise from trying to fix exchange rates without sufficient economic convergence.

Mitterrand responded that he had begun a close scrutiny of the British proposals and it seemed that they were not so far removed from French ideas as was originally thought. Major responded that the advantage of focusing on Stage Two rather than going all out for Stage Three was that if the intermediate phase succeeded in bringing about convergence, then the political, economic, and presentational difficulties of moving beyond it would become easier. There had been a perception that Britain was trying to block the whole process of EMU. Mitterrand replied that other EC countries had indeed thought that Britain was determined not to board the train. The Prime Minister's approach was not necessarily more reassuring, only more adroit.

Was John Major as opposed to EMU as Margaret Thatcher had been and simply more deft and sinuous at expressing British views without provoking a political crisis with Britain's partners? I think he started from a different place. She disliked EMU on sovereignty and economic grounds and believed that the project was a folly that should be resisted. Major saw that, in some form, it was inevitable and he was not going to fight an unwinnable battle to prevent Britain's partners from going ahead if they were so determined. He knew that the sovereignty argument did not resonate with them; they had gone beyond that point in their own reasoning. But he also knew that, if EMU did go ahead, it would profoundly affect the British economy, even if Britain did not participate. He hoped the practical economic arguments about convergence, in which he in any case profoundly believed, would have some influence. He was not indifferent to the political arguments against EMU. He saw no political attraction to EMU. But he took a practical view of sovereignty as being a commodity to be used for national advantage, not some untouchable heirloom to be hoarded at all costs. So he could see that circumstances might arise in which Britain's economic well being required her to come to terms with an EMU. He did not expect it to happen. He did not want it to happen. But he was not going to rule out the possibility in all conceivable circumstances. This policy was caricatured in the media as weak and dithering "wait and see". It would have been better described as the sensible safeguarding of British interest. Somewhat repackaged, it has been the policy pursued ever since.

There were other issues besides EMU on Mitterrand's mind. However good Franco-German relations were, he told John Major, Germany had different goals from France. It was a pity that France and Germany had been compelled to take so many bilateral initiatives in the EC. He would like to see that extended to the UK. He was particularly interested in defence. One of the ideas which were current at the time was to bring the WEU within the EC Treaties. Britain could not accept that but did see the WEU as an instrument for enhancing Europe's defence capacity, not least because its Article 5 guarantee of help for any of its members who came under attack, similar to that of the NATO Treaty, could only be honoured, in the event of such an attack, by NATO. The WEU was therefore, for the British, a ready-made vehicle for enhancing European defence, wholly compatible with NATO and unlikely, therefore, to alienate the United States.

At their meeting in January 1991, Mitterrand said to John Major that he saw no point in wasting much time or energy on WEU if it was simply to be an appendage to NATO. In that case, NATO would be enough. But the day would come when Europe would have to defend itself and we must start to prepare for that. Paradoxically, the ambition of the United States to influence Europe seemed to grow larger as they gradually moved away from Europe. President Bush and Secretary of State Jim Baker had suddenly discovered that, with the end of East–West confrontation and the diminution of the American presence, they were losing leverage and influence. Their response was a frenzy of ideas. But the Americans could not be both less present and more present. He was very much in favour of NATO even if he occasionally satirised it. He approved of the friendship of the United States. But Europe and America were bound to grow apart and this was why he wanted to see a solid core of European defence, with independent decision-making. So he favoured a WEU which would move ahead as part of the process of political union in Europe, rather than just as an appendix to NATO.

John Major responded that Britain was edgy about giving the EC a defence role. When one looked at the attitudes towards the Gulf of some EC members, it was clear that they did not have the same strengths and resolve as France and the UK. Britain wanted to build up a European capability through WEU but under the NATO umbrella. Mitterrand said WEU should be alongside NATO with bridges between the two organisations. John Major said that that idea could be considered but we must do nothing that gave the United States any excuse for minimising its commitment to European defence. Mitterrand said that that was already happening. It was not a case of WEU being either part of NATO or 100% independent. One had to be empirical.

Mitterrand concluded by saying that he was very happy with John Major's approach to European issues and his readiness to try to resolve problems. He would like to see the approach carried through into practical progress. He was fully open to the idea of a fuller UK role in Europe. At present, there was a tendency to think in terms of the Six plus Spain. And that was an incomplete Europe. Italy was all very well, but had no tradition as a nation. Germany was a people, not a state or a nation. The only countries which had a historic experience of nationhood to match that of Britain and France were Spain and Portugal. But Britain must help to give more concrete form to ideas for Anglo-French cooperation. He knew there was no obstacle of principle on the British side but somehow the machinery never seemed to rev up. We had to change that. EMU, political union, WEU, cooperation on the next generation of nuclear arms, were all matters where we should work together. John Major said he thought this a very positive approach and would respond in similar spirit.

Whether such cooperation could have been possible then, or later under Tony Blair when it was more systematically attempted, will be discussed later. In this particular instance, while relations between Mitterrand and Major remained good, the differences of perceived interest between the two countries were too great on the two key issues of monetary union and political union, including the defence aspects. Then, as now, the British Prime Minister was also concerned to do nothing to undermine the relationship with the United States.

John Major's relationship with Helmut Kohl, like that with Mitterrand, got off to a good start and remained amicable, even when the paths of the two countries diverged within Europe, apart from a brief spell around Black Wednesday when Britain withdrew from the ERM. After a meeting between the two leaders in March, Kohl spoke generously at their joint press conference about Britain's role in liberating Kuwait. He said:

The last month has shown that there is no alternative at all to a politically strong Europe and to a very close alliance and partnership with our American friends ... You have liberated Kuwait of a brutal occupation, you have fought for international rights and you have made enormous sacrifices so that we Germans too may live in a peaceful world.

Kohl spoke of the "almost universally friendly" relationship that had developed between Major and himself: "I can only say that the personal chemistry between the two of us works excellently."

John Major responded in similar terms. Britain was playing a full part at the very centre of the EC. It was perfectly possible for the UK to maintain the very close relationship that it had with the United States even "as geography and instinct determine we should be absolutely central to the development of the European Community". John Major, already espousing the cause of the countries of Eastern and Central Europe as future members of the EC, expressed himself as adamantly opposed to a two-speed Europe, not least in the context of EMU:

I will not equivocate about this. I think that would be fatal for Europe if we were to go ahead in that fashion. I think it would be fatal because it would be extremely difficult for those countries that did not go ahead in that inner core to subsequently become part of that inner core and I also think it would make it infinitely harder for those nations whom you [a journalist] referred to as staying in the waiting room ever to be able to join in the Europe of the future. It may be attractive in building a short term goal. It seems to me to be unattractive in terms of building the wider and better Europe that I would like to see over the next twenty-five years.

There was still perhaps a hope that the other eleven member states would not go ahead with EMU on their own. Former President Valéry Giscard d'Estaing told John Major in April that he disliked what he called "this eunuch monetary policy" and favoured a common currency. EMU, in his view, was really a combination of the single market and monetary union. A single currency might come at the end of the process but it was not vital. A common currency would itself exert pressure for convergence. A common currency, rather than the Delors approach, was the most sensible way forward.

Against that was set the knowledge that the eleven, technically and legally, could reach an agreement among themselves in a self-standing treaty that would be outside the Treaty of Rome but not inevitably in contradiction to it. Moreover, politically, the determination of the others was becoming ever clearer. The British ambassador in Paris, Sir Ewen Fergusson, sent a despatch to the Foreign Office in May 1991 in which he said:

It has become axiomatic in Paris that over the medium term a united Germany threatens to evolve into a European superpower. This unease over Germany translates into an almost obsessive anxiety to contain them within reinforced European structures as quickly and thoroughly as possible ... The clearest example is their determination to press quickly ahead with EMU as a means of getting a handle on German monetary policy before their economy recovers its former vigour and lest Kohl's Europeanist policies be replaced with more assertive nationalist ones.

At about the same time, French Prime Minister Michel Rocard visited London and told John Major that Europe had set in place a precious system of social organisation. What had happened in Latin America showed how dangerous the capitalist system could be without social institutions in place. We needed, said Rocard, increasingly to bring together our separate contributions to world events and that was why France had decided to work for a federalised Europe. He had told Mrs Thatcher that there would be a Federal Europe in fifty years. Mrs Thatcher had said: "A thousand years."

EMU, European defence, and the Social Europe of which Rocard had spoken, were the main British preoccupations in the IGC. The Secretary of State for Employment, Michael Howard, warned the Prime Minister in a minute he sent him in the spring that it had become

increasingly clear that the other member states will ultimately be willing to accept extensions of competence and QMV in such critical areas as the collective and industrial rights of workers. We could not accept that without undermining our labour market, trade union and industrial relations reforms of the last twelve years and facing, within a very few years, the prospect of substantial and uncontrollable increases in employers' costs. Accordingly, my assessment remains the one which OPD [the foreign affairs sub-committee of Cabinet] accepted in December—that there would be clear disadvantages for this country in any extension of QMV in the social field.

John Major agreed that this was probably an area where "we would have to hang tough". This perception was confirmed by the UK Permanent Representative to the EU, Sir John Kerr, who warned the Prime Minister that the social area was the one where we would face, in the IGC, the biggest problems. The Prime Minister was clear that we could not accept the proposals on compulsory worker participation or on living and working conditions.

At the heart of these difficulties was the issue that had beset Britain's relationship with her partners from the start of her membership of the EC: where to fit into a Community dominated by the relationship between France and Germany. It was the practice at the time for the senior members of the British embassies in Bonn and Paris to meet once or twice a year for a discussion of the issues with which both were grappling. Such a meeting took place in Baden-Baden in May that year.

Setting the scene from the Paris perspective beforehand, Sir Ewen Fergusson wrote that the speed of German unification had come as a shock to France.

The general public reacted calmly (opinion polls continually showed majority support for German unity). But the unexpectedly rapid pace caught the political class by surprise, here as elsewhere. I need hardly refer to the meeting of minds between our Prime Minister and the French President. Mitterrand's early hopes of Soviet resistance (the Kiev meeting with Gorbachev in December 1989) were disappointed. Franco-German relations went through a decidedly tense phase in the early part of 1990 and were only rescued by the Ottawa agreement (2 + 4) and by the self-discipline which both sides impose when the strain becomes too perceptible. French officials freely voiced their concerns to us about the dangers of German militarism or pacifism (sometimes in the same breath). Journalists went overboard in predicting an immediate rebalancing of power in Western Europe (and the eclipse of France). The three questions uppermost in French minds were: could France's economy compete with that of a united Germany? What would greater Germany's assertiveness mean for France's international standing (e.g. nuclear, UN status)? Would Germany drift eastwards out of France's (and Western Europe's) loving embrace?

Fergusson continued:

Six months after unification these questions are no longer being so openly posed. There are three factors: (i) the German economy is finding it more difficult to absorb E. Germany than many had predicted; (ii) Germany is not internationally assertive. The Gulf War showed that Germany remains a second class military and political power; (iii) many Frenchmen still believe that on the Franco-German tandem, France continues to steer and Germany to pedal. But, despite the almost palpable sense of relief that unification has not immediately upset the balance of the bilateral relationship, no one in Paris seriously doubts that in the medium to long term Germany will become the dominant European (a quasi super power). Germany remains the focus of French policy towards the Community. Concern about the future direction Germany may take has resulted in France trying to tie Germany into reinforced European structures as quickly and as thoroughly as possible. It lies at the heart of French enthusiasm both for EMU and CFSP [Common Foreign and Security Policy]. Nearly thirty years after the Elysee Treaty the Franco-German relationship still appears artificial. It is a marriage of reason, not of love, even among the younger generations whom the structures of the Elysee Treaty have brought so much closer together . . . But the relationship is neither superficial nor weak . . . Nor need it mean that the relationship does not have the power to adapt to new circumstances. But the process will be difficult for France. Germany's search for post-war respectability and low profile in foreign affairs are not constants. France cannot count on continuing to play the role of the senior partner in the equation. The balance will change in France's disfavour. This is why the French government sees itself in a race against time to shape European structures which will enable France to exercise continuing, if not decisive, influence over German policies.

In its response to Fergusson's analysis, the British embassy in Bonn noted that while, for the French, the Franco-German relationship had ultimately been about managing Germany,

for the Germans the Franco-German relationship has also ultimately been about managing Germany . . . The solutions adopted for "managing" Germany are likely to be increasingly to German taste and diminishingly to French . . . The Germans take the view that to compensate for and to conceal the fact that France is no longer unchallenged top country in Europe, Paris has swung European policy virtually totally to the service of co-managing Germany. The cover story, European integration, provides a very good alibi...Germans know that their increasing weight in Europe does scare neighbours, whatever they say politely when invited to tea. The Adenauer recipe of embedding Germany and German nationalism in a greater Europe still holds good for the German leadership...To return to your "tandem" metaphor, we here think that places are being swapped. But it is not clear whether the Germans know how to do the steering...

The Bonn embassy continued:

Our position in relation to both parties is improving somewhat. The French see us a useful counterweight to Germany while the Prime Minister has been able to re-establish a normal, even-keel, relationship with the Chancellor...The Germans instinctively like frameworks and organisations. We instinctively shy away. It has yet to be revealed how much beef there is in the better atmosphere of Anglo-German relations. As compared with a year ago, a lot of substance has gone, most notably our four-power status...These days the quality of Anglo-German relations is, if not exclusively, then very largely, dependent on the quality of our cooperation over European policy. At the early stages of the NATO restructuring/European pillar debate the Germans were alongside us in our thinking about the role of the WEU and they hoped, with it, to bring about further French military rapprochement to NATO. Then CFSP hove into sight and after only brief hesitation the Germans, led by the Chancellery, marched in the direction of defence as a component without which European union would not be complete.

On EMU, the Bonn embassy advised that price stability was the nearest thing to a national creed among ordinary Germans.

This then will be one of the hardest areas from which to extract concessions from the Germans and, for this very reason, will constitute an acid test of French pulling power. The French will be wrong if they imagine they can get concessions over EMU while conceding nothing, or virtually nothing, over the European Parliament. No one here, probably including Kohl, knows quite what the Chancellor means when he links the outcome of European Political Union and EMU. It seems inherently improbable that Kohl would turn down a good EMU treaty, if this were on offer, because the European Political Union treaty fell short. But in such circumstances, [we] can imagine him insisting that there would be no further cession of sovereignty and thus no entry into Stage 3 without further negotiation leading to a further major advance in reducing the "democratic deficit".

The sense of France and Britain and Germany and Britain trying to find common ground during this period comes through very strongly from the official papers and tallies with my own recollection. John Major wanted a constructive relationship with both, but it had to be subject to the severe constraints of domestic interest and politics.

When John Major and Helmut Kohl met on 9 June 1991 at Chequers, Major told him that the British were by temperament the least European of the present Community countries. This was for reasons of history and geography, our position as an island, and the fact that we were appalling linguists. We had trailed behind in the development of European ideas. He felt strongly that the Community should develop beyond its present membership. That Austria and the European free-trade area (EFTA) countries would join seemed very likely. We should begin to frame our European policies on the basis of Poland, Hungary, and Czechoslovakia—and maybe others—joining as well. This might be a long way off but we ought not to frame our policies in a way that made it more difficult for these countries to join. John Major identified two things as being necessary to carry the British along: (i) we should move a step at a time; (ii) we must find some policies on which Britain could give a lead and not just be dragged along in the tail coat of the Community. He did not see the parliamentary handling of a treaty on political union being more or less difficult after the next General Election [due in spring of the following year at the latest] than before. He and Kohl were at one in working for a conclusion to the IGC in December.

Kohl said he understood the political constraints. The important thing was that the Prime Minister should indicate that he was for Europe. Major replied that he was for Europe, as far as he could go. There was no point in agreeing to a treaty if he could not deliver the necessary votes for it in the House of Commons.

Helmut Kohl then set out his vision of political union. He looked for parallel development in the two IGCs. The most important point was that the direction should be clear and, from the German perspective, irreversible. Sweden, Austria, and Norway were likely to join the Community by the end of the decade, perhaps Finland too. Poland would probably be the laggard but, by the end of the decade, Hungary and Czechoslovakia would be negotiating for membership. Following these accessions, there would probably be no more for a long time. This sort of progress was necessary. Germany needed it more than others. He had no illusion about a Germany of eighty million people given her history and the economic power she wielded. There was no point in being coy about it. Fears about Germany would always be an item on the agenda. The view of Germany held by Mr Ridley [the British Cabinet Minister under Margaret Thatcher who had to resign after writing an article suggesting that Germany had not left her Nazi past behind] was not peculiar to him. It was not hard to find similar views in the French foreign ministry. The Dutch too had their fears. He wanted Germany's neighbours to see her fully integrated into Europe. That was why he wanted decisions taken this decade. Kohl went on to reflect wryly on his arguments with Margaret Thatcher over short range nuclear forces [whose deployment had been particularly controversial in Germany]. She had got in her tank and driven straight at him with the Union Jack flying. The crucial point was that, from today's perspective, the argument could as well have taken place a hundred years ago, as two years ago. He would never do anything anti-American. At the same time, we had to get a European dimension.

Kohl went on to say that there were two main ingredients of this European dimension as far as Germany was concerned. He wanted the new treaty on political union to refer to the "federal goal" of the EU. He was also set on going beyond the "ever closer union" of the Treaty of Rome.

The notion of a federal goal for the EU was unacceptable to the British but the British embassy in Bonn subsequently reported that they judged Kohl might settle for "confederation" or "confederate structures". Later in the year, Kohl himself sought to explain what Germany meant by federalism. Germany was working, he said, for a Europe characterised by diversity, in which the traditional—particularly regional—identities would have their place. He went on:

We do not want a Europe that causes nations and regions to lose their identity in a melting pot; the opposite is true. We are committed to federalism as an ideal for the structure of Europe . . . The Europe we envisage is a Europe in which being rooted in one's own area and taking the broad view will be able to exist side by side as perfectly natural. In the process of creating the United States of Europe it will be of particular importance to safeguard the traditions of local self government as a structural principle for our democratic federal system.

The reference to a United States of Europe was enough to set British alarm bells ringing while the fact that Kohl's European model followed closely the German federal model was of no consolation.

The second ingredient for Germany was democratic control through the EP, an institution of which successive British governments had been very nervous because democratic power exercised through the EP was democratic power not exercised by MPs at Westminster. This fear, wrapped up in an attitude of studied contempt, was shared in spades by President Mitterrand though Mitterrand's concern for the detail of negotiation was distinctly lofty. Robin Renwick recalls, when he was dealing with these issues for Margaret Thatcher, that he and his French opposite number Pierre de Boissieu, came up with an idea for conceding a minimal change in the EP's powers. When Mrs Thatcher told Mitterrand that she accepted the Boissieu plan, Mitterrand expressed himself delighted, adding: "What is it?"

On both these issues, France was prepared to go along with Germany. That was why the French Europe Minister, Elizabeth Guigou, was able to make a speech in Washington describing EMU as "well within the scope of this march towards a federal Europe". In return, the Germans went along with French ideas on European defence despite their own attachment to the integrity of NATO.

In 1991, Pierre de Boissieu was the official in the Quai d'Orsay in charge of French European policy. Four years later, when I became UK Permanent Representative to the EU, Boissieu was my French opposite number. A great nephew of de Gaulle, Boissieu dominated the Committee of Permanent Representatives (COREPER). While John Kerr, my predecessor, was there he had been given a run for his money but neither I nor any of our other colleagues could match Boissieu's brilliance. He was subtle, eloquent, ingenious, and irreverently funny: both a French patriot and a convinced European. As I got to know him, I came to appreciate that, along with the brilliance, came real strength of character and of purpose. He was a hero to the people who worked for him in the French Representation, frequently a thorn in the flesh of fellow officials in Paris who resented his independence of mind even as they were often unable to follow the ingenuity of his ideas and tactical sense. President Chirac had the good sense to listen to him.

In 1991, Boissieu outlined to his British opposite number, Michael Jay (later a successful British ambassador in Paris and then Permanent Undersecretary in the Foreign Office), his thinking on European defence, thinking that was to be reflected in his, and the wider French, approach consistently over the years that followed. "It was unthinkable", said Boissieu, "that Austria [a neutral country] should in due course join the European Community without also becoming part of the European defence structure. If an artificial division was created between European Union and European defence, it would not be long before the Germans were drifting into neutrality." Jay responded that, for the UK, it was essential to retain a single transatlantic structure for the defence of NATO territory. Britain could not accept the division of potential members of the WEU into those who would be entitled to join as full members by virtue of their membership of the EC and those who would be relegated to some kind of cooperative arrangement or associate membership because they were not EC members.

To the British this smacked of first and second class members of NATO with the Turks, for example, who had been supportive during the Iraq War, relegated to the second tier. The British also feared that there was a hidden French agenda to weaken NATO (in whose command structures the French did not participate) by compromising NATO's sole responsibility for territorial defence. The French were certainly somewhat schizophrenic in their attitude to NATO. There were times when the French defence chiefs tilted towards full participation in the NATO command structures and, when he became President, Chirac was thought for a time to lean in the same direction. At other times, French policy seemed to stem more from their self-imposed exclusion and their traditional dislike of US hegemony.

Pierre de Boissieu, thinking ahead as usual, was, I believe, though I did not see it in 1991, concerned at what would happen as Europe developed a security capacity. What he feared was a situation in which those member states which had the will and capacity to act militarily would be prevented from doing so by the veto of those who would have both the liberty not to contribute to the European security effort and the luxury of obstructing effective action by others. Defence was to become a key British preoccupation as the Maastricht deadline approached.

The other concession the Germans were ready to make to the French (though they scarcely saw it as such) was over social policy which became, and has remained, a key element in the French conception of Europe. Hubert Vedrine, later French Foreign Minister, was Secretary General of the Elysée in 1991. In talks with the British Cabinet Secretary, Sir Robin Butler, Vedrine explained that:

for France the construction of Europe was a necessity and France was prepared to accept the constraints that came with the positive aspects. For the last twenty to thirty years France had recognised the need to build Europe and wanted to ensure that there was strong public support for this within France. Public opinion had swung from indifference to enthusiasm when President Mitterrand raised French consciousness of Europe. Now, however, a nationalistic strain and a fear for French national identity were rising. The Community was becoming less popular again. The government felt that the social dimension of the Community was correspondingly more important. French public opinion needed to be assured that European Union would raise the standards for all member states to those of the best in all areas including social aspects. In general, France did not want to see regulation and increased bureaucracy in the social area but to increase negotiation and dialogue.

Robin Butler replied tersely that the UK could not accept extensions of competence which would bring into the scope of QMV proposals which would have intolerable costs.

Central to the overall argument were the rival concepts of Europe as a tree or a temple. In other words, there were those, such as the Dutch, Belgians, Italians, and the Commission who wanted the EU to be a single tree in which all policies would, in the end, be dealt with under the Community structures in which the Commission had the sole right of initiative and in which the EP would play its full part, with the ultimate arbiter of the law being the ECJ. This approach implied that, in due course, competence for issues such as justice and home affairs and foreign policy would become matters of Community competence. The idea was anathema to Britain and, de facto, to France though the French were sotto voce about it because the Germans were quite tempted by this approach.

The British favoured the so-called pillared approach under which the provisions of the revised treaty covering a CFSP and cooperation on justice and home affairs would be based on intergovernmental cooperation outside the Treaty of Rome and, therefore, outside the structures which allowed for the Commission's sole right of initiative, the intervention of the EP and the jurisdiction of the ECJ.

The Luxembourg presidency, under the low-key leadership of the Luxembourg Prime Minister, Jacques Santer, brought forward in June a draft treaty which followed the pillared approach. There would be a Treaty of European union covering common provisions, amendments to the original Treaty of Rome (encompassing the traditional Community method), provisions on CFSP and on cooperation in home affairs and judicial matters (intergovernmental in nature), and final provisions.

This approach suited the British well. The main substantive British reservations on the Luxembourg text were its reference to the EU's "federal goal", its provisions for Union citizenship, and the proposals for social policy, including decision-making by QMV. John Major's dislike of EU citizenship was not unlike Jack Straw's dislike of the notion of a European Foreign Minister ten years later. Just as Straw argued that a Foreign Minister, by definition, was the minister of a country, so Major argued that citizens, by definition, belonged to a country.

The Luxembourg presidency over, Europe went to the beach as it always does (its internal crises invariably suspended for Christmas, Easter, and August), and the Dutch took the chair. When normal European business resumed at the beginning of September, the Dutch presidency put forward a new text on political union. It was a bombshell. Submitting a summary of it to ministers, the EC Department of the Foreign Office noted that: "we need to kill the latest Dutch text" and gave four reasons:

- The text removed the pillared structure.
- It allowed the Community gradually to extend its competence over CFSP and gave the Commission more powers to represent Europe externally.
- It further extended the powers of the EP.
- It gave the Community competence over all aspects of employment.

John Major told the Dutch Prime Minister, Ruud Lubbers, when they met two weeks later, that he knew the French believed that the British always banged the table but came round in the end. He would not put on great displays. He wanted an agreement as much as anyone and would negotiate where practicable. But we would not sign up to proposals we could not accept or recommend to the House of Commons.

The Germans were quite attached to the new Dutch text. Dietrich von Kyaw, Michael Jay's opposite number in the German Foreign Ministry and later Germany's Permanent Representative to the EU, told him in early September that Germany had had hopes that a halfway house between the Luxemburg and Dutch texts might have been possible. If that was not so, then he doubted if agreement would be possible in December.

But the Dutch had miscalculated. They had mightily offended their Luxembourg predecessors as presidency by ditching their text, so it was the Luxembourg Foreign Minister, Jacques Poos, who was the first to attack the new draft when EC foreign ministers met to discuss it. Even the Italian Foreign Minister, from a country which could normally be relied on to support proposals for a Federal Europe, disliked it. And when the German Foreign Minister, Hans Dietrich Genscher, said that while he might have preferred it, it was clear that it would not run, the Dutch were forced into a humiliating climb down. For a long time, that day was known in the Dutch foreign ministry as Black Monday. It is a measure of the water that has flowed under the bridges of Europe since that the federalist Netherlands of 1991 was the same country that voted against the Constitutional Treaty in 2005.

While the form of the draft treaty was back in a shape congenial to Britain, the content remained a source of concern. Moreover, as the moment of decision approached, so did the habit of mutual concessions between France and Germany. Not only did this fit the pattern of Franco-German cooperation of the past thirty years, but also it was logical, given the French determination to bind Germany into an EMU of which Britain would have no part and German determination to balance EMU with political union. Kohl's diplomatic adviser, Peter Hartmann, told Britain's ambassador in Bonn, Sir Christopher Mallaby, in October 1991 that the German public needed to be sure that progress towards EU was irreversible, since otherwise the creation of a European currency would not be justified. The disappearance of the Soviet threat strengthened this line of argument: that threat had been an influence for unity in Western Europe and there could now be a tendency to greater nationalism in the foreign policy of, for instance, France. Mallaby had for some time been arguing that a reunified Germany would have less need of, and interest in, Europe than before and Hartmann agreed with him: German foreign policy would be bound to become more national and assertive if the trend towards a common foreign policy in the Community was reversed.

In Paris, the British Embassy reported, Mitterrand was up to his eyes in domestic problems. His Prime Minister, Edith Cresson, had proved to be "a damp squib"; the economy was in poor shape, and the feel-good index showed more pessimism among the electorate than for many years. Mitterrand had let the genie of Le Pen out of the bottle to undermine the Right but Le Pen was now making inroads on the Left as well. Worried about the shift in the centre of gravity of the relationship with Germany, Mitterrand wanted to go down in history as the leader who had bound Germany into a strengthened Europe still dominated by French design. So the French would not have many "bottom lines" in the negotiation. If paying a price to the British would make agreement with Germany more difficult, then that price would not be paid. In any event, the French still believed that the UK would give ground when push came to shove.

It was against this background that France and Germany brought forward, in October/November, detailed proposals for European defence which included a Franco-German corps which, to British eyes, implied that a brigade made up of forces that were not integrated into NATO could become the kernel of a WEU structure. The WEU in turn would become "an integral component of the European unification process" and, over time, the "defence component of the Union". The declared objective was "to strengthen the Atlantic alliance overall by reinforcing the role and responsibility of the Europeans and by creating a European pillar in their midst".

This rang alarm bells with the British government and there were extensive discussions between British officials and their French and German colleagues in a vain attempt to find common ground. To British eyes, there was an element of deliberate double-speak in the French and German plan: endorsing NATO while setting in place new arrangements which would, in practice, undermine it. The fact that the US government seemed relatively relaxed about the proposals was a further frustration and strenuous efforts were made by the British Embassy in Washington and by officials in Downing Street to alert the Americans to the danger to their interests. These efforts bore fruit somewhat belatedly and American lobbying of the Germans was to contribute to the relatively modest outcome on defence in the eventual agreement reached at Maastricht.

John Major wrote to President Mitterrand to express his concerns, which covered four main points: (i) the proposal that CFSP should include all questions relating to the security and defence of the Union; (ii) the portrayal of the WEU as simply the executive arm of the EU; (iii) the provision that the Council of Ministers should organise relations between the Union and WEU, that is, the implication that WEU was not autonomous; and (iv) a weak statement that the provisions on CFSP should not affect the obligations of members of the WEU and NATO. This was contradicted by the earlier provisions which clearly *did* affect the position of NATO members.

Mitterrand's reply may have been intended to reassure, but failed to do so. The President wrote:

It seems to us fundamental that the political union we wish to bring about ... should give itself the means to have a real foreign and security policy with the perspective of a common defence in due course. In the WEU we have at our disposal a mechanism to begin to put this security and defence policy, defined at the highest level of the European Council, into practice. There must be a direct organic link between the political union and the WEU. The latter will also establish a closer cooperation with NATO. It is clear that the sum total of this approach is progressive and that progress towards a common defence will take place in stages ...

The conclusion to Mitterrand's letter illustrated the internal inconsistency of the Franco-German position as seen by the British:

I want to stress the point that I have never questioned the need to preserve the security links between Europe and the United States of which the Atlantic Alliance constitutes the guarantee. It follows that the common European defence, whose scope should not be limited a priori, will of course be compatible with that being followed in the framework of NATO.

Any remaining ambiguity was removed in talks between the British Europe Minister, Tristan Garel-Jones, and his French opposite number, Elizabeth Guigou. Garel-Jones argued that we could not accept any erosion of NATO's effectiveness. Guigou agreed but added that there could be no question of placing the WEU midway between NATO and Europe's CFSP. Unless the WEU was closer to the EU, Europe's defence policies would continue to be subject to a US veto expressed through NATO. In other words, so it seemed to the British, a key intention behind the Franco-German plan was to take European defence out of the sphere of influence of the United States. That looked a recipe for disaster, first because Europe's armed forces and their equipment were inadequate on their own and secondly because the British government wished to do nothing that would make it easier for those in the United States who wanted to pull back their forces.

In November, one month before the Maastricht European Council, John Major set out his European views at the annual Lord Mayor's banquet. He began by noting the City of London's longstanding support for British membership of the ERM. Events had amply justified Britain's membership: our inflation rate had been more than halved and interest rates had been cut eight times while sterling had remained stable. For the first time in fifty years, we were in a position to achieve on a lasting basis that greater certainty that the business community needed.

He went on to set out his vision of an enlarged EC. I once heard Ted Heath say that John Major favoured enlargement in order to weaken the EC. That was not his motivation. He wanted a more diverse Community, one less driven by the impulsion towards Brussels-led integration, and in that respect the prospect of enlargement was welcome. But what he said to the Lord Mayor's banquet represented his deep conviction:

If we are to avoid the tragedy of Yugoslavia on a larger and more dangerous scale, we have to adapt the political structures of the West to accommodate the new democracies of the East ... We have to hold out to the countries of Eastern Europe and perhaps some of the new republics within the Soviet Union as well, the prospect of closer association with the Community and, in due course, membership of the Community ... We will never create a genuine European Union if we exclude those countries that most want to join, countries which for the first time since World War II are free democracies ... It would be tragic if, twenty years from now, there was an economic iron curtain across Europe, an iron curtain forged by the wealthy member states to keep out our democratic neighbours to the East.

If, now, the argument seems too self-evident to need making, it did not appear like that at the time. EC membership for the countries of Eastern and Central Europe was scarcely more popular across the Community than membership for Turkey is today. Only Britain and Germany were champions of enlargement. In one conversation with John Major, President Mitterrand asked him whether he thought the countries of Eastern and Central Europe might become members by 2010. "Who knows?", said John Major. "I know," said Mitterrand. "There is no way those countries will join by 2010."

Mitterrand's comment that the countries of Eastern Europe would not be members by 2010 was a reflection of his wishes, more than of objective assessment. Paradoxically, given subsequent developments, the one French politician with whom John Major was able to make common cause in pressing the case for enlargement was the then Mayor of Paris, Jacques Chirac, who saw in it an opportunity to tweak Mitterrand's tail.

One issue which John Major touched on in his speech at the Guildhall, where the issues at stake then have not been resolved in the intervening period, was trade. The GATT negotiations were in train. Margaret Thatcher had tried in vain to get GATT put at the top of the agenda of the European Council in October 1990. Now, John Major set out the British view:

If you give a man a fish, you give him food for a day. If you teach him how to fish, you give him food for a lifetime. But if you teach him how to fish and then stop him selling his catch, you create injustice, hardship, and resentment, and we should not do that. There is as much at stake in the GATT talks as there is at Maastricht.

Fourteen years later, at the same venue, Tony Blair found himself still having to make the same argument.

Finally, John Major set out his view on EMU:

To move to a single currency without the convergence of national economies would be an economic catastrophe. That is why we are negotiating a treaty which would ... allow the British government and the British parliament to take the decision on whether to join such a single currency when the option is a realistic one ... It would be wrong now to decide to join a single currency but it would be equally wrong to decide now that in no circumstances will we ever do so.

That same month, the Foreign Office produced a note of "areas where we have fended off demands from others" in the negotiations on a new treaty. The Dutch proposals for a unitary treaty structure had been rejected: "the UK took the lead in achieving this outcome". Germany and others had wanted to bring all areas of interior and justice cooperation, including asylum, police cooperation, and Europol within Community competence. A majority had not wanted this, at least for now. French ambitions, supported by Spain, Greece, and Belgium, to introduce a mutual defence commitment into the Treaty of Rome had been rejected. A majority of member states had "firmly rejected" the Commission's proposal to give themselves wide-ranging powers across the whole range of EC external policies. A proposal by Germany and the Commission to give the EP full co-decision on all Community legislation had been rejected in favour of a more limited "negative assent" procedure. A German proposal to give the EP the right to elect the European Commission had been rejected in favour of a more modest proposal whereby the EP would have the right to approve the nominations to the Commission of individual member states. Finally, Belgian proposals to extend QMV to fiscal harmonisation had been rejected "though they are still trying to slip this in by the back door".

That document is characteristic of many written by the Foreign Office during treaty negotiations over the years. It shows the success of British negotiators, armed with a brief to fend off determined efforts by a number of partners and the Commission to extend Community competence. It explains why, when the House of Commons debated Europe on the eve of the Maastricht European Council, the Leader of the Opposition, Neil Kinnock, was able to quote from the *Daily Mail*, which was then pro-European: "As so often in the past, our Government are stuck in the defensive mud. Grabbing a begrudged compromise here; clutching an opt-out clause there. Devoting maximum diplomatic effort to dilution and delay. This is a dreary, demeaning, and ultimately self-defeating posture. It is playing for a draw."

Neil Kinnock then, as Tony Blair was to do later, belittled the need for a specific opt-out clause for Britain on EMU on the grounds that no one doubted that Government and Parliament would take a decision when the time came. But for the Government, it was not that simple. They knew that Parliament would not accept a treaty that provided for automatic moves to EMU provided certain economic conditions were met. They certainly doubted whether their own supporters would do so and, only months from a General Election, the Prime Minister could not afford to have a divided party or to have his policy carried in the House of Commons only thanks to the votes of the Opposition.

John Major had to pursue the dual track of both stressing the positive and setting out clearly what he would not accept when he opened the debate on 20 November. He was clear that the other eleven member states could, if they wished, go ahead with EMU if they so chose. So, under the principle known in government as "no veto, no imposition and no lock-out", Major insisted that: "even if the requisite majority of member states decide to embrace full EMU with a single currency and a single central bank, Britain will not be obliged to do so. Whether to join—not just when to join—will be matters of separate decision by government and by Parliament." He then set out the principles that should guide the British approach to EMU in the longer term:

If the convergence conditions set out in the draft treaty are not met, we would certainly not wish to be part of an economic and monetary union with a single currency. But if they are met, our successors may wish to take a different view. A single currency could be the means of safeguarding anti-inflationary policies for the whole of the European Community. That would be a great prize. But the House knows that there is a price to pay for that prize. The price is that it would take from national governments the control of monetary policy. That would be a very significant political and economic step for Britain to take. We cannot take that step now, but nor should we exclude it.

John Major then described the various commitments made over the years to European union. The purpose of the new treaty was to define what political union would mean in practical, legal terms.

For many of our Community partners the definitions are not as important as they are for us. For many of them the diminution of the power of national Governments and national Parliaments is not an issue. They accept the idea of a European federation. We have never done so. When we joined, we accepted that Community law would take precedence over national law, but for that very reason we have always been concerned about the scope of Community law—precisely because it took precedence. In these negotiations, we have shown ourselves ready to discuss individual changes in the role of the Community where these are in the national interest, but we are not prepared to accept wholesale changes in the nature of the Community which would lead it toward an unacceptable dominance over our national life.

In words that would be echoed on a number of occasions by Tony Blair, John Major said: "There are, in truth, only three ways of dealing with the Community: we can leave it, and no doubt we would survive, but we would be diminished in influence and prosperity; we can stay in it grudgingly, in which case others will lead it; or we can play a leading role in it, and that is the right policy."

The government carried the day in the House of Commons by a majority of 101 with only 6 votes against from Tory MPs. They were less confident of carrying the day at Maastricht itself. John Major had separate meetings with Kohl and Mitterrand and other European leaders in the run-up. Kohl was concerned about the trend since German reunification. First of all, since reunification, he had, he told John Major, had sight of some of the files of the former GDR, including records of conversations as late as January 1990. It was interesting to see who had been trying to prevent reunification from taking place, Italian Prime Minister Andreotti being one of the fiercest opponents. Kohl said that he always defended Margaret Thatcher as the only person who had been honest about her views in public.

For Germany, said Kohl, the situation had become much more difficult since unification. With the diminution of the risks of East–West confrontation, nationalism had become a more significant force. In the Soviet Union, it had been suppressed by Stalin, who had continued the policies of the Romanovs. Now, with self-determination, we were seeing nationalism at work, including in Poland and Slovakia [the latter determined on the break-up of the unitary Czechoslovakia]. These nationalistic forces were at their least virulent in Germany but he wanted to prevent them recurring. We had a unique opportunity to make progress on both German and European unity. If we did not do it now, it would be another twenty or thirty years before we had another opportunity. In the meantime, we would have a very different, and not desirable, type of Europe. Unless it was set in the context of political union, EMU would lose its dynamism.

Kohl was also concerned about developments in the United States where, he feared, domestic issues would soon come to dominate. Bush was pay-ing the price of Reagan's policies. These basically had been Friedmanite and Friedman had nothing to do with human beings. In Germany, Chancellor Erhardt had been the most successful exponent of market economies but had always spoken of the social market economy. He, Kohl, would like to prick the social conscience of big business and encourage them to make smaller profits. That was not realistic, so he advocated the social market economy instead. He was also still a child of his Church, even though he agreed less and less with the present Pope [John Paul II], and had told him so to his face.

Kohl also saw the shape of NATO changing. We had to do everything in our power to link ourselves to the Americans. At the same time, we did not want to be at risk if the nature of the US President changed. The US constitution was perfect in all but one thing, namely the way it chose its presidents. The Franco-German position was of the utmost importance because of history. This was something Mrs Thatcher never understood. He wanted Britain along even if on certain issues we needed more time. Germany was not more European because Germans were more intelligent, but for historical reasons. If Germany's situation had been different in 1945, opinion in Germany on Europe might not be so very different now from that in Britain. He himself was a model that would not be much longer in production. There was a middle generation but the young people took for granted many of the things we were preoccupied about. His son, Peter, had studied in Glasgow and lots of his British friends, as well as friends from the Massachussetts Institute of Technology (MIT), often came to the house. They spoke a quite different language from the older generation.

John Major responded that it was for many of the reasons that Kohl had given that he believed German unification had been a good thing. The majority in the UK welcomed it and he was only sorry it had not happened ten years earlier. He had no doubt about the direction towards what might be called Europeanism.

With President Mittterrand, on the eve of Maastricht, the discussion focused more on the detail of the treaty. Major argued against an opt-out clause from EMU that was UK-specific. But Mitterrand was resistant. He did not want to see Britain isolated but nor did he want to offer a temptation to others to open up the issue again in a few years' time.

On European defence, Mitterrand argued that, with the possible eventual disappearance of the threat from the East, he doubted if the Americans would be able to resist forever the economic, press, and congressional pressures to bring their troops home. It would be perfectly possible for him to say that this was a problem for the distant future and for his successors, but that was not his way. He wanted to take a first step to make European public opinion aware that they must do more for their own defence: at the end of the day it was always France and Britain that had to bear the burdens.

On foreign policy, John Major explained British support for the concept of binding joint actions, as well as our reservations about majority voting for implementing measures, which might be the thin end of a wedge leading to pressure for majority voting on foreign policy in principle. Mitterrand was unmoved. Giving a Gallic shrug, he said he had read the text and it contained lots of safeguards.

By contrast, Mitterrand was concerned at the German proposal that Germany should have more MEPs to reflect the size of the united country. Mitterrand argued that the principle of proportionality had never been accepted. On that basis, if Nigeria were to join the Community she would have more MEPs than anyone else. We should maintain equality of representation.

When Major explained that the issue was not one that aroused much concern in Britain, Mitterrand advised him not to be so relaxed about it. He feared contagion as between the EP and the other institutions. Moreover, once the EP had more competence, it would also have more weight and that would be a step in the wrong direction.

The position John Major faced as he went to Maastricht was, in his own words, dire. As he put it in his autobiography, if he withheld agreement to the treaty, huge ill-will would be caused across Europe, the Conservative Party would be split, and the once-internationalist party would be perceived as being incapable of doing business in Europe. An unsatisfactory agreement might earn goodwill on the Continent but would split the Cabinet, be repudiated by the Conservative Party, and might fail in Parliament. Within six months, a General Election would have to be held. Success or failure at Maastricht would be a significant factor in determining the result.

7

Success Turned Sour: From Maastricht to Mad Cow Disease

"Game, set, and match" was a slogan invented at three o'clock in the morning at the end of the Maastricht summit by an over-enthusiastic Press officer. Like the phrase "Crisis, what crisis?", which Jim Callaghan never used to describe the winter of discontent of 1978, "Game, set, and match" were not words that ever crossed John Major's lips and were not consistent with his own non-triumphal presentation of the outcome.

While it jarred with Britain's partners, "Game, set, and match" did not, in domestic terms, seem a far-fetched description of John Major's achievement at Maastricht. The substantive achievement was matched by the operation to manage the news handling of it. John Major was determined to get his strike in first. Every Cabinet Minister woke up to find a briefing paper on their fax or doormat describing the Maastricht outcome. Now, what was done may seem commonplace. Then, the paper written by Major's head of policy, Sarah Hogg, and distributed to all Cabinet ministers in London before the Prime Minister himself had even left for home, was the first time anything like it had been attempted, especially remarkable considering that, in a pre-digital age, many copies had to be distributed by hand. The document is, of course, a piece of spin but it accurately reflects the mood:

The deal agreed in Maastricht was a great success for Britain and a personal success for the Prime Minister ... It very much reflects the Prime Minister's tough but courteous style of negotiating. There were five crucial areas for Britain: (i) we had to be free to decide whether, and not just when, to join EMU; (ii) we had to be free to determine our national foreign and defence policy; (iii) the Social Chapter on the table was unacceptable; (iv) we would not accept the phrase "federal vocation"; (v) we would not give up control over our immigration policy. No social chapter. The proposals on the table would have threatened British industry with heavy new regulatory burdens. The Prime Minister said he would not sign it and it was removed from the Treaty. Instead, the other eleven agreed under a protocol to pursue the 1989 social charter, which we never signed. This should make us, as Jacques Delors suggested, a haven for American and Japanese investment.

The British government is, of course, committed to a comprehensive social policy that safeguards the rights of our workforce. Of the 32 measures in the Social Action programme, eighteen have been adopted, and only Britain has implemented all eighteen. But what we could not accept was putting jobs at risk by undoing all the hard won trade union reforms of the 1990s. Costing British workers their jobs is not good for British workers. And some of the rights enjoyed by British workers—like free health care on the NHS—are the envy of many Europeans.

Maastricht was a serious success for John Major. He was *"suaviter in modo, fortiter in re"*. That part of him that was the boy from Brixton and the young Lambeth councillor who had duelled with Ken Livingstone could read the body language of his opponent and duck, weave, and jab with the best of them. But the iron fist was concealed in the velvet glove. He could score points without humiliating the person he had scored them from. He was a serious student of the official brief. Like Margaret Thatcher, he probably knew more of the detail of the issue under discussion than most others in the room. Unlike her, he did not make sure the others had their ignorance paraded.

The achievement of the Maastricht opt-out on EMU had been a long time in preparation and, by the time of the meeting, Britain was reconciled to an opt-out drawn up specifically to meet its needs. What Britain's partners had not expected was the detailed legal text drawn up by the Treasury's Nigel Wicks, and only tabled when Major judged that it was too late for others to try to rewrite it. Nigel Wicks was the best kind of civil servant: clever, loyal, and decent. He had served as one of Jim Callaghan's Private Secretaries and later as the British representative on the International Monetary Fund (IMF) and International Bank for Reconstruction and Development (IBRD) in Washington. He understood the requirements of negotiation: knowledge, patience, tolerance, ingenuity, and—a quality not in huge supply in Her Majesty's Treasury—judicious compromise. He later became Head of the EU's Monetary Committee, and was re-elected by his colleagues from the other member states for a second term. The Monetary Committee was the financial equivalent of COREPER, the most senior official body responsible for preparing the discussions of EU finance ministers, including on EMU. Against that background, the willingness, indeed enthusiasm, of Nigel's colleagues to serve under his chairmanship was a remarkable tribute to his wisdom, dexterity, and impartiality.

It is just possible that Britain might have signed up to some form of Social Chapter. Officials in the Department of Employment had tried their hands at a draft which their Secretary of State, Michael Howard, had never allowed them to put forward. Had they done so, perhaps the text on the table at Maastricht would have been less problematic. John Major's own instincts on the subject were robust but, in so far as he wanted to have some room for manoeuvre, there was no way Michael Howard was going to allow him to have it. During the three days of the summit, in frequent telephone discussions with Sarah Hogg, Michael Howard made it subtly, but plainly, clear that this was a resigning matter.

When the Dutch Chairman, Ruud Lubbers, offered John Major an opt-out from the Social Chapter, which would otherwise be incorporated in the new treaty, Major declined. It was hard enough to get some Conservative backbenchers to accept that the EMU opt-out was not simply a backdated surrender notice. He did not want the same argument over the Social Chapter. His calculation, that Lubbers would not allow his treaty triumph to collapse on this issue, proved correct. Lubbers came back with the offer of a protocol to the treaty which the other eleven would sign. Britain would have no part of it and would not be implicated in any of the administrative expenditure involved in implementing it.

The Maastricht Treaty was attacked in the House of Commons by Neil Kinnock, for the Labour Party, as the act of "a double opt-out government who have isolated Britain on the most vital issues of economic and monetary union and the social charter". He was joined in his criticism by Paddy Ashdown for the Liberal Democrats who accused Major of being the Prime Minister "who said he wanted to be at the heart of the [integration] process [but] has instead condemned this country to be semi-detached from it". But the agreement was well received by middle-of-the-road Conservatives and aroused little criticism from Euro-sceptics.

In retrospect, the decision not to put the legislation necessary to implement and ratify the Treaty to Parliament before the General Election was a bad call. But it was potentially time-consuming, with no guarantee of completion before the election was due to be called, and the safe course seemed to be to let a sleeping dog alone so that the Conservative Party would be able to focus all its resources on a campaign which most of the pundits, and most of us who worked in Downing Street, expected the Conservatives to lose. The Conservative leadership based their decision in part on their knowledge of the middle-of-the-road MPs in the 1987 Parliament. In the event, many of those MPs stood down and were replaced, in the 1992 election, by more ideological products of the 1980s. Had the party leadership known in advance the European views of the likely new intake, they might have taken a different decision.

The Conservative manifesto for the General Election in April 1992 was buoyant about Europe: "The Conservatives have been the party of Britain in Europe for 30 years. We have argued when argument was necessary, but we have not wavered nor changed our views. We have ensured that Britain is at the heart of Europe, a strong and respected partner . . . The Maastricht Treaty was a success both for Britain and for the rest of Europe." Unusually, there was an entire section devoted to the British Presidency of the EU, due in the second half of 1992: "The British Presidency comes at a turning point in the Community's history. It gives us the opportunity to shape the direction of the Community and to establish its priorities. We shall use it to promote our vision of an outward looking Community based on free enterprise."

But Europe featured little in a campaign which had Labour well ahead in the opinion polls almost to the end. In its last week, support started to shift away from the Labour Party and, by election day, John Major thought he would win although he was not confident of having an overall major- ity. Governing political parties lose elections but, for that to happen, the electorate must both have lost faith in the government and found faith in the Opposition party which will replace them. John Major was liked, had reversed the worst perceived excesses of Thatcherism (especially the Poll Tax), and was thought more competent than Labour would be at running the economy. There were nonetheless enough negatives for him very probably to have lost if, on the other side of the political divide, Labour had completed the reforms that Neil Kinnock had begun. But they were a work in progress and Neil Kinnock himself still carried baggage from his left-wing past which could be used against him. Even so, few people expected the tide to turn back to the Tories in the last days of the campaign as significantly as it did. Expectation being all, a Conservative majority of 21 in 1992 was seen as a triumph, while a Labour majority of 66 in 2005 was seen as a portent of doom.

John Major, though buoyed by his victory, was aware of problems to come. When I congratulated him on having achieved his own mandate, he replied: "You wait. This is where my troubles really begin." At the time, I put it down to an inherent tendency to picture the worst as a way of fending off the hubris that lies in wait for any successful leader. But he realised very quickly that the size of his majority was only just workable in the best of circumstances and that there were, even then, probably more Euro-sceptic Conservative backbenchers than the total of his majority. Over the following months, it became clear that many of those people were more interested in the integrity of their anti-European struggle than in the survival of the government. They were to be given hope by the failure of the Danish referendum on Maastricht in June 1992 and invigorated by "I told you so" self-righteousness after UK's withdrawal from the ERM in September.

On 21 May 1992, two dozen Conservative backbenchers voted against the second reading of the Maastricht Bill. Ten days later, the Danish people, contrary to the optimistic predictions of their own government, voted in a referendum to reject the treaty and, as Douglas Hurd put it in his memoirs, the

British government was "holed beneath the water line". Progress on the Bill in the House of Commons was suspended and Britain began to face up to the fact that dealing with the Danish "no" vote would be the principal preoccupation of her forthcoming presidency. With ratification complete in most member states, there was little sympathy across the Community for the view that the Danish vote could actually be allowed to prevent the Maastricht Treaty from coming into force even though, legally, that was precisely its effect. I later learned from a Belgian colleague that he had advised his Prime Minister that this was a good opportunity for the rest of the EC to "let the Danes go". The Danes themselves seemed all too ready to contemplate just such an outcome, not because it was what their government wanted, but because they felt the breath of some of the larger member states aggressively hot on their necks. Part of the British government's task, therefore, was to shore up the Danes and to ensure that either their "veto" was respected, or some accommodation found that did not require a renegotiation and re-ratification of the Maastricht Treaty.

The French were due to vote on the treaty in a referendum on 20 September 1992. It looked like being a close-run thing. By then, Britain was in the chair of the Community, and responsible for keeping the flag of ratification of the treaty flying bravely from the European battlements. In private, faced with their own domestic difficulties over the Maastricht Bill, the strong sense in the Whitehall corridors was that everyone from the Prime Minister downwards was praying for a French "no".

It was because of the real possibility of that happening that a group of ministers met in Admiralty House, under the Prime Minister's chairmanship, on the morning of Wednesday, 16 September. Admiralty House was the temporary home of the Prime Minister for several months in that year while extensive work was done on Number 10 to make it bomb proof following the Irish Republican Army (IRA) mortar attack of 1991. The work was effective. Some months later, I sat apprehensively at my desk in Number 10 one night waiting for an IRA bomb, placed in a hijacked taxi at the end of Downing Street, to explode. When it did, only the chandelier above my head gave a nervous shiver. The reinforced fittings and fixtures exhibited a good deal more *sangfroid* than I did.

Because of the subject matter, the Deputy Prime Minister, Michael Heseltine, Douglas Hurd, Ken Clarke (the Home Secretary), and a number of others, including myself, were present. But the meeting was soon joined by Norman Lamont, the Chancellor of the Exchequer, with the first report that the efforts he had been making to shore up the pound in the developing currency crisis were not working. Not long before what came to be known as Black Wednesday, John Nott, the former Defence Secretary, had called on John

Major. John Nott had gone into banking and one of the things he said to the Prime Minister was that there was a young man in his bank who moved more money across the exchanges in a day than the entire reserves of the Bank of England. If there were a crisis, we would not stand a chance.

Those words were prophetic. The currency crisis when it came caused turmoil all over Europe. It hit Britain and, as the reserves melted alarmingly away, successive rises in interest rates to all-time record levels did nothing to staunch the flow. Temporary withdrawal from the ERM began to seem the only realistic option. At one stage in the various discussions that dominated the morning, John Major took the view of everyone in the room as to whether we should seek a realignment of sterling within the ERM. As I recall, I was the only person who argued that we should but it was a suggestion born of desperation rather than calculation. It would have been too little and much too late.

Others present have said it already: there was no panic in the crisis. Norman Lamont, not surprisingly, appeared increasingly anguished as the traditional measures to shore up the pound were swept away by the tidal wave. But his advice, and that of the Governor of the Bank of England, was clear, if not cool, and the Prime Minister dealt with each phase in his typically methodical way (hence the examination of whether a realignment remained a realistic option). Characteristically, the Chancellor, Ken Clarke, summed it all up with a "bon mot": "Well, it is another good argument for a single currency!" It was received in silence.

In the early afternoon, the Prime Minister spoke to the French Prime Minister, Pierre Beregovoy, and, after he had been allegedly "unavailable" for some time, to Chancellor Kohl. Major and Beregovoy liked each other: there was a particular solidarity between Heads of Government who had been finance ministers. Beregovoy was sympathetic but powerless to help. The franc was itself coming under heavy pressure just days before the French referendum on Maastricht. In a subsequent crisis, the franc would also have had to leave the ERM but for massive German currency support. In Britain's case, Kohl refused that support, pleading the independence of the Bundesbank and his powerlessness to influence it. Careless, perhaps deliberately careless, Press comments by the Head of the Bundesbank, a few days earlier, had contributed to the run on sterling. The Germans could have acted if they had wanted to. Perhaps we paid the price of our less-than-wholehearted commitment to the European project as France and Germany conceived it. The Anglo-German relationship was not worth heroic measures on Germany's part. And the Germans had been seriously irritated by Norman Lamont's attempts, as chairman of an informal meeting of finance ministers in Bath earlier in the month, to put pressure on them to reduce their interest rates.

I do not believe that the Germans were influenced by continued irritation at our failure to consult the Monetary Committee of the EU in Brussels over the exchange rate at which we had entered the ERM in October 1990. We had entered at the market rate (DM2.95 to the pound) and the Bundesbank at that time had favoured a rate only marginally lower, while the Banque de France wanted a higher rate. As John Major recalls in his autobiography, the rate at which we joined was around the average rate for the previous decade. So that was not really an issue.

In one of the lulls between these international phone calls, I found in the Admiralty House bookshelves a memoir by Malcolm MacDonald, son of Ramsay MacDonald. MacDonald had been a member of the Attlee government and a distinguished Secretary of State for the Colonies. He was a friend of my parents-in-law and I went once to his house in the country where, for fear of burglars, he kept a Turner on the back of his bedroom door under his dressing gown. The book contained a story about Churchill. In Churchill's last period in office, the grandees of the Tory Party decided that the time had come for the old man to go. Lord Halifax, the Willie Whitelaw of his day, was sent to tell Churchill that, after his years of heroic devotion, the time had come for him to lay down the burdens of office. According to MacDonald's account, Churchill listened politely. Then, blowing rings of cigar smoke in Halifax's direction, he said: "My dear Edward, I have always made it a rule of my life never to leave the pub before closing time." He remained Prime Minister for another two years.

Soon after Black Wednesday, John Major felt that "closing time" had come for him. The story of the resignation broadcast that was never made has been told by John Major in his autobiography. I argued with him then that he should stay and, for what little contribution I made to his decision to do so, I am glad that I did. But he correctly saw, as I did not, that his own credibility, and that of the government, had taken a fatal knock. He was thereafter never certain that to resign would not have been the correct decision. The subsequent success of the Government's management of the economy and the buoyancy of the finances by 1997 were not enough to recreate trust and confidence. From Black Wednesday can be dated the demise of the view that only the Conservatives could competently manage the economy.

The extent of the debacle was clear when Parliament was recalled on 24 September to debate the crisis. The government did not want to commit themselves to rejoining the ERM, but nor could they rule it out. They had identified "fault lines" in the ERM which would need to be addressed before Britain could consider going back into a reformed system. The principal fault line was the economic fall-out from German reunification and the need for high interest rates across Europe due to a mechanism geared to the Deutschmark at a time in the economic cycle when Britain needed the exact opposite. I still believe that, had we not gone into the ERM, we would never have found the discipline to put an end to the inflationary "stop–go" policies that had bedevilled the management of the economy throughout my life and which largely accounted for our relatively poor economic performance for twenty years from the 1960s onwards. But the public political impact of our withdrawal from the ERM haunts us still. Just as the humiliation of Suez explains why crossing the US government has generally been bad politics in Britain, our withdrawal from the ERM helps explain the persistent hostility in Britain to the single currency. We linked our currency to those of our partners and were forced into what looked like a humiliating defeat. Thereafter, our economy prospered and for most people in Britain the logic of joining the euro zone looked very counter-intuitive.

In his autobiography, John Major describes the performance of the new Leader of the Opposition, John Smith, in the debate on the ERM as a "brilliant debating performance . . . Presented with an open goal, he joyfully smashed the ball into the net". So it seemed at the time and so the debate still reads to this day. John Smith's task was made easier by the fact that, less than a week before Black Wednesday, the Prime Minister, more in an attempt to shore up the markets than in total conviction, had publicly stated that there would be no devaluation and no realignment. In truth, the storm that hit sterling was like a tsunami: a cataclysm whose possibility is acknowledged while its likelihood seems unthinkable. The Opposition had fully supported the decision to join the ERM. While they mocked the indecision of the government on whether to seek re-entry, John Smith, when challenged, was careful to make no promises: any decision would have to be taken in the light of circumstances at the time. If John Major's policy could be called that of "wait and see", then so could John Smith's though, politics being an unfair business, it was not.

The failure of the ERM strategy was grist to the mill of Euro-sceptics and others who were in various ways disgruntled. I have heard John Major make the point, obvious when you stop to think about it, that the longer a government is in power, the greater the hostility to it from within the ranks of its own supporters: the pool of those eligible for ministerial office gets smaller, the ranks of those dismissed from office gets larger, and the hopes of those languishing on the backbenches grow dimmer. In the case of John Major's government, these problems were compounded by the disloyalty of Margaret Thatcher and her court. If Margaret Thatcher herself had suffered from the grumpy carping of Ted Heath, she seemed determined to outdo him, rather than avoid the same destructive tendency. Her criticisms started as dinner table scuttlebutt, invariably reported back to John Major. They soon graduated to overt opposition, especially on Europe and the Maastricht Treaty. I once suggested to John Major that he should be bold on some aspect of EU policy. "You forget", he said, "that I am standing astride a crack in the Conservative Party that is growing wider by the day."

It was against that background that John Major again set out in the House of Commons his policy on Britain's place in the EC. He said:

There are broadly three schools of thought about our membership of the Community. The first—it is spread thinly across each political party—is that we should leave the Community; that we should never have joined. It is a minority view, often disguised by rhetoric affirming support for the principles of membership while actions speak the opposite. There are people who, in their hearts, would prefer it if we were not in the Community, who trade under false colours and who do not address their arguments to the implications of non-membership for jobs, prosperity and the future.

The second school of thought is that European development is inevitable and goes inexorably in one direction: that sooner or later a centralised Europe is inevitable . . . I do not share the belief in the desirability or inevitability of a centralised Europe. Each country in the Community at times of crisis will inevitably look first to its own national interest; each will pool some of it in the common interest, but none will sacrifice it. Just as the interests of France and Germany will always come first for them, so the interests of Britain must always come first for us. I understand the fears about a centralised Europe, but I think they are fanciful, for we will not have one.

The third school of thought, the one for which I stand, is quite different. It is that it is in the interests of Britain—our interests, our objectives and our prosperity—for us to be part of the development of our continent. By part, I do not mean a walk-on part; I do not mean simply being a member. I mean playing a leading role in the European Community . . . We will need to compromise on some matters, but so will every nation state in Europe unless we return to tribalism right across the European Community.

Intense activity can sometimes be a useful diversion. After the debacle of Black Wednesday, the Government called a special meeting of the European Council for 16 October in Birmingham. The ostensible aim was to address the fault lines in the ERM, to look at the issue of subsidiarity, that is, less centralisation, and to map out a way of dealing with the Danish no vote in the referendum on Maastricht. The underlying rationale was to recreate a sense of direction and authority in the British Presidency.

As part of the preparations, John Major met President Mitterrand in Paris at the end of September. Mitterrand's prostate cancer had just been made public, though it had been diagnosed some time earlier. John Major expressed his sympathy. "So far so good", said the President. He had got to the age of 75, the age when many people died, without any serious medical problems. Now he had spoiled his record but he would try in the time available to do what was necessary. One needed a very solid constitution, he said, to tackle European problems.

Turning to the French referendum, which had been narrowly won, Mitterrand said that he had expected a 52% yes from the very start and had been wrong by only 1% [I recall him telling John Major when he had first called the referendum that he expected an outcome of 55% in favour]. In 1974, he had been beaten by Giscard d'Estaing, who had a majority of only half the size of the margin in the referendum. He had observed the difference between victory and defeat. Mitterrand felt that the "no" voters in France had been people who did not really know what they wanted and whose views were dominated by day-to-day issues.

The Prime Minister said that many of the grievances which had come to the fore in the referendums on Maastricht reflected complaints which, in the UK, were long-standing: that the Community was too centralist, about the lack of consultation over EC legislation, and over loss of national identity. On a wider point, he believed it was right for the UK to play a major role in Europe. He was prepared to take great risks for that. But the President should know that, if he was defeated on the Maastricht Bill, he did not believe that any Prime Minister, whether himself or another, would be able to go down the same road for a long time. Defeat on the Maastricht Bill would leave a political legacy which would take a long time to overcome. There was no way he was seeking a row with Germany, but he had wanted to explain to the President the degree of bitterness that was felt in London [over the comments by the Head of the Bundesbank which, it was felt, had helped trigger the run on the pound].

Mitterrand said that he could have hoped for greater European solidarity early on, both for Britain and for France [whose currency had also been under severe pressure]. Fortunately, Kohl had seen the seriousness of the situation and the risk of the damage going very much wider. So things had stopped there. That would remain the case because he and Kohl had built a serious agreement.

Mitterrand said that there was no doubt that the Commission (he excepted Delors who was a friend of his) had made excessive use of its powers. Power should lie more with the European Council and less with the Commission. Maybe we would get to more supranationality in future but now anything other than full respect for subsidiarity would be fatal for Europe.

John Major said that he hoped the European Council at Birmingham would make a declaration on:

- Greater openness
- More Commission consultation, for example, Green Papers
- Greater involvement by national parliaments
- Rolling back some legislation
- Showing how the Maastricht Treaty affected people's lives

John Major added that he did not see how the ERM could work properly unless it was a policy more appropriate for all of Europe and not just for Germany. We should look at reforms of the ERM such as intramarginal support. Just as currencies at the bottom of the band had to buy their own currency and put up interest rates, so currencies at the top should be obliged to sell their currency and lower their interest rates. This did not find favour with Mitterrand, who commented that he did not see the majority of EC countries, who had remained within the system, making deep changes. Finance ministers had already opposed what Britain was suggesting. By contrast, he was attracted by the declaration that John Major had outlined, though he hoped we would not subject the Commission to too much flak. The Prime Minister said we would not, with one or two exceptions. Did those exceptions include Sir Leon Brittan [a particular bête noire of the French because of his rigorous pursuit of EC competition policy for which he was then responsible]? asked Mitterrand. The Prime Minister, wisely, did not respond. A few years earlier, Mrs Thatcher and Mitterrand had had a similar conversation in which Mitterrand had commented that all Commissioners "went native" in Brussels— except of course—the British. "Especially the British", Thatcher had replied, with feeling. Mitterrand concluded by telling Major that he did not want to see Britain uselessly isolated with Denmark. He would help us to use Birmingham to put balm on burns that remained all too sore for the time being. He believed that the Prime Minister had shown great courage over Maastricht in the way he had led public opinion. He had seen him at work and had been struck by his honesty in difficult situations. Britain would not be put at a disadvantage by France.

At the time, the Birmingham European Council felt like one of those events to be got past and forgotten. It was memorable mainly for the long absences from the meeting of President Mitterrand, whose health was problematic, and John Major's distraction due to the mysterious disappearance, in London, of the Chancellor of the Exchequer. Norman Lamont had been worsted in a discussion at the Star Chamber (a meeting of ministers to try to resolve wrangles over departmental budgets in the annual expenditure round). He had walked out and vanished. No one knew whether he had simply gone to cool off or to resign. He eventually showed up but, in the meantime, John Major spent as much time on a phone outside the meeting room (there were then no mobile phones) as he did in the chair, trying to track the whereabouts and intentions of the errant Chancellor.

As Mitterrand had predicted, British efforts to identify and correct the fault lines in the ERM made little progress. Rather more was achieved on the other issues on the British shopping list. The Birmingham Declaration, as Major reported to the House of Commons, recognised:

the importance of national identity. It acknowledges that the Community can act only where member states have given it the power to do so in the treaties. It lays down that action at the Community level should happen only when necessary. It calls for new guidelines so that when the Community action is taken it takes the lightest possible form. It introduces better consultation by the Commission before proposals are brought forward. It calls for a greater role for national Parliaments in the work of the Community. The declaration provides, for the first time, a proper framework for the practical definition and implementation of subsidiarity.

Public reaction was not generous. The Dutch Press dismissed the Birmingham declaration as containing little of importance. The problems surrounding the Maastricht Treaty were no nearer solution and the general lack of confidence in Europe felt by her citizens remained. In Germany, one newspaper (*NRC Handelsblad*) was even starker in its analysis, not just of the failure of Birmingham, but of the European leaders as a whole:

Instead of seeking a reason for the recent monetary crisis, and making a start on formulating policy to ensure that a similar situation does not occur again, the leaders in Birmingham have tried to represent the derailment of Europe as the result of a misunderstanding between people and politicians as though that is a small breakdown that can be remedied by public relations exercises.

In the House of Commons, John Smith dismissed the summit as being typical of the British Presidency as a whole: "indecisive and largely irrelevant", while the Liberal Democrat leader, Paddy Ashdown, dubbed it "the summit that never was".

Fifteen years later, much of the agenda set out in the Birmingham Declaration is still a work in progress. But it is an active and quite successful agenda and Birmingham was its birthplace. In that respect, the Birmingham summit was not unlike the one-day summit at Hampton Court called by Tony Blair during the British EU Presidency of 2005. At the time, that summit was dismissed by the Press as a public relations exercise designed to distract attention from Britain's isolation on the issue of her budget rebate. But the EU's Energy policy, which later dominated much of the agenda, was set in train at that meeting.

The Dutch Press were right to say that Birmingham did nothing to resolve the underlying crisis over the ratification of the Maastricht Treaty. In Britain, that crisis was now acute. Following the Danish "no" vote, the government had suspended work on the Maastricht Bill in the House of Commons until the intentions of the Danish government became clear. This was logical, since, in legal terms, a Danish failure to ratify dealt a terminal blow to the treaty. But Denmark was hardly the most influential member of the Community. They were seen as being as sceptical as the British but without the clout that comes from being a big player. A French "no" in September would have let the British government off the hook, just as the French "no" in 2005 let Britain off the hook of its promised referendum on the draft constitution. But the French had voted yes and Britain had little option but to try to resume the ratification process in the House of Commons. In November, the Government sought to revive the Bill via a paving debate which would be a prelude to the start of the committee stages.

Opening the debate, the Prime Minister once again stressed the importance for Britain of playing a central role in the Community, but this time the argument was couched in somewhat more combative terms, reflecting the extent of opposition to the Maastricht Treaty in the Conservative Party and the open hostility to it of Margaret Thatcher, Norman Tebbit, and others:

There are important decisions to be made, now and in the immediate future, about the way in which the Community develops. We can develop as a centralist institution, as some might want, or we can develop as a free-market, free-trade, wider European Community more responsive to its citizens. I am unreservedly in favour of the latter form of the Community, and I believe that that is the overwhelming view of this country. But there is only one way in which we can bring that Community about, and I believe that it is this—by Britain playing a full part in the Community, by arguing its case, by forming alliances, by exercising its influence and authority, by persuading, by pushing, by fighting for its interests and, sometimes, by digging our toes in and saying no as we did over the social chapter and the single currency... A centralist Community is most likely to develop if Britain has no influence in the Community, if it is sidelined, and if we do stand aside and let others run Europe while Britain scowls in frustration on the fringes.

Later in his speech, Major stressed the significance of the so-called pillared treaty structure achieved at Maastricht:

One of the matters that concerned us most in the run-up to the negotiations was that, hitherto, each and every development in the Community could only go through the central institutions—the Treaty of Rome and the Commission, and justiciably through the European Court of Justice. At Maastricht, we developed a new way, and one much more amenable to the instincts of this country: cooperation by agreement between Governments, but not under the Treaty of Rome. It covers interior and justice matters, foreign affairs and security, and the option is available for it to cover wider matters in future. Some member states—I make no secret of it—had ambitions for that cooperation to go through the traditional route. We resisted that, and in doing so set a pattern for further cooperation.

The result in the House of Commons was a close-run thing. The Government carried the day by three votes after doing a deal with one of its backbenchers in which he was given a promise that the Bill would not receive its third reading unless and until the Danes, who were edging towards a second referendum, had voted in favour of the treaty.

The Foreign Secretary, Douglas Hurd, was not consulted about this last ditch manoeuvre which put Britain's own ratification of the treaty at the mercy of the Danes and meant Britain would, in all circumstances, be the last country to ratify. The following day, when the Prime Minister and Foreign Secretary met to reflect on what had been done, it was clear that Douglas Hurd was deeply discontented with the decision. He had a key ring, featuring a silver horse's head, which had been given him by Prime Minister Andreotti of Italy (an entirely appropriate gift from a politician who was later convicted of conspiracy with the mafia). Douglas Hurd always used the key ring as his version of worry beads, but usually in a rather carefree fashion. That morning, the key ring was being twirled in a decidedly agitated manner.

It was tempting to act as if the whole deal had never been made. But Douglas Hurd said forcefully that that would not do. In any case, the backbencher in question, doubtless realising that last night's suitor might, in the cold light of day, rue the shotgun engagement, quickly made the details public. So it stuck. It turned out to be a passing embarrassment both domestically and among our partners. It had, after all, saved the day, the Bill, and the treaty. Months later, the Bill passed into law.

There was never any question in John Major's mind of going back on the commitment he had entered into when he had negotiated the treaty. He would doubtless have heaved a sigh of relief had the French voted against it. But he was always adamant that Britain's international credibility would be destroyed if she did not stand by a treaty freely negotiated, especially one whose details had been effectively approved in advance by the House of Commons and whose outcome had been enthusiastically welcomed. If the treaty had not been ratified, John Major would have resigned, as he would have failed to meet his treaty commitment to his European colleagues. His view was that if you entered into an agreement and did not discharge it, no one would subsequently trust you, and therefore you could not properly do the job. By the same token, our non-ratification would have provoked a much greater European crisis. Had the treaty not been ratified by Britain, we would have been less easy than Denmark to intimidate into trying again with the, mostly cosmetic, safeguards that eventually enabled the Danes to win a second referendum.

In the European farm, some animals are more equal than others. The founding members, and those seen to play the game wholeheartedly, undoubtedly have more leeway with their partners than do those who are perceived to be back markers. Had Britain failed to ratify, the Maastricht Treaty would have been stopped in its tracks. Britain's partners would have allowed her time for reflection and reconsideration but not, I think, renegotiation. The determination of the other members to proceed with EMU would have led them in due course to a separate treaty and, as Douglas Hurd commented in his memoirs, to "the nightmare which had always alarmed our predecessors: a continental union influencing British lives at almost every turn over which we had no control".

The British Presidency of 1992 maintained the tradition by which our generals lose every battle but the last. The last "battle" was the Edinburgh European Council in December. However, while it was intricate, tense, and intense, it was one of the least bad-tempered of the many last-chance, one-minute to midnight negotiations I attended. It had to put together a deal for the Danes which would allow them enough changes to the negotiated Maastricht Treaty to justify, and win, a second referendum. It had to agree an increase in the overall ceiling of the Community's Own Resources without, from the British perspective, undermining our budget rebate. The increase in the budget ceiling had to be small enough not to dismay the Germans and large enough to allow for increased structural fund spending in the poorer member states. Of these, Spain, under Felipe Gonzalez, was the most deter-mined and uncompromising.

With John Major, Michael Jay, and Gus O'Donnell (the Prime Minister's Press Secretary), I had been part of the small group which flew by RAF plane, day after day, to almost every EC capital in the run-up to Edinburgh. Felipe Gonzalez knew little of the ins and outs of the structural funds or of the proposed cohesion fund designed to help the four poorest countries in the EC (Spain, Portugal, Ireland, and Greece) with transport and energy infrastructure projects. But he knew the amount of money he wanted and dug in hard. His Portuguese opposite number, Anibal Cavaco Silva, was a man after John Major's heart. He had studied economics at York University, was as determined as Gonzales but had mastered all the minutiae of the funds. He would score on points while Gonzalez went for the knock-out blow. It was on our visit to Lisbon that John Major told Cavaco Silva that it was his intention to nominate me as the next British ambassador to Portugal. Cavaco Silva passed the word to his Foreign Minister, Jose-Manuel Durao Barroso, who replied, as he told me three years later: "What have we done wrong?" It did, incidentally, take all of us who worked for John Major a little time to decipher the identity of two people on the European scene whom he clearly rated highly and whose names appeared to be Annabelle and Juliana. British Prime Ministers and the pronunciation of foreign names are not easy companions. In the run-up to Britain's entry into the EC, Ted Heath broadcast in French on French television. "Excellent speech by your Prime Minister", said our French friends, "What language was it in?" The combined linguistic skills of Jay, Wall, and Gus O'Donnell eventually worked out that "Annabelle" was Anibal Cavaco Silva and "Juliana" was Giuliano Amato.

John Major describes the Edinburgh summit in his autobiography as, Maastricht aside, the most successful he attended as Prime Minister and he expresses pride at having been in the chair. He pulled off a remarkable success. He was under domestic pressure on Europe. The Maastricht Bill was still hanging fire. Major told one of the Heads of Government that, in a free vote, up to 40% of the parliamentary Conservative Party would vote against the Maastricht Bill. And a significant number of tricky issues had to be brought together.

Timing is a huge ingredient in the success or failure of European negotiations. Agreement is usually reached, not when the Heads of Government or the Press have declared a crisis—for on that measure, the EU is in crisis most of the time—but when the Heads share a sense that, if they do not reach agreement, there will be serious consequences. In 1984, Margaret Thatcher secured a good deal for Britain over the budget rebate because the EC's finances were about to run out and could not be increased without Britain's agreement. In 1985, agreement was reached on the SEA because the Italians, by cleverly outvoting Britain on calling an IGC, had instilled in the British a fear that, if we did not compromise, we would be left behind by the other member states and that our real interests would suffer. In 1991, it was the knowledge that our partners could, and probably would, go ahead with their own treaty establishing a monetary union if Britain were to veto the draft on the table that led the British government, from quite an early stage, to seek a compromise which would allow the other member states to go ahead and Britain to join later, or not to join at all. The majority used their leverage on Britain to induce us to compromise. We used our veto over the draft treaty to extract concessions favourable to Britain which would not have been available had we pushed the issue to the point of rupture. In December 2003, the Italians were unable to reach an agreement on the draft EU constitution. Six months later, the Irish succeeded in doing so with a package that was substantially little changed. The Irish skilfully built up the pressure in the cooker in their six months in office. In 2004, the Luxembourg Presidency failed to pull off an agreement on the EU budget, including the UK abatement. Six months later, Tony Blair, as Chair of the Council, secured an agreement which, in financial terms, was not hugely different but which, in political terms, represented a new ball game. In his case, he used the impending sense of crisis in different ways: he built up the pressure on others to believe that Britain was more likely to compromise during her Presidency than after it. At home, he fended off pressure from the Treasury to hold out beyond our Presidency by arguing that we would get a better deal from ourselves as Presidency than from any other member state, given that only one country, the UK, wanted the abatement to continue while all the other twenty-four wanted it to be abolished. He was also able to use the growing sense of grievance against Britain on the part of the new member states to argue that Britain's real interests in those countries would suffer if we allowed the argument to persist beyond our six months in the chair.

The other issue of timing is that of when to put proposals on the table. At Maastricht, John Major had held back the British detailed opt-out protocol until a stage in the European Council when our partners were too close to the finishing line to have time or energy to argue over the detail. Had the opt-out protocol been tabled on day one, it would have been subjected to death by a thousand cuts. In 2005, the British Presidency held back its proposals for the budget until just before the final European Council, keeping up their sleeve the sweeteners for individual member states and a substantive concession of their own. If those concessions had been plucked out of the hat too soon, they would have become, not the basis for a resolution, but the starting point for a whole new phase of negotiation.

John Kerr, Britain's Permanent Representative to the EU, played a similar game in 1992. It is the Presidency's strongest card: however irritated and querulous your partners become, however much they may criticise your behaviour, they cannot force the Presidency's hand. So, on the British budget rebate, in particular, the British Presidency held its ace close to its chest. Fifty pages of text on the budget had been discussed in COREPER before Edinburgh, with all but one sentence (on the British abatement) agreed and eighteen blanks left—those covering the crucial numbers.

John Major faced, in 1992, similar pressure to that faced by Tony Blair in 2005. The Chancellor, Norman Lamont, and his senior officials wanted to postpone a deal on the budget (including the issue of the British rebate) until after the British Presidency, arguing that we would not then be constrained by the obligations of being in the chair. John Major, however, agreed with John Kerr that it was better to settle while we were in control of the agenda. Norman Lamont was not pleased when Major came down against him, but that decision was vindicated by events.

A number of things helped produce the success at Edinburgh. The choice of venue, both Edinburgh and Holyrood House, were good ones. The city was looking like the set from the film "Tunes of Glory"; the appeal of meeting in a Palace which was known to be not a tourist attraction but the Queen's home was irresistible and the reversal of the normal order of the agenda helped create a friendly atmosphere. Normally, the Heads of Government have an opening session of the Council in the morning, then go to a formal lunch with the Head of State of the host country and work through the afternoon and evening, which includes a working dinner. At Edinburgh, the Heads worked through lunch and the formal meeting with the Queen was over a dinner in the evening on the royal yacht *Britannia*. As I recall, this was done to fit in with the Queen's own programme and there was some tutting about it at the time on the grounds that it would disrupt the flow of serious business. But, in many respects, it is better to do business during the working day rather than when people are tired at the day's end. The Heads of Government were seduced by the welcome they had on *Britannia* and, in that pre-digital age, the Palace pulled off something of a coup. Before dinner on *Britannia*, the Heads had their group photograph taken with the Queen and Prince Philip. By the time they disembarked from *Britannia*, a few hours later, each had been given a silver-framed copy, signed by the Queen and the Prince. No combination of courtesy and showmanship will be enough to produce an agreement where the substantive ingredients are not right. But they can certainly help create the right mood.

In the days when more meetings of the European Council were held in the capital of the Presidency country than in Brussels, Margaret Thatcher used to argue that the dreary grimness of the Charlemagne building in Brussels made it harder to reach agreement there than elsewhere in the Community. I spent some of the happiest hours of my professional career in the Justus Lipsius building which is now the home of all formal meetings, including of the European Council, and I am probably the only person who has a good word to say for it. I would change only one thing. Still being an inquisitive 10-year-old at heart, I could not resist, as I walked out of the building one day, rapping my knuckles on the splendid bronze bust of Justus Lipsius, a Flemish Renaissance worthy, which dominates the front entrance. The bronze turned out to be made of hollow plastic. Whatever symbolism one chooses to read into that, even I would not claim that the Justus Lipsius building is a piece of architecture destined to induce a sense of history, destiny, or compromise in those who negotiate in its soulless rooms.

The series of interlocking issues that were eventually resolved at Edinburgh were the need to find a solution to Denmark's inability to ratify the Maastricht Treaty following her failed referendum; the financing of the Community until the end of the century (including the place of the British rebate within that); the need to remove the block on the opening of enlargement negotiations with Sweden, Finland, and Austria (which in turn depended on finding additional resources for the "poor four" member states who would most feel the stiff wind of competition—or so they argued); the issues of subsidiarity and openness dear to the heart of the British government; and the vexed question of the site of a number of EC institutions.

At lunch on the first day, 11 December, the division between what the British Presidency were trying to achieve and the approach of some partners was evident. John Major told his partners that, if the Heads got it wrong and the Danes lost a second referendum, the political reality was that the other eleven member states could not just go ahead and ratify the treaty. There would have to be a new negotiation which would be a huge setback. Nor did he believe that an agreement based on the eleven, leaving Denmark behind, would get through the British Parliament. They would argue that, if Denmark were left behind now, who would be left behind next?

Chancellor Kohl said that, if Denmark was forced to separate from the rest of the membership, then Germany would want to go further. Mitterrand agreed. France would continue with those who were willing. The Prime Minister replied that, on that basis, there was no doubt that the British position and the Franco-German position were not compatible in the event of the treaty failing. The stakes were very high.

Poul Schluter, the Danish Prime Minister, said that he hoped to have a basis for a new Danish referendum. The consequences of another "no" would be that Denmark would cease to be an ordinary member of the EC.

Quite a lot of the menacing language from Mitterrand and Kohl was deliberately designed to make Danish flesh creep: they wanted the Danish government and people to realise that a second "no" would have serious consequences. There was a warning to Britain too that the option of burying the treaty in a Danish graveyard was not acceptable.

After the flesh creeping, member states rallied round the plan that had been in gestation for some weeks of providing an interpretation of the treaty which would, as the Council's legal adviser, the clever and inventive Frenchman Jean-Claude Piris, advised the Heads, clarify the treaty provisions for Denmark. It was an intergovernmental act with binding legal consequences. However, that "did not mean, either in national law, Community law, or constitutional law that it needed to be ratified".

Denmark's "no" vote was the first time in the history of the EC that a member state had been unable to ratify a European treaty. But then, the Maastricht Treaty was only the second significant treaty change since the original Treaty of Rome. Later, the Irish failed to ratify the Nice Treaty first time round, and France and the Netherlands lost their referendums on the Constitutional Treaty. As the EU enlarges, securing national ratification for controversial EU treaties is bound to become harder. Whether this presages the kind of parting of the ways foreshadowed by Kohl and Mitterrand in Edinburgh, or greater caution in approaching treaty change in the first place, is an issue so far unresolved.

John Major had to pay one small price for his success at Edinburgh: as part of a complex package on the site of EU institutions, that is, which EU body is headquartered in which EU capital, Mitterrand secured binding reassurance that the EP would remain in Strasbourg and that eleven plenary sessions a year would be held there. Anyone who fears that we are about to be swamped by a federal Europe should listen in to the debate among Heads of Government as they fight, like stags in rut, over whose country should have the privilege of hosting the European Cross-border Widgets Institute. It is not an elevating spectacle.

There is a scene, in a BBC television documentary made at the time, which shows the British delegation at Edinburgh spontaneously applauding John Major as he leaves at about 2.30 in the morning at the end of the Council. It had been a bravura performance. It was the high point of the Presidency, which thus ended in success, and it was the high point of John Major's engagement with the EU.

The following year, with the ERM again in crisis, John Major sat on a hillside overlooking the Douro valley in Portugal and composed an article for *The Economist* in which he wrote that, if the response of the EU to the crisis that had almost brought the ERM to its knees that year was to continue with EMU as if nothing had happened, then that would have all the quality of a rain dance and about as much potency. I was involved in that draft and agreed with it. The comment irritated Helmut Kohl, caused anguish in the Foreign Office, and was later seen as showing how out of touch the British government was with what was happening in Europe. In retrospect, it was certainly provocative. However, those in the EMU project did postpone its start date from 1997 to 1999, and the Stability and Growth pact was negotiated as a reassurance to Germany of financial rigour. John Major's preoccupation with convergence, later shared by Gordon Brown, looks less obsessive now than it did to his partners then. The economic reform needed to compensate for the absence of national decision-making on exchange rates and interest rates still eludes some member states and is one reason why the euro zone has not been as successful as it otherwise might. But it is also true that determination not to be excluded from the euro zone empowered finance ministers all over Europe, including Italy, to get belts tightened and debt, deficits, and inflation down. Against that background, it was not perceptive of many in Britain, myself included, to cling to a belief that, in the end, EMU might not happen. In fairness to them, some in the Treasury and Sir John Kerr, the UK Permanent Representative until 1995, were consistent in their view that it would happen. In my own case, it was not until I got to Brussels as Kerr's successor in 1995 that I appreciated the truth of what he had been saying.

By then, the Conservative government's dwindling majority at home, and the rising tide of Euro-scepticism in the Conservative Party, had reduced John Major's room for manoeuvre to zero. Sullen dissent flared into open conflict in the crisis over BSE, Mad Cow Disease, in 1996. It was one of the unhappiest,

though blessedly short-lived, chapters in Britain's relationship with her partners. It was an issue where fear skewed objective judgement on both sides.
It led to a feeling among Britain's partners, subsequently reinforced by the
Government's approach to the Amsterdam Treaty, that perhaps even the UK's
commitment to EU membership was in doubt.

The BSE crisis had been slow to build up but sudden to break. The risk
to cattle from feed made up of mashed-up sheep parts had been recognised
and measures to ban the use of such feed put in place. But the enforcement of
the ban had been very patchy and the extent of the disease among the British
herd came to light belatedly and with devastating speed. Douglas Hogg, the
Minister of Agriculture, told his ministerial colleagues that the entire British
herd might have to be destroyed. That would have been economically devastating and politically unsustainable. From then on, from my viewpoint as
Britain's ambassador to the EU in Brussels, the measures that the government
took to tackle the crisis were an uneasy compromise between the scientifically necessary and the politically deliverable. When the European Commission, who had been inadequately informed of developments at the outset,
banned exports of British beef throughout the world, the Euro-sceptics in
the Conservative Party saw it as an opportunity to declare war on Brussels.
A subsequent decision by the Standing Veterinary Committee to maintain a
ban on British exports of gelatine, semen, and tallow, despite a Commission
recommendation that the ban should in due course be lifted, prompted the
British government's policy of non-cooperation.

The Government saw the decision of the senior EU vets as a blatant piece
of political and commercial discrimination. I had met all the senior EU veteri-
narians at my house in an attempt to persuade them of our case. They found
themselves in an invidious position. This was not an area where the science
was absolutely clear. If they took a decision in our favour, their governments
would face huge criticism at home, not just from farmers who feared for their
herds, but from a population who feared for their lives. The decision of the
Standing Veterinary Committee to maintain the ban was a response, not born
of a desire to punish the British or to secure commercial advantage, but of fear
of taking a decision that might end up harming the health of their citizens and
their herds. It was not received as such in Britain where it aroused fury on the
Conservative benches and led the government to doubt if they could retain the
support of the House of Commons.

In response, the government devised, in haste, a policy of non-cooperation
whereby any decision in the EU, in whatever forum, that required the unanimous consent of all member states would be vetoed by the British. The first
minister called upon to implement it was the Development Minister, Lynda
Chalker, a former Europe minister and a lifelong supporter of the EC. She dis-
played a clear sense of reluctance and embarrassment. Even the Euro-sceptic

Home Secretary, Michael Howard, was embarrassed to find himself having to veto in the Council a proposal which had been a British initiative in the first place.

Our partners, and the Italian Presidency, bore with us. They had little choice in the short term. But it soon became clear that, if the policy of non-cooperation were sustained, our national interests would start to suffer: our partners would not allow their interests to be overruled and would look for ways of getting round the British veto or of retaliating. At a meeting of the General Affairs Council, the foreign ministers one after the other took Britain's Foreign Secretary, Malcolm Rifkind, to task. It was reasoned argument but the basic message was that the British government had to find a way of meeting the very real concerns of its partners about the inadequacy of our response to the biggest animal health crisis in the Community's history. While, in Britain, the government felt that our partners were playing politics with our predicament, on the Continent, our partners felt that Britain was allowing political self-interest to get the better of scientific judgement and effective remedial action.

John Major himself quickly realised that the policy of non-cooperation was unsustainable. The EU, like any other organisation, depends on give and take. The European Commission is called upon to take decisions on the adequacy of the implementation of EU law by individual member states. It decides on the applications by member states to grant state aids for domestic projects. It determines the application of competition law in mergers and takeovers. In all these areas, the Commission and the member states are obliged to follow rules. But in every decision on whether to take a country to the European Court or to deny its state aid application, 90% may be the rule book but 10% will be political judgement. If the Commission decided to go 100% by the rule book and to allow no room for negotiation with the member state concerned, then life could become pretty tough for that country. That is the situation Britain would have found herself in if she had persisted with the policy of non-cooperation. There would have been nothing in the behaviour of the Commission that we could legitimately have complained about, but we would have felt our position becoming more and more uncomfortable in areas where we depended on good will.

The Italian government, whose presidency was being held to ransom by our action, had every interest in helping Britain to find a way out. Once he realised the gravity of the situation, Commission President Jacques Santer also put his mind to finding a solution. That solution was the development of a rigorous, scientifically based programme of actions, going further in terms of the culling of animals than the British government wanted, which all member states could sign up to and which did take the politics out of the subsequent progressive lifting of the ban. It is a measure of anti-European sentiment in the UK that the United States, which maintained a ban on the import of UK beef products for much longer than the EU, received very little of the hostility that had been directed at Brussels.

The ramifications of the affair stretched in time well into the Blair government as the French government of Lionel Jospin continued to deny British exports access to French markets after every other member state had accepted the judgement that there was no longer a health risk. Their attitude was a blend of Jospin's generally uncooperative attitude towards Tony Blair; traditional French commercially inspired hostility to British meat imports; and a residue of genuine anxiety following the scandal over tainted blood that had beset an earlier socialist French government. In the end, Commission action against France at the ECJ, a clear ECJ judgement against France, and the threat of swingeing fines if France failed to comply with the judgement led the French government to back down. It was an excellent example of the usefulness of supranational structures in providing a framework in which disputes can be handled and resolved. Had it not been for that framework, Britain and France would probably have got into a series of tit-for-tat retaliatory actions which could easily have spiralled into a serious bilateral dispute.

By this time, 1996, the EU was again in the throes of treaty negotiation. At Maastricht in 1991, the Heads of Government had agreed to a provision in the treaty convening a new IGC in 1996 "with a view to considering . . . to what extent the policies and forms of cooperation introduced by this Treaty may need to be revised". The British government had gone along with the provision because the language used at Maastricht in principle left open whether treaty amendment would actually prove necessary. But the terms of the Maastricht agreement in practice meant that social policy, justice and home affairs, foreign and security policy, and the powers of the EP were all on the agenda. After a months-long preparatory phase led, for Britain, by the Europe Minister David Davies, the negotiating conference itself was conducted mainly at official level. As the UK representative on the negotiating group, I was on a very tight rein. Every week, before each negotiating session, I would receive pages of minute instructions from the Foreign Office, personally authorised by David Davies. The Foreign Office could have saved themselves a lot of trouble by sending a one-line instruction: "Just say no." There was virtually nothing on the agenda that was palatable to the government.

Malcolm Rifkind, the Foreign Secretary, gave advice to John Major before a meeting of the European Council in Dublin in October 1996 where progress in the negotiations was to be discussed:

You may wish to make your intervention constructive but robust. You are keen on early progress so as not to hold up other more important negotiations like enlargement. The best way of achieving this would be to concentrate on the changes which are actually needed at this juncture to prepare for enlargement; to overcome manifest deficiencies demonstrated, in practice, in the present treaties; and to make the EU more relevant and acceptable to people ... The scope of majority voting or the powers of the European Parliament and questions like new rights of citizenship are neither relevant to enlargement nor reflect any demonstrable need for change ... Treaty language on coordinating Member State employment policies is not the answer to people's real concerns on jobs. You might also register the UK's determination to develop a real European Security and Defence identity, anchored within the North Atlantic Alliance.

There was much in this that was eminently sensible. But the issues that Britain wanted to avoid had been placed on the agenda as long ago as Maastricht and constituted a hymn sheet that most of Britain's partners were happy to sing from. To their ears, the British agenda sounded unimaginatively familiar.

In his intervention at Dublin, John Major put forward proposals for flexibility in decision-making in the enlarged Europe. There was a school of thought in the British Cabinet, led by Michael Howard, that wanted flexibility to take the form of what our partners saw as Europe à la carte. In other words, Britain would not prevent her partners from going ahead with any policy which had achieved the necessary majority for approval but she would have the right not to participate. This would have been un-negotiable as an across-the-board provision and would have given scope to others, by the same token, to opt out of swathes of policy where we wanted to bind them in, most notably the Single Market. John Major never seriously entertained it. But he told the European Council that, outside the core disciplines (especially the Single Market), there should be a readiness to allow those who wished to cooperate more closely in certain areas to do so, subject to conditions. Those conditions must include the rights of those member states who did not participate in a particular action. Equally, it would be wrong to force member states into obligations which might build up resentment.

Of equal concern to the government was how to make progress on European Defence. As in 1991, the concern was to allow the evolution of a greater defence role for the EU, especially in the peacekeeping tasks which were rightly predicted to be the area where demand would grow, without undermining the primacy of NATO. Once again, the British government saw the WEU as the vehicle whereby European action and NATO primacy could be reconciled.

Two illustrations highlight the political pressure the government found itself in as its majority dwindled with every by-election. By the end of 1995, the government had conceded that there would be a referendum on EMU entry if the Cabinet should ever decide to recommend it. In the same year, John Major had indicated in an interview with David Frost that any agreement by the government in the IGC to QMV being extended might be cause for a referendum on the resulting treaty change. It took two years of discussion before Cabinet could agree on a referendum on EMU entry. John Major, while in general unenthusiastic about referendums, had come to the conclusion that since EMU entry, if it went wrong, could destroy the political party that took Britain in, it would be prudent to get support from the public. But a number of Cabinet members, notably Michael Heseltine and Kenneth Clarke, were for a long time opposed.

Early in 1997, Malcolm Rifkind embarked on a tour of EU capitals to present the British case. In Bonn, on 19 February, Rifkind told his audience:

Part of what disturbs people in Britain, and many elsewhere, is that they see a constant transfer of power in one direction only. They see all the footsteps leading into the cave and none of them coming out. So they doubt whether it is wise to go any further inside themselves. Where does it end? The conclusion that many draw is that, logically, this process will end in a European state. Mistaken or not, that is a political fact. And this is associated especially with Germany. We hear political leaders in Germany tell us that after Maastricht II we should look forward to Maastrichts III, IV and V. We do not know what might be on the agenda for those conferences. But it is enough to look at the agenda for Maastricht II. The German government is making the following proposals:

1. More majority voting;
2. More co-decision with the European Parliament;
3. Communitisation [i.e. bringing within the ambit of EC law] large areas of justice and home affairs;
4. A common electoral system for the European Parliament;
5. A European police authority;
6. Movement towards common defence;
7. Development of the European Court of Justice in the direction of a supreme constitutional court.

All of these proposals seem to point the same way: a transfer of power from the member states to the European institutions. At least this is further centralisation. To many people it looks like an agenda for creating a European State. Helmut Kohl makes clear that he for one does not foresee a United States of Europe. I am glad to hear that. But people in Britain ask how does a United States of Europe differ from the proposals made by Germany and others for ever closer integration? How far down the road of integration do leaders in Germany and elsewhere think that Europe should go? It is no good saying that the convoy must not go at the pace of the slowest ship. We are not talking about convoys. We are talking about democracy.

Kohl was livid and was only just persuaded not to complain formally. The German Press, doubtless briefed by the German government, laid into the man the *Franfurter Allgemeine Zeitung* called "The Jew, Rifkind". *Die Welt* said this was "not the way for a gentleman to behave". It was, the paper continued,

a piece of British electioneering in Germany aimed at German ideas for a united Europe. The British normally take matters of style and etiquette more seriously than almost any other nation in Europe. How desperate must be the situation of Major's Conservative government for a Foreign Secretary to commit such a breach of etiquette for election purposes and to please British populists.

In the same month, John Major came to Brussels and made a serious and thoughtful speech about economic reform in Europe. It received little attention. By some quirk of IT eccentricity, over a year later, a copy of the UK Representation's telegram reporting John Major's speech found its way into my daily telegram distribution. Before I realised what it was, I thought I was looking at a report of a speech by Tony Blair. There was no difference of substance between the positions of the two men.

I recall John Major's visit for two other reasons. Knowing my obsession with motor cars, he had brought with him, and gave to me, a beautiful model of a Model T Ford, which had been made by Ford apprentices at Bridgend and which had been on display in the Prime Minister's flat in Downing Street. I also noticed that he was no longer wearing the fine watch that had been given to him by the Sultan of Oman, a watch of a value that meant he could wear it while he was Prime Minister but not take with him when he left. Nothing was said. But a General Election was to be held by May. I realised he was clearing the decks.

8

"A New Dawn has Broken has it Not?" New Labour and the European Union

Tony Blair was elected to the House of Commons in 1983 at a time when the Labour Party was committed to withdrawal from the EC. That was not his own view and, canvassing in Sedgefield in the General Election campaign that May, he discovered that it was not really the view of many of his future constituents either.

Following the defeat of 1983 and the election of Neil Kinnock as Labour's new leader, the policy of the party began to change. It has been a feature of British politics, from Macmillan's first application to join the Common Market, that British governments have been favourable to the EC and Oppositions much less so. The period from after the 1983 election until 1992 was one in which the commitment of both main parties to making a success of Britain's EC membership gradually converged. Neil Kinnock moved the Labour Party's stance from "withdrawal" through "withdrawal as a last resort" to a commitment to Britain's successful membership. Neil Kinnock's approach to the Maastricht Treaty in Parliament in 1991 shows the extent of the transformation. The main substantive point of disagreement between Government and Opposition was over the Social Chapter. Then, and later, Labour were able to make political capital from what they portrayed as an opt-out government putting Britain needlessly in a minority of one. In practice, both parties had promised a referendum on entry into the single currency and neither was ready to recommend membership. However, as the 1997 General Election approached, hostility to the single currency, and indeed the EU as a whole, grew in the Conservative Party while Labour's approach became more positive.

Nonetheless, what is interesting is the similarity, rather than the differences, between the manifestos of both parties for the General Election of May 1997. Both talked about avoiding a federal Europe, of a partnership of nations, of focusing on enlargement, CAP reform, the single market, and foreign policy. The Conservative manifesto kept open the option of joining the single currency while stressing the importance of the opt-out and of a referendum.

The Labour manifesto was not dissimilar on EMU. It talked of the "formidable obstacles" in the way of Britain joining in the first phase should EMU go ahead in 1999. It emphasised the triple safeguard of the need for a favourable decision by Cabinet, a vote in favour in Parliament, and then a referendum. The one significant difference in the manifestos was over the Social Chapter. The Conservatives pledged to maintain the opt-out secured at Maastricht. Labour pledged to sign up to the Social Chapter.

This caution on the part of the Labour Party reflected the lack of popular support for EMU, the need to avoid alienating the Murdoch press whose backing Tony Blair had secured when he visited Rupert Murdoch in Australia the previous year, and an unsurprising reluctance on the part of New Labour to believe that their lead in the opinion polls would translate into victory on the day.

This caution was reflected in the one speech Tony Blair made on foreign policy during the campaign in Manchester on 21 April. The speech was entitled: "A New Role for Britain in the World". On Europe, Tony Blair said:

There are three choices open to Britain. The first is leaving; the second is in but impotent; and the third is remaining in but leading...Of course we must stand up firmly for Britain's interests. And, as I have always made clear, we must be prepared to stand alone in support of those interests if necessary. But it is misguided to make perpetual isolation the aim of our policy...I want Britain to be one of the leading countries in Europe...This is a good moment for Britain to make a fresh start in Europe. For the other Europeans are not involved in a Gadarene rush to a European super state. In fact there is a good deal of unease at the pace and direction of integration in many continental countries, not just Britain. And if there were a desire for a super state, we would not hesitate to stop it in its tracks. We want a Europe where national identities are not submerged and where countries cooperate together, not a giant and unmanageable super state run from the centre.

It will be part of our negotiating position at Amsterdam that there should be agreement on our five key points for promoting jobs and prosperity [single market, enlargement, CAP reform, tackling unemployment and creating flexible labour markets, making a reality of foreign policy cooperation]...We will consider the extension of Qualified Majority Voting to areas where it is in Britain's interests to do so whilst retaining the veto in areas where it is essential...I believe we can use our membership of the social chapter to bring about change across Europe...The hardest question remains EMU. It is not yet certain that it will go ahead on 1 January 1999. I can see formidable obstacles to Britain joining in the first wave if it does go ahead, not least that Britain is at a different stage of the economic cycle to the rest of Europe...There must be genuine sustainable convergence between the economies that take part...We will have no truck with a fudged single currency. However, to rule out membership forever would destroy any influence we have over the process. Therefore we will keep our options open. And when we make our decision, we should do so on the basis of a hard headed assessment of our national economic interest … The issue between the parties is not the position on EMU. Our position and the formal position of the Conservatives are the same. The real issue is one of leadership and clarity. John Major's agonies over the single currency illustrate the real dividing line on Europe. It is not federalist or anti federalist—neither of us wants a federal super state. We agree on the maintenance of the national veto in vital areas like tax and treaty change. We agree on the single market. We agree on our attitude to the single currency and the referendum. The real dividing line is between success and failure. The fundamental differences lie in Party management, attitude and leadership.

A day later, writing in the *Sun*, Tony Blair said: "Let me make my position on Europe absolutely clear. I will have no truck with a European super state. If there are moves to create that dragon, I will slay it."

Once in government, New Labour had little time for reflection, as opposed to decision. The negotiation on the Amsterdam Treaty was into its last few weeks. The first thing the government had to do was signal its new approach to its partners. There had been considerable contact between the Labour Party in Opposition and like-minded fellow Europeans, especially the Dutch. Robin Cook, who became Foreign Secretary, was up to speed on most of the detail even before Election Day. In any event, given his capacity, unequalled in my experience by any other politician except Harold Wilson, to read fast and remember everything he had read, he was well on top of the brief by the time he held his first meeting with officials on the subject two days after the election. I recall Robin Cook's surprise that officials had prepared for him a draft minute to the Prime Minister about the negotiations that so accurately reflected the positions previously announced by the Labour Party in Opposition. Labour had been out of office for eighteen years. Cook himself had never been in government before. I think he expected to find a Civil Service that would try to persuade him to take Conservative positions, whereas what he in fact found was a Civil Service nervously anxious to satisfy its new boss.

Joyce Quin, who had been shadow Europe Minister, had, in the event, been made Prisons Minister in the Home Office. Doug Henderson, who, like Tony Blair, had a North East constituency and had been his companion on weekend train journeys back home from London, became Europe Minister and the man who, less than a week after the election, had the task of setting out the government's policy at a meeting of the group of member state representatives that had been negotiating the new treaty each week in Brussels. "I come to this meeting as the representative of a new government with an overwhelming mandate", he said. "One of the most important priorities we have identified is to make a fresh start to Britain's relations with the rest of the EU and draw a line under the recent past." He went on to tell Britain's partners that Britain would

- end its opt-out from the Social Chapter
- support an employment chapter in the treaty
- support enshrining a commitment to human rights
- be prepared to see the Petersberg peacekeeping tasks of the EU included among the issues covered by Europe's CFSP, with the WEU implementing decisions with defence implications

But Henderson warned his colleagues of some areas where the new government would have reservations. "We regard NATO as the primary framework for common defence for all members of the Alliance", he said. He described cooperation in Justice and Home Affairs as:

probably the area where we have most problems. If there is to be treaty change in this area, the UK will want to see explicitly recognised its right to maintain frontier controls in respect of third country nationals. We will also want arrangements which allow us to work together as fifteen member states whenever possible. In our view this should continue to be inter-governmental cooperation.

Henderson signalled areas where Britain was willing to see movement to QMV: industrial policy, some aspects of environment policy, regional policy, "and Article 216". This last was the Article governing the seats of the institutions and meant that the traditional British tease of the French, desperate to keep the article subject to unanimity and thus to prevent the abolition of Strasbourg as the seat of the EP's plenary sessions, was one element of continuity between governments.

The Social Chapter, and Britain's opt-out from it, had been the main reason why the Labour Opposition had voted against the Maastricht Treaty in the House of Commons. Labour was pledged to sign up to it, just as the Tories had been pledged to maintain the opt-out. But to sign up to the Social Chapter, and to the majority-voting decisions it implied in areas such as working time, was not without problems. The government had to establish their credentials as competent managers of the economy. They could not afford to alienate the Confederation of British Industry (CBI), who disliked the Social Chapter. Some ministers feared that the application of the Social Chapter could cause political and practical difficulties and one of the earliest decisions they had to take, and did take, was to stick to the manifesto commitment and to live with the risk. Against that background, what Henderson had to say was significant, not least because his words had largely been written by Robin Cook:

At today's meeting, Britain will take a historic step towards signing up to the Social Chapter. We will tell our European partners that we want the rights and benefits of the Social Chapter to extend to the people of Britain. We do not accept that the British people should be second class citizens with fewer rights than employees on the continent. We want our people to enjoy rights to information about their company, and parental leave with their family as good as those enjoyed by the staff who work on the continent, often from the same companies. The British people have demanded to share in the benefits of the Social Chapter in repeated opinion polls. Today's initiative is a democratic response to the wishes of the British people and the interests of British employees. The Social Chapter is not a threat to British industry or British jobs. Dozens of the largest companies in Britain have already broken the Tory opt-out and opted in to the provisions of the Social Chapter. Not one of them has sacked a single worker as a result. A partnership between innovative management and a committed workforce is key to a competitive company. We will test all future proposals for action under the Social Chapter by whether they promote competitiveness and help us to meet our goal of a skilled, flexible workforce. Today's meeting opens a new chapter in Britain's relations with Europe. It marks a fresh start in Europe for Britain, working with other member states as a partner, not as an opponent.

The new approach was welcomed by Britain's partners. They had begun to doubt whether the Conservative government would be able to agree to any changes at all in the Amsterdam Treaty and, indeed, whether British Euro-sceptic opinion might drive Britain to leave the EU altogether. At the same time, they did not see the approach of the British government as a radical reversal of the British position as they would have expected it before the final year or two of Conservative government had skewed things in a more negative direction. In other words, just as in Britain we have a conception of French or German policy on Europe which does not depend on which party is in power, so our partners had and have a conception of British European policy which transcends our own domestic electoral landscape. Indeed, the government had made clear, in Henderson's statement, that on defence policy, the "communi-tisation" of justice and home affairs, frontier controls and majority voting on tax, and social security, there was continuity of policy.

An Irish official, Bobby McDonagh, who was part of the group negotiating the Amsterdam Treaty, recalled in his book on the subject (*Original Sin in a Brave New World*) that the movement by the new Labour government was limited but concluded: "Overall there was a growing sense that a deal at Amsterdam was now on."

The EU Heads of Government met at Noordvijk, a Dutch North Sea resort, at the end of May for an informal gathering. It was noteworthy for the film star attention given to Tony Blair as, one after another, the Heads vied to be seen and photographed with him. But Blair was not slow to spell out the substance behind the smile. He addressed a meeting of European socialists in Malmo on 6 June. He said:

There can be a third way that manages security and flexibility...We will be using our Presidency of the EU next year to put jobs at the top of the agenda—cutting unnecessary bureaucracy for the small firms that are likely to be the main job creators, completing the single market, promoting welfare to work initiatives which bring real jobs within the reach of those now excluded from the labour market—and all the time keeping a watchful eye on the Social Chapter to ensure that it does not jeopardise more jobs than it creates...We do not believe that the Social Chapter means that Europe should seek to harmonise and regulate wherever it can. The crucial challenges to Europe are to be competitive internationally and to create jobs...Employment policy in each country should remain for each government to decide in its own particular circumstances...I want to help shape Europe's future...But am I satisfied with Europe? Frankly, no. Too many of its concerns and debates seem impossibly remote from ordinary people...How many of our citizens have even heard of the IGC, let alone have the first clue about what we are discussing...So we must find a way to change the focus away from process and onto substance...to stop talking about European theology and start doing things for which real people can see real benefit—jobs, the environment and international security.

These themes were to be something of a leitmotif of the next ten years: a Europe in touch with its citizens, a focus on economic issues, and moderate impatience with the agenda of institutional change that had become the staple fare of the EU. In emphasising the first two of those issues (relevance to the citizen and economic reform), Tony Blair was following a well-established British approach which had begun with Margaret Thatcher. A European audience would not have been in the least surprised to hear a British Prime Minister talk in those terms. They might have been surprised to hear the warning note that Blair struck about the Social Chapter and there was a hint there of difficulties to come.

One immediate difference between Tony Blair and his two predecessors as Prime Minister was that, while he had little inclination for the institutional debate, he was not instinctively averse to institutional change as Margaret Thatcher had been. Nor was the issue, as it had been for John Major, a bear trap ready to be sprung by obsessed backbenchers from his own party. Likewise, while Tony Blair had no natural sympathy for the EP (few members of national parliaments do), he was not preoccupied by it. This meant that the new government could approach the Amsterdam negotiation with a more open mind than their predecessors. They proceeded with caution because they did not want to stir up a media hornet's nest. They did not need to worry about the state of opinion in the Parliamentary Labour Party.

About a week before the Amsterdam meeting, Robin Cook sent a minute to his officials in which he wrote:

In the first phase of our strategy in relation to Europe we have transformed the negotiating climate. It is much more favourable to Britain, much more positive. We are now in the second phase which will climax at Amsterdam, which is tough bargaining to transform that improved negotiating climate into an improved negotiating outcome for Britain...I am quite confident that we are going to come away with a good deal.

So it proved. The addition of provisions on social policy and employment was easily agreed, though the new government, like its predecessors, signalled that it was not prepared to move to majority voting on social security measures or measures that would impinge on the national regulation of employment law. The pillared structure, created at Maastricht by the Conservatives, had proved only partly viable. Most member states wanted foreign policy cooperation to remain a matter for decision by governments but most felt that asylum and immigration matters should progressively be moved to the First Pillar, that is, made subject to the normal EC decision-making procedures, involving proposals from the Commission and decisions by majority. Some wanted this for doctrinal reasons; most for practical ones. Unanimity was the bane of decision-making. Moreover, any agreement reached intergovernmentally had to be ratified in some member states by lengthy procedures in regional assemblies as well as national parliaments.

This change was a relatively easy one for the government to agree to because Tony Blair banked the offer which had first been made some months before to allow Britain to retain her separate frontier controls. It was a concession which our partners were obliged to make in order to secure British acquiescence in what they badly wanted: the incorporation into the Community treaties of their own Schengen frontier agreements which had thus far operated outside the EU legal framework. So, Britain (and Ireland because of the common frontier between the Republic and Northern Ireland) retained her frontiers and, with it, the right to determine her own migration arrangements. But Britain also secured the right to opt into the individual frontier and migration measures which the other member states would make among themselves. At the time, it looked like the best of both worlds. In practice, the arrangement has given rise to some friction between Britain and her partners. But, even now, I doubt whether any British government would feel that the disadvantages of not being fully in the same decision-making loop as our partners in this field outweigh the political benefits of being seen to be able to take our own decisions on visa, migration, and asylum matters.

Some of the rationale for Britain's original position on this issue has in fact changed. The fight against terrorism and international crime is conducted at least as much through good intelligence as through vigilance at frontiers. Frontier controls are anyway largely ineffective in an age of cheap mass travel when citizens enjoy the right to move freely within the EU. But Britain's opt-out from the EU treaty provisions on frontiers has given the government the ability to take the measures it has thought necessary on asylum and visa policy. Moreover, politically, it would still be difficult for a British government to persuade the public that our frontier arrangements could in practice be no better than those of the least efficient member state with whom we shared a common frontier policy. If anything, the enlargement of the Union has made it harder politically to argue that Britain should join the common frontier arrangements.

The Amsterdam Treaty did one of the things that had featured on the list of warning signs of a European state with which Malcolm Rifkind had so irritated the Germans shortly before the General Election. It abolished the procedure whereby, in its relations with the EP, the Council of Ministers had the last word and, in its place, extended the co-decision procedure whereby the Parliament achieved a genuine power of equal participation in decision-making.

This development has caused a big shift in the balance of power inside the EU. Yet it is hard to argue that it has led to anything approaching a European state or that it has either paralysed or undermined effective decision-taking. The old argument used to be that democratic accountability was adequately assured by the Council of Ministers, consisting of politicians who were all elected parliamentarians from their own countries. But the procedures for democratic scrutiny of EU legislation in national parliaments have been, for the most part, slow and inadequate. And it is hard to accept that there should be a directly elected EP and then deny it the powers to do what it is elected to do: represent the interests of the electors. Theory apart, and accepting that the EP has faults, co-decision has led to a more professional approach to legislation by the EP. The quality of individual British MEPs is generally high as is the professional standard of their work. In areas such as financial services, a critically important British interest, the EP has helped advance the British agenda.

At Amsterdam, Tony Blair was cautious on Foreign Policy and Defence. Foreign Policy was excluded from the new arrangements for enhanced cooperation, that is, the ability of sub-groups of member states to cooperate ahead of the EU membership as a whole. At Maastricht, it had been agreed, and written into the treaty, that: "the common foreign and security policy shall include all questions relating to the security of the Union, including the progressive framing of a common defence policy which might lead to a common defence should the EU so decide." At Amsterdam, after a lot of argument, it was agreed that "the common foreign and security policy shall include all questions relating to the security of the Union, including the progressive framing of a common defence policy, in accordance with the second sub-paragraph, which might lead to a common defence, should the European Council so decide."

The "second sub-paragraph" gave a special role to the WEU. As at Maastricht, the position and obligations of NATO members were also explicitly recognised.

Textual exegesis of EU treaties is one way to go quietly mad, only exceeded as a route to hysteria by having to negotiate them in the first place. The nub of the argument lay around the degree of automaticity in the move towards the progressive framing of a common defence policy. As usual, the convoluted formula papered over a gap between those, led by the British, who wanted to ensure the primacy of NATO in European territorial defence and to limit the role of EU forces to peacekeeping tasks, and those such as the French who wanted Europe to assume greater autonomy in defence. The argument was the same as the one made by Mitterrand to John Major six years before.

At the time, this issue was top of the agenda and the one where Tony Blair proceeded with great caution. He did not want to risk a perception that New Labour was unsound on defence (an accusation that had dogged the Party in the early 1980s) or a disagreement with the United States. It was, though, an area where his own instincts told him that he could and should go further over time. He believed that the EU's perceived failure to match up to its responsibilities in Bosnia had seriously undermined its credibility with its own citizens. The ability to deal with Europe's internal peacekeeping problems, including by deploying military force, was not the same thing as undermining NATO's responsibility for defence in the event of external attack.

In due course, European defence was to become the area where Tony Blair moved British policy further than any of his predecessors. He did so out of conviction that Europe had to be able to take action in its own backyard. He was not so concerned by all of the institutional aspects that had preoccupied Britain in the past. And he needed an area where Britain could demonstrate leadership. This was particularly so after the decision in October 1997 that Britain would not join EMU in the first wave from 1999.

The circumstances of that decision and its announcement have been extensively aired in public. While the manner of the announcement was unfortunate, and a harbinger of things to come, the decision itself was not surprising given Tony Blair's earlier public caution. In retrospect, there was probably never a better time to hold a referendum on entry into the euro. But it remains questionable, even so, whether the moment was good enough. The argument that Tony Blair could, at that stage in the life of the government, "walk on water" overlooks the fact that the government had come within a whisker of defeat in the Welsh referendum on devolution, a less controversial issue than EMU. It would have been a very high-risk strategy for a government, newly elected for the first time in eighteen years, to put its authority on the line so soon and so riskily. To have tried and lost would have put at risk the credibility of New Labour as trustworthy managers of the British economy. It would have damaged its standing with Britain's European partners. As it was, those partners were disappointed but not altogether surprised. They still believed that the British government intended to join at some stage. Their willingness not to push Britain over difficult treaty issues such as tax harmonisation at Amsterdam, and later at Nice in 2000, was partly down to their wish not to make the prospects in a euro referendum harder than they already were.

It has also been argued that, by allowing the Chancellor to set five tests for British entry to the euro, the Prime Minister lost control of the EMU agenda. It is true that the five tests set a framework which gave the economic judgement of the Treasury more importance than if those particular criteria had not been set. But, in political terms, the five tests were no more than a confirmation of the obvious point that the Prime Minister and his Chancellor had to be in complete agreement for there to be any hope of a successful EMU referendum campaign.

I believe EMU was probably always going to be an issue for the second term, in the absence of a shift in public opinion that was never probable. There is equally no doubt that the Prime Minister hoped to take Britain into the euro in the second term. It was he who decided to announce to Parliament, shortly after the 2001 election, that the assessment would be completed within two years. The organisation "Britain in Europe" was established at the government's behest to campaign for the euro. Tony Blair made no secret, in discussion with other EU leaders, British business leaders, and trusted journalists that he was in favour of Britain's entry.

In late 2002 and early 2003, scenarios were prepared within the European Secretariat of the Cabinet Office covering, on different timing assumptions, the steps that would have to be taken to legislate for and organise a referendum and to get through the steps necessary to apply for EMU membership. There was never any question of fudging the five tests. But, at the end of the day, the tests were a way of measuring whether the British and Continental economies had converged sufficiently to make EMU membership successfully sustainable for Britain. And that was a matter of political as well as economic judgement. When the detailed research documents which underlay the tests were discussed by the Prime Minister and the Chancellor, there was a real debate between them, but I never believed that the issue was one in which the Prime Minister wanted to go ahead immediately and regardless, while the Chancellor did not want to go ahead ever, regardless. But what was clear was that, at the least, the watchword of the government ("Prepare and Decide") would have to be given some fresh interpretation and impetus if it was not to appear identical to the policy of John Major that had been caricatured as "wait and see".

In the end, the statement that was made to Parliament by the Chancellor on 9 June 2003 did go beyond "wait and see" but not as far as to indicate that the issue was now when, rather than whether, Britain would join. The Chancellor declared that, of the five tests, the one covering the competitiveness of Britain's financial services within the euro zone had been met. Of the remaining four, those covering investment and employment would, he said, be met if, as we had not, we met the tests for sustainable convergence and flexibility. Although the Chancellor spoke of flexibility in terms of the steps which still needed to be taken in Britain, it was actually the Continental economies he was talking about: "As the persistence of volatility in inflation rates within the euro area demonstrates", he said, "we cannot be certain that there is as yet sufficient flexibility to deal with the potential stresses."

It was largely because of the way expectations had been managed from 2001 onwards on both sides of the argument that the Chancellor's statement was seen by the Press and by Britain's partners as ruling out British membership during that Parliament. The road show on EMU which was announced never happened. The ministerial committee that was established to monitor progress on the various aspects of convergence to which the Chancellor had committed himself in the House was more virtual than real. After 9 June 2003, the necessary window for joining before spring 2005 was, in any case, effectively closed.

By the time of the 2005 election, the superior performance of the British economy, compared with that of most euro zone economies, meant that there was no scope for winning a euro referendum. The whole issue had also by then been overlaid by the argument about the European Constitution, on which the Prime Minister had promised a referendum. There was some confusion in people's minds (not discouraged by the Euro-sceptic press) as to whether a vote in favour of the constitution would mean that Britain had thereby signed up for the single currency. The government were obliged to make clear that the two issues were entirely separate and that the euro question would be decided by a separate referendum if the government and Parliament ever decided to recommend euro membership. In the meantime, it was clear that a referendum on the constitution was already more than enough of a challenge. The fact that Tony Blair had announced that he would not lead the Labour Party into the next General Election also contributed to the issue of EMU becoming business that would remain unfinished during his premiership.

At the end of 1998, as parities within the euro zone were about to be fixed irrevocably, we sent from UK Representation in Brussels our assessment of what euro zone membership would mean for Britain's interests. We estimated that the requirements of managing the euro zone economies would lead to coordination of policy across the board among the member countries. In other words, we would start to see those member states determining policy on transport, energy, and probably fiscal policy. In the event, it has not happened. That in turn has meant that there has been no pressure on the government to seek euro zone membership, either from interests within Britain, such as business, or from the other member states.

The decision in October 1997 not to join in the first wave was one of the factors which led Tony Blair to put more emphasis on European defence. It was a combination of conviction and opportunity. He needed to demonstrate to Britain's partners that he meant what he said about Britain being a leader in Europe. Defence was an area where, from conviction, he believed Europe could and should do more. Action on defence also fitted with his view of an EU effectively led and run by the larger member states. The declaration which Blair and Chirac issued in St Malo in December 1998, following an intervention Blair had made to acclamation at an informal EU summit a few weeks earlier, was seen at the time by France as a commitment to go further and faster in the direction of European defence integration than in practice was possible for a British government for whom doing nothing to weaken NATO, let alone the perception of Alliance interests on the part of the United States, was paramount. Yet, European defence is the principal area of European policy where the Labour government have moved British policy. Today, there is greater integration of European forces, a rapid reaction capability, coordinated planning at European level, and an embryonic headquarters arrangement. Much more importantly, EU forces are involved in significant peacekeeping operations in the Balkans and beyond Europe's frontiers. This has, not without difficulty, been achieved with the consent of the United States, and Tony Blair played a decisive part in assuring that consent.

The biggest test of Blair's willingness to move on European defence came in 2003. In April, in the wake of the Iraq War, the leaders of France, Germany, Luxembourg, and Belgium met in Terveuren, a suburb of Brussels, and issued a declaration which announced their decision to set up a joint headquarters to run European defence operations. The plan was declared open to other member states to join.

The plan was the brainchild of Guy Verhofstadt, the Belgian Prime Minister, and it immediately set alarm bells ringing in Washington and London. Hitherto, military actions had been run from headquarters which were either under the auspices of NATO or of a country with a significant military planning capacity, such as France or Britain. An embryo European headquarters, separate from NATO, looked like a deliberate ploy to set up France and Germany in particular as a rival pole of attraction to those countries which had not supported the military action in Iraq, or to those who were less preoccupied than the UK by the issue of NATO primacy in territorial defence.

The initial British response was to rally opposition to the plan that had emerged from what was dubbed "the Chocolate Summit". Most member states were wary of it, especially those like the Dutch and Portuguese, with a traditional Atlanticist bent, as well as the new member states such as Poland who had not formally joined the EU but were already participating fully in meetings.

Yet, in September 2003, Tony Blair set a new course. The divisions over Iraq between the French and German governments and their supporters on the one hand, and the British government and its supporters, including the governments of Spain and Italy, on the other, had left a fault line down the middle of the EU. Relations between Blair and Chirac, always on a knife-edge, had come close to breaking point. The much closer relationship between Blair and Schroeder had been placed under huge strain though both men sought to avoid Iraq infecting other issues.

So, in the aftermath of the Iraq War, when Blair and Chirac had a conciliatory meeting at the Elysée, Chirac proposed that the three governments—Britain, France, and Germany—should put their relationship on to a different basis. Chirac had clearly decided that France and Germany could not alone determine European policy: they had tried to do so over Iraq and had failed. Chirac was also convinced that the interests of the large member states would suffer in the enlarged EU. He had no time for the Spanish government under Aznar and a scarcely concealed dislike of Prime Minister Berlusconi of Italy. He saw Poland as an awkward partner and the smaller new members as irritants. He had famously given vent to his anger with the smaller member states at a summit under his chairmanship in Biarritz in October 2000. The ill-starred Nice summit two months later was marked by a greater large–small divide than had ever been seen before in the EU.

Out of this arose Chirac's offer to Tony Blair to work in a partnership of three on the key European issues. The idea had obvious appeal. Tony Blair did not share in any way Chirac's contempt for some of the new member states. But he did fear that the enlarged EU would be difficult to manage. He also felt that Britain had, for too long, suffered from not having a stable relationship with France and Germany. As a result, he argued, successive British governments constantly found themselves having to argue over every jot and comma of negotiating texts because that was the only way we had of defending our interests. France and Germany could be much less preoccupied by the minutiae because they could always count on each other to recognise and uphold a vital national interest.

No one in Downing Street was under any illusion about the difficulty of making such a policy work. France and Germany had a forty-year history of working intimately together at every level and of making real concessions to each other in the interest of agreement. Britain found such compromise much harder, partly because of our practice of micro-coordination, which made it harder for us than for others to change a policy once it had been agreed, and partly because of the lack of deep-seated public support in Britain for the European project. We knew we would have to proceed step by step and with circumspection vis-a-vis our other partners. There were doubts in the Foreign Office and elsewhere about the workability of the policy, not only because of the likely reaction of other partners, but also because of deep-rooted suspicions of French policy and motives. I recall writing from Downing Street to Whitehall departments explaining the policy and its rationale and the requirement to make a concerted effort to help it succeed. I saw it as risky, for sure, but an exciting opportunity to put our relationship on to a new footing.

Defence was the first test. Unless the three governments could reach agreement on the wording on foreign and security cooperation in the Constitutional Treaty which was then under negotiation, there was no hope of an overall agreement. France and Germany wanted to include in the Constitutional Treaty provisions which would have allowed a self-appointed group of member states to take action in the defence field in the name of the EU as a whole and without the approval of the entire membership. The idea owed much to the thinking of Pierre de Boissieu, first aired ten years before. Its rationale was, as then, that countries with a serious defence capability and the willingness to act should not be held back by those who were committed to neutrality. The British government was sympathetic to the argument but not the conclusion drawn from it. For Britain, it was essential that any European action in foreign policy or defence had the backing of all the membership. While it was unlikely that defence decisions would be taken without Britain, that was not a risk we were prepared to take, let alone try to sell to the House of Commons. The key to persuading the French and Germans to budge on this issue was to move towards them on the idea of a European headquarters which might, in certain circumstances, be used to control a European peacekeeping operation.

After weeks of intense negotiation, and quite a lot of sucking of teeth in the Foreign Office and Ministry of Defence (MOD), an agreement was reached. To Tony Blair then fell the difficult task of selling it to the United States. The Americans, as Mitterrand had warned years earlier, seemed to want to control more as they engaged less. They could not see why we were making concessions to the French, in particular, when a significant number of member states were suspicious of the "chocolate summit" outcome. Tony Blair's argument in reply was that hostility to the Franco-German scheme was broad but shallow. If Aznar lost power in Spain or Berlusconi in Italy, new governments in both countries might well embrace the scheme, in which case others would follow.

The drawing power of France and Germany should not be underestimated. It was better to turn their scheme into something acceptable rather than let it gather momentum beyond our influence. In the end, against the views of his advisers and his own instincts, George Bush agreed to trust Tony Blair's judgement. Having decided to do so, the US Administration backed Britain and resisted all efforts from the British media to persuade them to rubbish what had been done.

I believe Tony Blair's judgement on this issue has been borne out by subsequent events. Governments in Spain and Italy led by Zapatero and Prodi, respectively, would not have resisted the Terveuren plan. There would have been rival centres of attraction and the route to European defence would have been dangerously polarised. The United States too accepted the wisdom of the compromise.

After such an auspicious start, it was a disappointment that trilateralism failed to prosper. There were three main reasons. First, the UK was the junior partner in a relationship where France and Germany, not surprisingly given their longstanding partnership, determined their joint position before the British entered the room. Secondly, it was harder for Britain to make compromises on other issues in the Constitutional Treaty, especially on judicial and criminal cooperation where the Prime Minister would have had to exercise considerable leverage on Cabinet colleagues to move British policy in the French/German direction. Thirdly, the adverse reaction of the Spanish and Italian governments exceeded our expectations.

Tony Blair had established a close relationship with Jose Maria Aznar, the Conservative Prime Minister of Spain. Together with the Portuguese Prime Minister, Antonio Guterres, they had set in train the Lisbon process of economic reform. By the time trilateralism began, Aznar had already signalled his intention to stand down as Prime Minister at the next election. Even so, he reacted badly and I felt at the time that his relationship with Tony Blair never quite recovered. While Aznar seethed, Silvio Berlusconi erupted. For him, matters were made worse by the fact that Italy held the Presidency of the EU. He felt as a lover scorned, rejected, and humiliated. Interestingly, member states such as the Netherlands were quite relaxed about what had happened. They saw it as natural that the three largest member states should have a confidential relationship. They preferred the three in question to be getting along than to be quarrelling. They asked only that they and other member states should not be presented with outcomes over which they would have no say.

So, Tony Blair was forced to soft pedal. Then, at the European Council of December 2003, Chirac decided that he was not prepared to clinch an agreement on the European Constitution under Berlusconi's chairmanship. He and Schroeder treated Berlusconi with contumely. Although it was an

Italian Prime Minister who was on the receiving end of the bullying, it was reminiscent of the treatment meted out to Thatcher and Lubbers by Chirac and Kohl in 1988. It was clear to all of us that Schroeder and Chirac would put their relationship first. Thereafter, two issues dealt a death blow to the cooperation.

Chirac had half promised the French electorate a referendum on the Constitutional Treaty but clearly wanted to get out of any such undertaking. At a time when a referendum was not part of the British government's agenda, Chirac proposed a pact between France, Britain, and Germany under which none of the three countries would hold referendums. No pact as such was ever agreed but, since Germany has no constitutional provision for referendums, and Britain was not expected to have one, when Tony Blair did in the end offer a referendum, Chirac felt that he had been let down. On top of that, when Schroeder and Chirac sought to impose their choice of candidate to succeed Romano Prodi as President of the Commission, Tony Blair felt compelled, along with a number of other EU leaders to make clear that that candidate, Belgian Prime Minister Guy Verhofstadt, would not be acceptable. Chirac and Schroeder chose to ignore the many private warnings they were given that Verhofstadt did not command support. Able as he was, Verhofstadt was considered to be too much of a "federalist". In this, there were echoes of John Major's objections to Verhofstadt's predecessor, Jean-Luc Dehaene, who had been championed by Kohl and Mitterrand, and vetoed by John Major, in 1994. As a result of the Nice Treaty, there was no longer an individual veto on the appointment of the Commission President. The issue was for decision by majority vote. So, when they were told that Britain had no candidate of her own and would be prepared to consider a number of alternatives, the response was that France and Germany had decided that Verhofstadt was to be the next president of the Commission and would push the issue to its conclusion. They did and they lost, very publicly. That was the end of trilateralism.

The experiment in trilateral partnership with France and Germany was the most prominent example of a consistent effort by the Labour government to put Britain's relationship with her partners on to a new footing. The policy of "step change" as it was known was inaugurated shortly after the 1997 General Election. All Whitehall Departments, as well as British embassies around the EU, were involved in a concerted effort to find areas of new, substantive cooperation with other member states. The work was overseen by a committee of ministers from across Whitehall under the chairmanship of the Foreign Office Europe Minister, and known as Minecor. While the policy did not deliver dramatic results, it did achieve a significant thickening of the relationship in a number of cases. The extent to which joint articles appeared in the European Press co-authored by Blair and another EU Head of Government became something of a running gag across the Union. But others started to emulate it. And the very effort of sitting down to find the common ground for a joint article set in train a process of mutual accommodation and understanding that was valuable. The fact that the British government had made the effort was noted. In the case of Ireland, where relations had been cool for obvious historical reasons, the initiatives which Britain took served to break the ice and remove suspicion.

As with all such initiatives, the long-term success of the "step change" policy will depend on the commitment of each generation of ministers and officials. Direction from the top is important. Tony Blair's negotiating style was different from that of his predecessors. The traditional British negotiating method, especially on issues where Britain had a veto on what others wanted which would be given up only in exchange for concessions by them to us, was to plant the flag, form the thin red line, and hold out against all comers. As one British diplomat put it, Margaret Thatcher would take the wheel of the European car and drive it at full speed to the cliff's edge, confident that the others would lose their nerve before she did.

This tactic had worked well, but at some cost in personal relationships. Tony Blair, by contrast, was prepared to show his hand earlier in the negotiating game and to use his skill at networking and at riding several horses at once to deliver a result. The technique usually worked. It in turn required a change of tactics by British officials. It also occasionally required officials to interpret what had been said by the Prime Minister for the benefit of foreign colleagues who had not latched onto the new tone. Our EU partners were used to British Prime Ministers who said "no", either with overstatement in the case of Margaret Thatcher, or moderation in the case of John Major. It took some time for them to get used to the fact that, for example, a comment by Tony Blair that he was not keen on the idea of majority voting for tax issues meant, not that he was open to persuasion, but that he would duck and weave his way to a victory on points rather than seek the knock-out blow.

To be liked is not sufficient, but it helps. Personal relationships at the level of Head of Government are not the key to successful negotiation, but they are important. Margaret Thatcher had few, if any, friends among her fellow Heads of Government. Tony Blair made a concerted effort, especially with the leaders of the other large member states. In the case of Spain and Italy, he found leaders who shared many of his political and economic beliefs. In the case of Germany, he believed that Schroeder was, like him, a Third Way politician. When the two governments produced a joint document on the subject, which bombed in Germany, the limits of cooperation became clearer. Schroeder rarely repaid the personal and political investment Tony Blair made in the relationship.

I have no doubt that Schroeder liked Blair but, in the end, the importance of the Franco-German relationship took precedence. Even after the negotiation of the Nice Treaty, when Schroeder felt that Chirac had traduced him by not agreeing to increase the number of German votes in the Council of Ministers to make them commensurate with the increased population of the united Germany, the two men made a conscious effort to repair their relationship. They were, Schroeder and Chirac, birds of a feather. They gave the impression of being in politics because politics was what they were good at, not for what politics would allow them to achieve. In any event, both in France and Germany, being on good terms with one's most important neighbour was good politics, just as being the closest friend of the United States was good politics in the UK.

Nicolas Sarkozy, admittedly not the most impartial witness, reportedly said of Chirac: "Avec lui, on n'est toujours qu'un ennemi ou un esclave." Franz-Olivier Giesbert's book *La Tragédie du Président*, from which that quotation comes, paints a picture of Chirac as a politician paralysed before the economic and social problems confronting France, a leader of the right with instincts of the centre left, a man who, having won 82% of the popular vote in his final re-election to the Presidency concluded that, having achieved the support of virtually all French men and women, he should make a point of doing nothing to offend any of them.

Chirac is a man who rarely forgave those who crossed him and there were times when Tony Blair did cross him. But he seems to have taken against Blair from the start, probably seeing in him the leader Chirac might himself have been: attractive, popular, and with a programme of action he was determined to implement. Blair, without seeking it, readily stole the thunder of the old guard. Moreover, his vision of Europe was one in which the economic reform which he practised at home was to be sold as a project to the EU as a whole. The Blair government was active in Africa and the Middle East, regions where Chirac saw himself as the elder statesman.

Iraq was to prove the most divisive issue between the two men. Chirac disliked George W. Bush from the start, though he had been something of an admirer of his father. A reflex anti-Americanism would probably have led him to oppose the war in Iraq even if his own knowledge and judgement about the region had not led him to predict much of what subsequently happened. But it was not just the British action in support of the United States that riled him. It was the fact that Blair could carry with him around half the rest of the membership, including the governments of Spain, Italy, and Poland.

Before then, there had been the famous quarrel in October 2002 when, at a European Council in Brussels, Chirac turned on Blair, accused him of being the rudest man he had ever met and proceeded publicly to cancel the forthcoming Anglo-French bilateral summit. At the time, most commentators thought that the argument arose because Britain had been wrong-footed by Schroeder and Chirac who had, without consulting Britain, fixed between themselves the budget for agriculture up to 2013.

It is true that the two men had done just that, as the price France was prepared to pay to allow enlargement to go ahead. It is also true that Schroeder had been out-negotiated by Chirac and that the British government was presented with a fait accompli which could have been overturned, if at all, only by putting the enlargement at risk. If we made a mistake at the time, it was in not appreciating just how far mutual self-interest would lead Chirac and Schroeder to put behind them the differences which had caused a breach between them at Nice two years earlier. But we knew there were contacts between the two governments to which we were not privy, and Tony Blair was right not to take on himself the blame for busting the Franco-German deal and thus, the enlargement of which Britain was the principal champion. However, when Blair arrived in Brussels and went straight to a meeting with Chirac, the latter was beside himself with satisfaction at the agreement he and Schroeder had just reached. There were, he said, three parts to it: the deal on agricultural spending, the necessity for Britain to give up her rebate and the postponement until the big budget negotiation of 2005/2006 of any agricultural reform. In other words, the big package of CAP reforms which the Commission had put on the table and which was due to be decided by majority vote, by agriculture ministers, in 2003 would be postponed by two to three years and then be determined by Heads of Government by unanimity.

I never saw Tony Blair lose his self-control in any meeting, although this was one occasion when those of us accompanying him were reaching for our jawbones which were somewhere near the floor and, in my case at least, hoping that, just this once, Blair might deliver himself of a Thatcher-like retort. He, probably wisely, refrained from doing so. But the following day, in the European Council, he set about resisting Chirac's brazen attempt to derail the reform of the CAP. He was forced to do so single-handed. The package he was defending was the brain child of the Commission but its President, Romano Prodi, was not prepared to stick his head above the parapet. By contrast, frantic messages came to the British delegation from the Agriculture Commissioner, Franz Fischler, begging Blair to fight the good fight. He was also privately encouraged by the German Foreign Minister, Joshka Fischer, who told Blair that Schroeder had put himself out of the game by his unwise deal with Chirac of the previous day, a deal that German officials had sought, without success, to renegotiate when they discovered the detail of what Schroeder had conceded.

Blair fought and won, using as part of his argument the fact that Chirac seemed ready to sacrifice the interests of the poorest countries for the sake of the CAP. This barb struck home and provoked Chirac's angry response. Less than a year later, the Agriculture Council agreed, by a majority, the reform package that Blair had saved, including the move to the single farm payment which was one of the most significant reforms so far achieved.

Given this episode, conducted in full sight of all the membership and there-fore of the media, and the way in which the anti-French card was played in the British media the following spring on the eve of the Iraq War, it is perhaps surprising that trilateralism was ever attempted and that it achieved even as much as it did. Its one notable success, the agreement on defence issues, would have aroused Press and political opposition in Britain had Tony Blair not been able to sell the project to the US President. For not until the referendums on the Constitutional Treaty did any other European leader have to confront the suspicion of the EU that dogged Tony Blair's time in office.

All of Tony Blair's speeches about the EU had in common the theme of Britain as a successful and leading member of the EU. That those speeches did not have more resonance or success is down to a number of factors: the scepticism of much of the British media, especially the Murdoch press on whose support the government had been able to count since 1996; the perceived differences on Europe between Numbers 10 and 11 Downing Street which meant that few other ministers were willing to speak on Europe for fear of offending either the Prime Minister or the Chancellor and the fact that, after the Iraq War, the political capital needed for a sustained campaign on Europe was in short supply.

Tony Blair was accused by the Press of speaking about Europe, and Britain's place in it, more frequently abroad than at home. But if he chose a foreign platform, as he did in Warsaw in 2003, it was to stress just how far Britain's interests were bound up with those of her partners. The Warsaw speech con-tained a classic Blair European rallying cry:

For Poland as with Britain, our strategy should be: get in, make the most of it, have the confidence to win the debate not be frightened by it. Do we believe that the Europe our people want is a Europe of nations not a federal superstate? Yes. Do we believe Europe must reform economically to succeed? Yes. Do we believe Europe and the United States of America should be allies? Yes. Are our arguments good ones? Yes. Can we win the debate? It is up to us. But great nations do not hide away or follow along, stragglers at the back. They win. They have the confidence that comes not from arrogance but from a true understanding of the modern world.

What was striking about the speech was its underlying theme, summed up in the sentence: "So: you in Poland, we in Britain, are once again contemplating our future in Europe." Poland was about to become a member of the EU and was facing up to the unknown. Britain had already been a member for thirty years.

Two years earlier, in Birmingham, Tony Blair had addressed the basic issues surrounding Britain's membership. He said:

The purpose of this speech is to argue: that Britain's future is inextricably linked with Europe; that to get the best out of it, we must make the most of our strength and influence within it; and that to do so, we must be wholehearted, not half-hearted, partners in Europe. We have a vision for Europe—as a union of nations working more closely together, not a federal superstate submerging national identity.

He went on to describe the many occasions when British governments had made the wrong judgements in their relations with their European partners and made what was probably the most direct statement about sovereignty since Macmillan's pamphlet, quoted in Chapter 1, of forty years before:

Those opposed to Britain's role in Europe argue about sovereignty: that the gains we have made are outweighed by the fact that in many areas sovereignty is no longer absolute. My answer is this: I see sovereignty not merely as the ability of a single country to say no, but as the power to maximise our national strength and capacity in business, trade, foreign policy, defence and the fight against crime. Sovereignty has to be deployed for national advantage. When we isolated ourselves in the past, we squandered our sovereignty—leaving us sole masters of a shrinking sphere of influence.

To this, however, he added a classic British codicil: "It is true that British governments have shared sovereignty over some decisions. But we have retained control over our immigration policy and national border controls, our tax, defence and foreign policies—and will continue to do so." But Tony Blair then returned to his earlier, bolder theme:

I want a sovereignty rooted in democratic consent. Rooted in being, in this century, not just a national power in shifting alliances, but a great European power in a lasting Union. A Union of nations, of democracies with shared goals, delivering shared peace, stability and prosperity for our citizens. Ours will be a sovereignty rooted in being part, not of a European superstate, but of a proud nation, proud of its identity and of its alliance in Europe.

Almost exactly a year later, in a speech entitled "A Clear Course for Europe", Tony Blair set out, again in greater detail than had been done by any of his predecessors, how he saw the relationship between the intergovernmental and the supranational in Europe:

We want a Europe of sovereign nations, countries proud of their distinctive identity, but co-operating together for mutual good. We fear that the driving ideology behind European integration is a move to a European superstate, in which power is sucked into an unaccountable centre. And what is more a centre of fudge and muddle, bureaucratic meddling, which in economic terms could impede efficiency and in security terms may move us away from the transatlantic alliance. So, for all these reasons, our attitudes have, historically, been characterised by uncertainty and that has bred in our psyche a feeling that Europe is something done to us by others, not something we do with others. Now we have an historic opportunity to put our relations with the rest of Europe on a more serious footing and choose not to hang back but to participate fully and wholeheartedly. Europe itself is about to undergo profound change . . . Europe's rules are having to be rewritten. At the same time, crucial debates on European defence and the European economy are under way. All these developments will have a vast impact on Britain . . . Now is a moment when isolation from decision-making is not just pointless but immensely damaging . . . First, we must end the nonsense of "thus far and no further". There are areas in which Europe should and will integrate more: in fighting crime and illegal immigration; to secure economic reform; in having a more effective defence and security policy. Britain should not be at the back of the file on such issues but at the front . . . Second, we should understand that our opposition to Europe as some federal superstate is not a British obsession. It is in fact the reasonably settled view of most members of the EU and, more importantly, of their people . . . Thirdly, however, the answer to the second point is not to reach for inter-governmentalism as a weapon against European institutions—again, if not a traditional British position, certainly perceived as such—but to recognise that Europe is and should remain an alliance of European and national Government. The very purpose of having a Council is to recognise that ultimately Europe represents the will of sovereign states. The key purpose of having a Commission with its own powers of initiative and a Parliament and Court organised on a European basis, is that we also recognise that we need supranational European institutions for Europe to work i.e. for that sovereign will to be implemented effectively. The two are not in opposition to each other. It is the two together which are necessary for the unique union of nations that is Europe to function.

Looking back, it is even clearer than it was at the time, that the Prime Minister, and a succession of courageous and relatively short-lived Europe ministers, were the only ministers speaking in these terms. Tony Blair did not carry single-handed the burden of negotiation in Europe: other ministers were deeply engaged. But it was he who bore the burden of trying to educate public opinion and to change it. This was especially hard in a media world where little was reported without first being spun, not by the government, but by the editorialists in the media itself.

Against this background, it is not surprising that the Constitutional Treaty risked becoming almost as much of an incubus for Tony Blair as the Maastricht Treaty had become for John Major.

In his speech in 2002, just quoted, Tony Blair spoke in favour of a proper Constitution for Europe, one which makes it clear that the driving ideology is indeed a union of nations, not a superstate subsuming national sovereignty and national identity. This should be spelt out in simple language. A new Constitution for Europe can bring a new stability to the shape of Europe—not a finality which would prevent any future evolution, but a settlement to last a generation or more.

A year later, in Warsaw, the Prime Minister explained why he was opposed to a referendum on the Constitution: "If the Convention or IGC represented a fundamental change to the British Constitution and to our system of parliamentary democracy, there would be a case for a referendum. But it does not. The truth is the argument...against a European superstate is being won."

In the spring of 2004, a few weeks before the EP elections in which the Conservatives were expected to make gains, Tony Blair decided to concede a referendum. He was persuaded by the argument that was put to him by Jack Straw, the Foreign Secretary, that when agreement was reached on the Constitution and that agreement was put by the government to Parliament in the form of enabling legislation, the Bill would be amended by the Conservative majority in the House of Lords to require a referendum before ratification could take place. The government, so Straw argued, would not have time to use the Parliament Act to overturn the vote in the Lords in advance of the next General Election. Labour would therefore go into the Election on the back foot on the issue while the Conservative Party would present itself as the party which trusted the people. If the government lost seats in the election, it might be forced to concede the referendum anyway. In other words, better to jump than to be pushed.

Whether a referendum on the Constitutional Treaty would have been winnable in Britain is one of the "ifs" of history. The polling evidence available to the organisation "Britain in Europe" with which I was associated after I left government service in the summer of 2004 suggested that, if twenty-four other member states had already ratified, then fear of isolation might induce the British electorate to vote in favour as well. But the odds were against a "yes" even so.

In the event, Britain was saved by the bell that tolled in France and the Netherlands in May 2005. But it was a bell that signalled the end of round one, not the end of the match.

It fell to the British government, in its Presidency of the EU in the second half of 2005, to try to pick up the pieces of the Constitutional debacle. Tony Blair's brilliant speech to the EP in June, in which he likened what had happened to the battle of Jericho, with the people of Europe sounding the trumpet at the city walls, was largely, like most of his speeches, his own work. Despite the hopes of some, it was beyond any one Presidency to repair the city walls and, in the event, Tony Blair, in his second and final Presidency of the EU, did what British Prime Ministers do best: he solved a budget crisis, preserving the British abatement won by Margaret Thatcher twenty-one years earlier, and he set the EU its most significant challenge of modern times: how to tackle the crucial issues of energy dependency and climate change. In that respect, the one-day summit at Hampton Court was much more significant than most allowed at the time. Just as Margaret Thatcher can claim, with Jacques Delors, to have done more than any other leader to put the single market on the European agenda, so Tony Blair can claim, with Jose Manuel Durao Barroso, to have done more than any other EU leader to put energy and climate change at the top of the European agenda.

The final word of this chapter about the Labour government and the EU should probably go to Tony Blair himself. In a valedictory speech on Europe in Oxford in spring 2006, he said that his vision of the EU was the same as that of the founders of Europe; "ever closer union among freely cooperating sovereign governments". In that misquotation of the provision of the Treaty of Rome and its call for "ever closer union among the peoples of Europe", Tony Blair summed up in a phrase what had been a remarkable continuity of view between him and the two Prime Ministers who preceded him. The last chapter will look at their legacy.

9

How the British Government's European Policy is Made

As I was writing this book, I remarked to a friend on the similarity between speeches made on Europe by Margaret Thatcher, John Major, and Tony Blair. My friend replied that that was hardly surprising since the speeches had, in each case, been written by people like me.

That view correspondents to the brilliant caricature in the TV series *Yes Minister* where the politically astute, but otherwise clueless minister, Jim Hacker, is led a dance by the cynical, self-serving, manipulative civil servant, Sir Humphrey. In the background, torn between his loyalty to his minister and his dependence on his bureaucratic boss for his future success, lurks the luckless Private Secretary, Bernard.

As with all good caricatures, it is recognisable enough to be plausible and far enough from the truth to be laughed at as parody. But the notion of policy made by generations of civil servants almost regardless of which political party happens to be in power is well ingrained. So too is the image of the power-hungry, self-interested politician for whom perception (spin) is more important than policy. The fact that politicians are collectively held in such low esteem owes much to this view. It is a view which reflects the black and white, un-nuanced rhetoric of political debate in Britain where the two-party system, and first past the post, create the kind of confrontational politics which marks out the House of Commons by comparison with other European parliaments where coalition politics are the norm.

At the other extreme is the view, sometimes found in otherwise brilliant and insightful studies, which portrays government decision-making as ordered, logical, rational, and predictable. In reality, the factors which make up the processes of government are an extraordinary, complex, and changing mixture of factors which include an inherited view of the British national interest, partisanship, personality, circumstance, public pressures, luck (or the lack of it), and, of course, a coherent, ordered, dispassionate effort to analyse what needs to be done in the national interest and a wholehearted and conscientious effort to turn declared policy into accomplished fact.

I spent nearly ten of my thirty-five-year career in the British Diplomatic Service as a Private Secretary. As such, I had a bird's eye view, or perhaps more accurately a worm's eye view, of how government works and of how politicians work and think. I became typecast as a Private Secretary.

The Private Secretary is the person who sees more of his or her minister than anyone else outside the minister's immediate family. Indeed, during the working week he or she may see more of the minister than the minister's family does. For the duration of your service as a Private Secretary, you kiss goodbye to anything remotely approaching a private life. You are the first person into the minister's office in the morning and the last one out at night. You are, though you advertise it at your peril, the last person to talk to your minister before he takes a decision and the first person to know when that decision has been taken. You are the one official in a department who can give advice to the minister entirely in private. Your advice may run counter to that of the department as a whole. If the minister accepts your view, then you have exercised more influence than your elders and betters think you have any right to do.

The Private Office, brilliantly analysed in Sir Nicholas Henderson's book of that name, is the interface between the Secretary of State and the rest of the department, be it other ministers, or officials. In the Foreign Office, it handles all the information that comes into the Secretary of State from officials in the Foreign Office, as well as all the recommendations that those officials make in the form of written policy submissions. It is also the interface with the rest of Whitehall, handling a huge volume of policy correspondence between government departments, not just on foreign policy issues, but also on other matters which the Foreign Secretary has to deal with as a member of Cabinet.

The Private Secretaries are the people who convey the minister's instructions, ideas, requests, and opinions to the rest of the department. It is they who will be telephoned by other officials keen to know what is on the minister's mind, anxious to interpret his or her wishes accurately or simply to work out how to manage an instruction which may have been easier for the minister to give than for his officials to execute.

What service in a private office gives you is a unique vantage point from which to see the character and ability of your minister, as well as the strengths and weaknesses of the departmental machine which serves him. It also brings you face to face with the political pressures which may determine policy, with conflicts of departmental interest, with personality differences, and, above all, with the almost inhuman workload and stress which we expect our political leaders to bear.

From 1977 to 1979, I was one of David Owen's Private Secretaries during his time as Foreign Secretary. I dealt mostly with African issues, especially what was then his central preoccupation: the future of Rhodesia. From 1988 to the end of 1990, I was Private Secretary to three successive Foreign Secretaries: Geoffrey Howe, John Major, and Douglas Hurd. From 1991 to 1993, I was the Foreign Office Private Secretary in Number 10 Downing Street, working for John Major in the days when there was only one such Private Secretary, handling foreign policy, defence, and Northern Ireland. From 2000 to 2004, I was Tony Blair's senior official adviser on the EU in Downing Street, as well as Head of the European Secretariat in the Cabinet Office.

All of those men were people of outstanding ability in very different ways. As with any profession, politics produces people of mixed abilities. But those who make it to the top are almost invariably extremely bright, exceptionally hard-working, and of superhuman stamina. They also give of their best in the national interest as they conceive it. I think that an otherwise sceptical public knows this even if it is reluctant to acknowledge it. If it did not, today's politician would not be transformed in the public mind into tomorrow's statesman. But I do not believe that anyone who has not experienced the life of a top politician at first hand can appreciate the relentless pressure and the constant stress which those politicians endure, in the midst of which they are expected to perform at the top of their game and to make good judgements based on careful and wise thought. The remarkable thing about the British political system is not how often it fails but how consistently well it delivers, given that senior ministers face each day the kind of pressures which few of the rest of us face ever.

David Owen would think nothing of flying to New York on the morning Concorde, going from there to Washington for a day of meetings with US Secretary of State, Cy Vance, back to London on the overnight flight from Washington (usually doing some hours' work on the aeroplane), and then driving straight from Heathrow to the Foreign Office for a full day's work. So, in a twenty-four-hour period, he might have worked for twenty hours. His experience as a junior doctor undoubtedly helped him and explained why he was still going strong while the rest of us wilted. Come the evening, he would take home three or four large boxes (black, not red) and work on them late into the night. At a time when his older son, Tristan, was seriously ill with leukaemia, Owen would get up in the night to tend to Tristan and put in some work on the boxes at the same time.

All ministerial days are filled from start to finish. When we were not travelling, Geoffrey Howe would often hold his first office meeting of the day at 08:00 and then have constant meetings, commitments in the House of Commons, maybe a speech or an official dinner, and get home at midnight. At which point, he would do a couple of hours' work on the official boxes, sleep for three hours, and then start again at around 05:00.

While John Major was Foreign Secretary, he lived during the week in one of the rooms at the top of the Foreign Office usually used by those officials (the Resident Clerks) who were on call out of hours. He might finish work in his grand Victorian office at 21:00, go to MacDonald's for a quick hamburger, and then return to work. As Prime Minister, he would often be up, working in his bedroom, at 06:00, frequently being badgered for decisions by people like me from very early in the morning. Privacy is not a commodity available to the Prime Minister living over the shop.

Douglas Hurd never wasted a moment. If he was in a car, or on a plane, he would be working, often dictating constituency correspondence (which was dealt with by a House of Commons secretary, not the Foreign Office). Whenever he got into his official car for a journey of more than a few minutes, we would put a box of work into the car with him. He went through it swiftly but rigorously.

The diaries of Alastair Campbell portray a similar pattern for Tony Blair.

This workload, amazingly, rarely seems to produce bad health. Sheer stamina is the first quality that marks out successful politicians from lesser mortals. They are helped by a huge drip-feed of adrenalin, a potent and addictive drug. Adrenalin masks fatigue but one of its side effects can be hubris. It is not surprising that a politician such as Margaret Thatcher found that life after Number 10 was not happy. Fatigue and adrenalin can also produce bad judgements and the effects of such extreme fatigue are cumulative. That is one reason why governments do not just run out of ideas, they run out of steam.

The higher you climb in politics and government, the greater the pressures, and the more important and urgent the decisions you have to take. A senior politician needs good judgement, combined with enormous self-confidence. Margaret Thatcher decided to launch the Falklands task force when her naval advisers were still unsure of the prospects of success. John Major publicly initiated the campaign for safe havens for the Iraqi Kurds even though he was not sure he would have the backing of the United States. Tony Blair led, within minutes of them happening, the response of the Western world to the bombings of 9/11.

In each case, the Prime Minister of the day reached his or her own judgement. They led from the front. But, on top of their form, these leaders tempered their own wishes with shrewd, often instinctive, assessment of the political environment.

In his autobiography, Nigel Lawson says that recklessness characterised Margaret Thatcher's last months in government. And it may be so. Yet anyone who reads Margaret Thatcher's own autobiography can see the combination of robustness and care which she took in tackling the miners' strike. There was nothing reckless about her behaviour then. She had strong instincts about the ERM but was obliged to temper them in the face of a united front by Geoffrey Howe and Nigel Lawson.

On one occasion, when I encouraged John Major to take some bold step over Europe, he reminded me that he was "standing astride a crack in the Conservative Party that is getting wider every day".

Tony Blair decided, against his long-held and unchanged conviction to the contrary, to offer a referendum on the draft European Constitution because of his reading of what the domestic political situation required. That decision was taken on the eve of elections to the EP and ostensibly for related political reasons. But I doubt if he would have taken that decision had his domestic standing not taken a battering over Iraq.

In other words, all three leaders had to temper what they wanted to do to fit with what they could in practice accomplish at any one time. It sounds obvious. But it is often not predictable.

The reckless Margaret Thatcher, as observed by Nigel Lawson at the end, was recognisably the same person who, seven years earlier, had kept one of my colleagues sitting up until three in the morning in the British embassy in Rome while, over a whisky or three, she laid into the EC and all its ills. But she knew when, at Fontainebleau, she should compromise to reach an agreement with the other member governments of that same disliked Community. In other words, her European policy was shaped by strong instincts, but tempered by careful assessment of the national interest. If that care deserted her at the end, it was not just hubris. I am sure that cumulative fatigue required ever increasing doses of adrenalin and adrenalin, like other drugs, can distort judgement and undermine performance as well as enhance it.

John Major who nearly lost a vote of confidence over the Maastricht Bill was the same leader whose success in negotiating the Maastricht Treaty had been hailed by virtually every member of the Parliamentary Conservative Party only a few months before. On the face of it, he should have had more authority, having won a General Election, against the odds, in between. But he knew, as soon as the election was over, that while he had a majority of twenty-one he also had more than that number of Euro-sceptic backbenchers prepared to imperil the government for their beliefs.

Since all political parties believe that their policies are the best ones in the national interest, there is nothing cynical about the fact that most governments implicitly regard it as their first duty to stay in power if they possibly can. All governments, in my experience, seek to take decisions on an informed and rational basis in the national interest but all are subject to the pressures, human and political, I have described. To describe the machinery and process of European decision-making is therefore to describe how, but not always why, European decisions have been taken by British governments over the last twenty-five years.

Successive British governments have used a model of decision-making on EU issues which is often envied by other member states and has been emulated by not a few. It is a model which has usually meant that if ten different British government ministers are asked by their EU opposite numbers about the British view of a particular issue, outside their own area of expertise, all ten ministers will give the same answer. This seems so obvious to anyone used to our system as to scarcely rate mention. But it is a system rooted, not just in thoroughgoing preparation on all issues but, above all, by the sharing of information.

This passion to share information with colleagues across government departments is an almost uniquely British quality. It is one of the benign consequences of a system that does not produce coalition governments in which the foreign minister from one party will not necessarily trust his fellow finance minister from another. I had constant dealings with my German opposite number in Chancellor Schroeder's office during my four years as Tony Blair's EU adviser. I was often told things which I was enjoined on no account to allow to fall into the hands of the Foreign Ministry. Not ours; theirs. The Germans accepted that I would, as a matter of routine and duty, brief both our embassy in Berlin and the Foreign Office in detail about what had passed between me and Schroeder's adviser. This meant that the British ambassador in Berlin might know more about what was on the mind of the German Chancellor than did the German Foreign Minister.

The other key ingredient of the British system is coordination among officials and ministers. Ever since Britain joined the EC in 1973, the Foreign Secretary has been the senior minister responsible for the coordination of EC policy across government, reflecting the fact that the EC was seen as primarily a foreign policy responsibility as well as the fact that in Brussels it was the General Affairs Council, consisting of the foreign ministers of the member states, who were responsible for coordinating the work of other, specialist Councils, as well as for negotiating on institutional issues. Thus, every IGC on treaty change, from the SEA onwards has been negotiated, at least in theory, by the EU's Foreign Ministers.

Every Foreign Secretary has chaired a subcommittee of the Cabinet responsible for coordinating European policy. The regularity with which the committee has met has varied over the years. But it is within the framework of that committee that differences of view among ministers on EU business are thrashed out.

Working to the Foreign Secretary (and to the Prime Minister) is a secretariat in the Cabinet Office called the European Secretariat which, today, consists of over thirty people under the leadership of someone of Permanent Secretary rank who is also the Prime Minister's EU adviser. Until the General Election of 2001, the Head of the European Secretariat was always a Deputy Secretary and always drawn from the Home Civil Service. And the European Secretariat was somewhat smaller than it is now.

Throughout the 1980s, there was an elaborate, formal structure of official-level committees which met regularly under the chairmanship of the European Secretariat. These committees considered papers prepared by the lead government department, according to the subject, on issues to be negotiated in Brussels and officials would try to thrash out an interdepartmentally agreed view of what Britain's substantive position, and negotiating tactics, should be. Since much of the business of the EC was subject to unanimous voting until the passage of the SEA, substance and tactics were often one and the same that is, Britain could afford to hang tough if she so chose.

The outcome of these meetings was very often agreement between departments at official level. In that case, the officials of the lead department would make a formal recommendation to their minister based on the conclusions of the meeting. If the minister agreed, he or she would then write to ministerial colleagues recommending the course of action already discussed at official level.

If officials at working level had been unable to agree, the issue might go to a higher-level meeting, but still a meeting of officials. The most contentious and topical issues were discussed each Friday in the Cabinet Office, at a session chaired by the Head of the European Secretariat and attended by other senior officials, including the UK Permanent Representative to the EC in Brussels.

Today, the system is still recognisably the same though it has changed over the years. The hierarchy of official-level committees no longer exists. Plenty of meetings of officials from across Whitehall still take place, chaired by the Cabinet Office, but they are organised according to need; each department determines the level at which it wants to be represented and the officials in the UK Representation in Brussels no longer routinely cross the Channel to be present. They participate by a secure video conference link.

The Friday meeting, attended by the UK Permanent Representative, still takes place though not every week and its importance has diminished in recent years. This is partly because of the speed and informality of communication via e-mail, partly because of fewer fundamental disagreements across Whitehall on tactics, and partly because, on some key issues, transparent discussion between the Treasury and other government departments has been problematic, leaving some issues for resolution between the Prime Minister and the Chancellor of the Exchequer alone.

If tactics are less controversial than they were twenty years ago, that is down to two factors: the huge increase in EU expertise across government departments and the increasing use of QMV. In the 1980s, there were three or four government departments with day-to-day experience of negotiating in Brussels: the Foreign Office, the Ministry of Agriculture, the Department of Trade and Industry, and the Treasury. Departments such as the Home Office and the MOD had no reason to have such expertise: Brussels hardly impinged on them at all.

In the intervening period, the increase in EU involvement in the issues of environment, migration, asylum, terrorism, international crime, security, and defence has meant that virtually all government departments have had to acquire expertise in EU law and negotiation. All of them send officials to working groups where draft legislation is negotiated between the member states. All of them have had to learn how to build alliances since most of their legislation is decided by majority and they need those alliances either to create a majority to ensure the passage of laws or to forge a blocking minority to prevent their adoption.

This same combination of factors has reduced the direct involvement of Britain's embassies in EU countries in the resolution of EU business. Our embassies still play a part in lobbying on behalf of the government on EU issues. Britain does more of such lobbying than any other member state. When I was British ambassador in Lisbon from 1993 to 1995, we found that, quite often, our lobbying alerted the Portuguese government to some esoteric issue on which their attention had not hitherto alighted. Unfortunately, their gratitude to Britain for alerting them to the matter did not always result in their deciding to vote on the same side. Our embassies lobby effectively on behalf of the British position. They also offer to British ministers an insight into the domestic economic and political factors which underlie the position of their host government. But negotiation as such takes place in Brussels or through the ministers and officials in the Whitehall department concerned telephoning their opposite numbers across the EU and thrashing things out directly. The evolution of English as the second language of most European Ministers and officials has made this much easier.

It is still down to the Foreign Secretary, as chairman of the European Committee of Cabinet, to sum up interministerial correspondence on a particular EU issue, to try to adjudicate where there is disagreement, and to chair a meeting of the committee where his word alone is not enough to resolve a dispute. Jack Straw made particularly good use of the committee when Britain was faced with an interpretation by the ECJ of the Working Time Directive that risked driving a coach and horses through the government's policy on the working hours of doctors. He used the committee to alert other departmental ministers to the problem, to generate defensive action across government, and to organise a lobbying campaign which, even by British standards, was on an unprecedented scale.

The continuing importance of the Foreign Secretary as interministerial coordinator of government policy on Europe in London has not been matched by the role of foreign ministers collectively in Brussels. At one level, their work-load has increased as the EU has developed its foreign policy and, increasingly, its security and defence policy. But the foreign ministers, even though they still meet as the General Affairs Council, cannot claim any role either as coordina-tor or court of appeal. The work of the numerous specialist councils, dealing with agriculture, fisheries, environment, competition, industry, justice and home affairs, transport, energy, and finance, is too detailed for foreign minis-ters to have time to master it. Nor are the ministers in those specialist coun-cils ready to accept the superior jurisdiction of foreign ministers. The only example I can recall of the General Affairs Council successfully intervening in the affairs of another Council was when the Dutch EU Presidency in 1997 contrived with some difficulty to get the issue of leg-hold traps taken from the agenda of the Environment Council and put on that of the foreign ministers. Environment ministers, understandably given the cruelty of leg-hold traps as a means of trapping animals killed for their fur, wanted to impose a ban on the import of fur from animals caught by such traps. Such action would have launched a trade war between the EU on the one hand and the United States, Canada, and Russia on the other. Foreign ministers decided that EU interests would suffer disproportionately if the ban were imposed by the EU alone.

The decline in importance of the General Affairs Council has also under-mined the prestige and significance of the COREPER. This committee of Permanent Representatives meets weekly in two formations: COREPER I and COREPER II. This being the EU, COREPER II consists of the Permanent Representatives and COREPER I their deputies. This allegedly led, during one Italian Presidency when members of both COREPER formations were on an official visit to Sicily, to the deputies being lodged in five star comfort while the ambassadors were housed in a local *pensione*. Maybe this was symbolic because it is the ambassador-level committee which has declined more noticeably in significance. The two formations of COREPER divide the work of the Council of Ministers between them but it is COREPER I that deals with most of the substantive EU legislation on issues such as energy, environment, and transport.

Draft legislation, introduced by the Commission, who retain the sole right of legislative initiative under EU law, goes first to working groups where middle-ranking officials from all the member states try to hammer out agreement on the text before them. They may refer the matter up for guidance from COREPER several times before the issue comes substantively to the COREPER agenda in the hope that, at that level, the remaining difficulties can either be ironed out, or narrowed down so that ministers in the Council have only a few key points of difference to resolve. Therein lies COREPER's importance: it is the point at which, in all but formality (since only the Council of Ministers can actually vote), most issues get resolved. It is also the body regularly charged by ministers with sorting things out when the politicians find that they cannot after all resolve outstanding differences. Unfortunately for the Permanent Representatives, however, on almost all the issues for which they are responsible (Foreign and Security policy, Justice and Home Affairs, the work of the EU Finance Ministers) the primacy of "their" COREPER is challenged by other senior-level committees which in practice do much of the work before matters reach ministerial level in the Council.

This trend was evident during my time as the UK Permanent Representative from 1995 to 2000 and has continued. A senior committee (the Political and Security Committee) now meets full-time in Brussels to discuss foreign policy and security issues. It has replaced the occasional meetings of Political Directors who would fly into Brussels ahead of the meetings of foreign ministers but were not necessarily in the right place when a crisis blew up. That development has meant, in turn, that most member states now send as their representatives on the committee people of ambassadorial rank. In some cases, those ambassadors are not subordinate to the Permanent Representative or disposed, therefore, to seek guidance from him or her. This is not the case in the British Permanent Representation and the job of Permanent Representative remains a hugely important one. It is simply that the focus of activity of the Perm Reps, as they are known, is no longer centred on the weekly meetings of COREPER with the same intensity it once was. The main exception to that is the negotiation of treaty changes in an IGC where, in practice, it is the ambassadorial members of COREPER who do most of the negotiating spade work.

By contrast, COREPER I (the deputy heads of the Permanent Representations) deals with the bulk of legislation in the fields of industry, the single market, and environment, all of which is decided by QMV and all of it subject to co-decision with the EP. As a negotiating forum, COREPER I is more demanding than COREPER II, has a huge schedule of late-night negotiations, and spends much of its time in exhausting, but politically challenging, negotiation with the EP.

What to do about the decline of the General Affairs Council is one of the hardy annuals of Brussels debate. One idea, frequently floated, usually by Europe Ministers, is to have a committee of ministers (Europe Ministers, needless to say) meeting virtually full time in Brussels. The problem with this idea is that it is most unlikely that those ministers would be empowered to take the decisions now taken by their senior colleagues, the foreign ministers. So they would end up becoming an over-graded COREPER doing work which is essentially suited to civil servants, not politicians. For, contrary to the mythology, decisions are not taken by COREPER members, winging it with no political control. Anyone who negotiates in COREPER does so under political instructions from their government. If you are lucky, you will either be given, or manage to carve out, sufficient tactical flexibility to enable you to duck and weave to secure the result your government wants. But the outcome you are aiming for is one that, ultimately, has been set by ministers. What the Whitehall system described in this chapter does give to the UK Permanent Representative is the opportunity to make an input to each phase of the process by which policy is set. In that sense, the UK Representation, whose 130 or so UK staff are drawn from every government department, is unlike most bilateral embassies whose input to policy is less intravenous.

So, in essence, the system continues in Brussels as it has always done. But all Permanent Representatives from all member states have found that it is more difficult for them than it used to be to be regarded in their home capital as the representative of the government as a whole, rather than as that of the foreign ministry. In their turn, the foreign ministers have found that their clout, outside the field of foreign policy, is strictly limited. As a result, the role of the Heads of Government, meeting at least four times a year in the European Council, has grown. The European Council spends some of its time setting the strategic direction of the EU and even more as the final court of appeal (and therefore the forum of negotiation) for issues which cannot be resolved lower down.

Not surprisingly, the role of the offices of Heads of Government has grown too. Most EU Heads of Government have a (usually quite small) team of people in their office dealing full-time with EU issues. Any Presidency trying to put together a deal in a difficult negotiation will negotiate with the representatives of the Head of Government from the problem countries, as well as continue the more formal negotiations in COREPER.

In Britain, some see the development, under Tony Blair, of EU and foreign policy teams in Number 10 Downing Street as somewhat sinister. They fear that, if the Prime Minister of the day has an independent capacity in EU and foreign policy, the role of the Foreign Secretary and of Cabinet government will be undermined.

Tony Blair did not invent, he inherited, the long-standing system whereby there are two "foreign" secretariats in the Cabinet Office: the European

Secretariat, responsible for coordinating EU policy across Whitehall, and the Overseas and Defence Secretariat, responsible for servicing the Overseas and Defence Policy Committee of the Cabinet (a committee traditionally chaired by the Prime Minister of the day) and for coordinating foreign and defence policy issues likely to come to that committee.

When I first started dealing with EC business in the Foreign Office in 1983, the Head of the European Secretariat was David Williamson, a Deputy Secretary on secondment from the Ministry of Agriculture. In her autobiography, Margaret Thatcher describes Williamson as "perhaps the mainstay" of the "truly superb official team" she had to help her. Twenty years later, I did the same job as Williamson, albeit less competently, but sitting in a grand office in Number 10 Downing Street and with the even grander title of Permanent Secretary to go with it. But the job was exactly the same job and my real influence and importance no different from that exercised by Williamson. If anything, my efficiency was marginally diminished when I moved from the Cabinet Office itself into Downing Street because I became physically removed from the team I headed. Over the years, the influence of the European Secretariat and its head, and their closeness to the Prime Minister of the day, has depended more on the personalities involved, on both sides, than on the character of the structures.

The Foreign Policy team which was set up by Tony Blair in Number 10, also under the direction of an official of Permanent Secretary rank, was somewhat different. When I was John Major's Private Secretary in Downing Street, I was one of a long line of Foreign Officials who had filled the job of Foreign Policy Private Secretary to successive Prime Ministers. My immediate predecessor, Charles Powell, had done the job under Margaret Thatcher for an unprecedented seven years and, because of his extraordinary ability and stamina and his closeness to Margaret Thatcher who led from the front more than is habitual even for Prime Ministers, had become a powerful figure, resented by some in the Foreign Office. But the system was designed so that, however able, ambitious, and needless of sleep, the person concerned was just one person working a minimum of sixteen hours a day and usually at weekends. When I did the job, it would range from drafting a letter from John Major to a police widow in Belfast whose pension payment had gone awry (for the Foreign Policy Private Secretary was responsible for Defence and Northern Ireland too), to speaking to the US National Security Adviser, Brent Scowcroft, at midnight on the secure telephone to discuss the next day's bombing raid on Saddam Hussein's missile sites in Iraq, to briefing John Major before every meeting he had with an overseas visitor, to taking and disseminating the record of each of those same meetings. There was no way I could substitute for the Foreign Secretary or the Foreign Office, even if I had wished to do so.

I could not have provided the service the Prime Minister required without the policy and practical input which I received from the Foreign Office, MOD, and Northern Ireland Office hour-by-hour every day. But the system placed a huge burden on one person. My family paid a higher price than I had any right to demand.

It was no more than common sense therefore for the Prime Minister to have a small team dealing with foreign policy rather than a one-man band. The team in Downing Street depended as critically on input from the Foreign Office and the MOD as their predecessors did. What is also true, however, as I have heard Douglas Hurd argue, is that the team, headed by an official who was as senior as the most senior official in the Foreign Office, had a greater capacity for independent origination of ideas, for negotiation on the Prime Minister's behalf, and for implementation of policy than existed before. The risk in this lay not in the structures themselves but in how they were used within the overall framework of Cabinet government. The Foreign Policy team in Number 10 was a product of Tony Blair's working methods, not the cause of them. I believe it to be in the interests of good government to have a foreign policy team in Number 10 that is not quite as potent as the one created by Tony Blair. But it would be a mistake, in terms of the efficiency of the Prime Minister's office, to go back to the system as it was before Tony Blair took office.

The structures of Cabinet government, if fully used, offer protection against bad decisions for, if a policy paper goes to Cabinet Ministers forty-eight hours before the meeting, there is a good chance that members of the Cabinet who are not directly involved in the subject, will have time to read and reflect and bring their political wisdom and experience to bear. It is not a foolproof system. Cabinet, after all, backed Suez. But Cabinet also pulled the plug on the expedition. Would Eden otherwise have continued on a potentially disastrous course?

It was opinion in Cabinet, as well as the advice of the Defence Chiefs on the huge military risks, that led John Major to avoid direct military engagement in Bosnia. Given the advice of the Chiefs at the time that the war could not be won from the air and that a huge commitment of ground troops would be needed, with a very uncertain prospect of winning, the decision was exactly the one Cabinet was designed to take: cautious perhaps but placing weight on the balance between Britain's desire to stop bloodshed in the Balkans on the one hand and the responsibility of ministers to safeguard British lives on the other. It was also frequent debate in Cabinet that enabled John Major to keep the Euro-sceptic members on side because they were given the chance to air their views and, even more importantly, to appreciate that those views were not shared by the majority of Cabinet members.

Much of the time, the Prime Minister and Foreign Secretary are called on to make judgements in EU negotiations without benefit of immediate Cabinet advice and without the time to consult. For it is the two of them who are alone at the table in meetings of the European Council when crucial decisions come to be taken. And once the conclusions of the meeting are finalised, there is no going back. The Presidency will not change what has been agreed because a particular Head of Government did not grasp the point at issue at the time.

The membership of the European Council (Heads of State or Government and Foreign Ministers) is laid down by treaty. Largely because the British insisted, finance ministers are sometimes admitted when their business is at issue. And in 1999, under the first Finnish Presidency of the EU, interior ministers were admitted since it was their business that was under discussion though, in the British case, Foreign Secretary Robin Cook occupied the second UK seat throughout while the Home Secretary, Jack Straw, waited, with commendable patience, outside the room.

A British Prime Minister will have established the framework of Cabinet tolerance within which he or she is operating. Before the Maastricht European Council in 1992, John Major had set out his negotiating stance in detail before the House of Commons in advance in order to ensure that he had political cover. Even so, it was up to him to decide, on the spot, whether or not to accept the Social Chapter which was about to be agreed by the other eleven member states and which was problematic for him. I think it most unlikely that John Major would have accepted the text on the table in any circumstances. But a variant of the Social Chapter, acceptable to the UK, was not inconceivable. Indeed, the officials of the Department of Employment had drafted just such a text some time before. What constrained John Major's negotiating room, his own instincts apart, were the frequent and insistent telephone calls from London from the Employment Secretary, Michael Howard, who made it plain, without ever using the word so far as I know, that this was a potential resigning matter for him.

At Fontainebleau, in 1984, Margaret Thatcher had to decide whether or not to accept the deal on the British budget rebate that was then on the table. She, and ultimately she alone, took the decision that the time had come to settle, even though she knew that Treasury officials wanted her to hold out for more. For her, the key point was that she had the support of Geoffrey Howe, former Chancellor as well as current Foreign Secretary. And, in the event, she had the support of her current Chancellor, Nigel Lawson, although she did not consult Lawson before taking the decision to settle.

Tony Blair had to make a similar judgement when, during the UK Presidency of the EU in 2005, it fell to him to negotiate a budget settlement for the

EU as a whole, while also getting a good deal for the UK on the level of the British rebate, then under attack by all the other member states. Tony Blair had to make a judgement on the level at which to settle, despite the wish of the Chancellor of the Exchequer to hold out beyond the British Presidency and despite the reticence of his two Foreign Office ministers, Jack Straw and Douglas Alexander, about the kind of deal he was prepared to do. He made his own judgement, calculating, correctly I believe, that he might well not get a better deal later and that, in the meantime, Britain would be held responsible for plunging the EU into a crisis, in which Britain's good and privileged relationship with the new member states from Eastern and Central Europe would have been damaged.

So, the Prime Minister has to calculate what is best for Britain in the circumstances, as well as what he or she can sell back home to the rest of the Cabinet, to Parliament, and to the Press. So long as the Prime Minister is the unchallenged instrument of electoral success for the Party, he or she is likely to be given considerable leeway. Margaret Thatcher's intemperate comments in the House of Commons in October 1990 and her outright hostility to EMU might, in any circumstances, have provoked the resignation of Geoffrey Howe. They would not necessarily have provoked a leadership challenge but for the much more serious erosion of the government's popularity caused by the poll tax.

The formation of policy advice by civil servants is governed first of all by the declared policy of the governing party. This seems too self-evident to need saying. But political parties coming to power after a long time in opposition, as Labour did in 1964 and 1997, genuinely believe that the Civil Service has been hijacked by their predecessors over such a long period in office. In 1996, Robin Cook told the then Permanent Undersecretary at the Foreign Office, John Coles, that when Labour won the election, I was to lose my job as UK Permanent Representative to the EU. The first I knew was when I read of my forthcoming demise in a British newspaper. Robin Cook's reasoning was that I had been too close to John Major and would be unable to articulate the new government's new approach to Europe. Very soon, Robin Cook realised that I, along with all other civil servants, would work loyally for the new government, as we had done for the old. Robin Cook may have been surprised that I could work for him, having been John Major's Private Secretary and having been appointed by Major to Brussels. His surprise would have been as nothing compared with John Major's shock had I told him that I did not think I could work for a Labour government. John Major rightly expected that, whatever my feelings of affection for him, and they were and are strong, it was my duty as a civil servant loyally to serve the government of the day. There are civil servants who are lifelong voters for one or other political party. Most are, however, little different from the rest of the population. In 1964, when Labour returned to power after thirteen years in opposition, roughly the same proportion of civil servants voted for the Labour Party as the proportion of the population as a whole. This was despite the belief of the Labour Party that the Civil Service had become the creature of the Tory Party.

Civil Servants are also imbued with the ethos of their parent department about Europe, as about other things. It is undoubtedly true that the Foreign Office has, since the 1960s, been a "pro-European" department. The lessons from the judgements made in the 1950s, when Foreign Office officials made the same judgements as their political masters about the significance of the establishment of the EC, were learned and passed on to successor generations. That tradition is now being tested by the Foreign Office's nervousness at the implications for national policymaking of the EU's CFSP.

The Foreign Office view was also born of experience, not of "going native" but of realising the significance of the EC for British interests and the need therefore to negotiate from within, rather than carp from the sidelines. This pro-Europeanism is, I would argue, no more than sensible realism. In the same sense, the Ministry of Agriculture could also be said to be a pro-European department because, from the beginning of our membership, it has had to work with the fact that most of Britain's agricultural practices are set by negotiation in Brussels.

In general, however, one feature that is common to most Whitehall departments, and which goes wider and deeper than their individual ethos, is an instinctive dislike of EU legislation.

"No unless" is the common response of Whitehall departments to a piece of proposed EU legislation, compared to the "yes if" reaction of most of our partners. In this, officials are undoubtedly responding to successive ministers, of both main parties, who have been nervous of the domestic political reaction to legislation originating in Brussels. But they readily share that suspicion. They do not have to be taught it. It is rooted in our national psyche, the psyche of an island nation which has lived by resisting Continental encroachment; whose sixteenth-century Reformation was about politics as well as worship; which fought against the very countries who are now our partners to establish its imperial supremacy in the eighteenth and nineteenth centuries; which did do something remarkable for European liberty in 1940, and which, unlike much of the rest of Europe, emerged from war in 1945 with its pride in its national institutions enhanced. However flawed it may have often been in practice, England was *the* model of liberal political philosophy until the newly born United States of America took on the mantle in the late eighteenth century. Margaret Thatcher's claim that, in her lifetime, all the problems of the world had come from Continental Europe and all the solutions from the

English-speaking world, was a characteristically insensitive expression of a view probably held by a large proportion of her fellow countrymen.

The other determining factor in Whitehall's view of the EU is the political instinct of a Department's Secretary of State and, even more importantly, the views of the Prime Minister. Margaret Thatcher's instincts about Europe, and therefore about majority voting, political union, the single currency, and European defence were the main determinants of the government's policy. As has been shown earlier in this book, some of those instinctive reactions might occasionally be challenged by the Foreign Secretary but a head-on confrontation was rare. The process of persuading Mrs Thatcher that some movement to majority voting might be in Britain's interest if we wanted to see the completion of the Single Market took months of subtle effort by Geoffrey Howe and by officials. The same is true of the efforts made by Lawson and Howe, and later by Hurd and Major, to persuade her of the merits of joining the ERM. No Prime Minister can go against the strongly held views of a majority in the Cabinet. But equally, it takes a very determined group of politicians within the Cabinet to persuade a Prime Minister to do something he or she does not like. If, as in Margaret Thatcher's case, the position, in this case on Europe, sits well with public opinion, then the task is that much harder. And in Margaret Thatcher's case, she formed public opinion as well as being influenced by it.

While I was working in Downing Street for John Major, I helped a young academic who was writing a doctoral thesis on the SEA. His work was brilliant. But it advanced logical reasons, often based on theories of foreign policy, for all of the negotiating positions that the British government had taken. I had to tell him that, as often as not, we had taken a particular view because the Prime Minister had expressed a forthright opinion that had immediately become holy writ. In due course, my friend joined the Diplomatic Service and we later worked companionably together on European issues. He soon saw how rich a mixture of the systematic, logical, rational, instinctive, personal, reasonable, and sometimes unreasonable, went into the process of policymaking.

The final piece in the jigsaw of European policymaking in London is implementation: how the policy decisions of ministers are carried out. The systematic way in which policy is considered, and recommendations on it are approved, means not just that all ministers are likely to sing the same song from the same song sheet, but that they and their officials will not dare to depart from it. There are factors at play here that have a lot to do with the pressures of public, parliamentary, and press opinion and those are looked at in the last chapter. Whatever the causes, it is probably true that, until Spain joined the EC, Britain was seen by her partners as the most bloody-minded member state; the member state least likely to compromise on its national interests.

We have already seen how Britain is more systematic and rigorous in lobbying other member states on EU issues than any of its partners. The amount of effort which the UK Representation in Brussels puts into keeping alongside the Commission and the EP certainly exceeds that of most other member governments. Before each week's meeting of the European Commission, the British Commissioner's office, his *cabinet*, will receive written briefing from the UK Representation on issues on the agenda that are of concern to the UK government. Britain is not unique in doing this but is particularly assiduous in providing such briefing. The same procedure applies to MEPs. The British members are all entitled to, and receive, written briefing on the British government's position on the legislation before them. This written briefing, prepared by departments in London, goes to British MEPs regardless of Party. When I first arrived in Brussels as the UK Permanent Representative in 1995 under a Conservative government, Conservative MEPs were heavily outnumbered by Labour ones, who made a point of telling me how much they valued the British government's briefing because they immediately knew which way to vote: the opposite of what the government was recommending. Today's MEPs of all main parties are more sensitive to the national interest and more inclined to look at issues on their merits, helped by the fact that Conservative, Liberal Democrat, and Labour policy on EU economic issues does not these days differ greatly.

The large member states, Britain included, can obviously devote more resources to following EU issues than can the smaller member states. So it is not so much that we British care more passionately on particular issues than our partners. But we do care more passionately about more of them than do most of our partners. The Portuguese, for example, will fight like tigers where their textile interests are concerned but there are a lot of issues where, if they do not consider a vital national interest to be at stake, they will follow the Commission's lead, with an instinctive tendency to vote in favour of a Commission proposal. Our instinctive tendency is to be suspicious of Commission initiatives. Even where those initiatives respond to our interests, for example, over the single market in financial services for which Britain campaigned long and hard, we will take huge trouble to ensure that the detail is absolutely right from the British perspective.

This habit reflects in turn the seriousness with which Britain takes its EU obligations. Throughout the 1980s and most of the 1990s Britain, along with Denmark, was the member state which had the best record of faithful implementation of EC law. Our record is still one of the best, though others are more assiduous, and we are deliberately less conscientious, than in the past. Our system of transcribing EU law into domestic law partly accounts for our rigour. To implement EU law usually involves amending an existing statute, and Parliament's legal draftsmen are punctilious. The extent to which Britain is also more prone to "goldplate" EU legislation by using it as an opportunity to introduce domestic regulation and blame it on Brussels has achieved the status of urban myth. Successive studies have shown some evidence of it but not nearly as much as claimed by British business, which cannot always produce the evidence to support its complaints.

Whether Britain is more assiduous, not just in carrying EU legislation into law, but in enforcing it thereafter is another sore issue. There is certainly plenty of anecdotal evidence about the blind eye turned by the authorities in some member states to breaches of EU law. But the evidence of the annual reports of the Court of Auditors suggests that no member state is immune from the desire of quick-minded people to get round the system. The story of the same flock of sheep being driven from one farm to another to collect sheep premium is told of every EU country where sheep are bred. What is true is that Britain has a highly developed society of special interest, consumer, and other lobby groups who do not hesitate to complain to the European Commission if they see evidence of breaches of EU law. The Commission cannot ignore those complaints and it sometimes happens that Britain is the first country to be taken to the European Court for offences which may in practice be more widespread in other member states. Part of the answer should lie in the Commission having more enforcement staff. But, not least because of the widespread view in Britain that the Commission bureaucracy is already huge, the British have been among those governments least willing to increase the Commission's staffing budget.

Margaret Thatcher, John Major, and Tony Blair all had different techniques for getting their way. One of the reasons they, other British ministers, and their officials had to be tougher than anyone else was because Britain has found herself fighting alone on more issues than any other member state in the last twenty years. Did they inevitably find themselves alone or did they needlessly isolate themselves? That is a question for the final chapter.

10

A Stranger in Europe

Sir Thomas More held the office that, in sixteenth-century England, came closest to that of Prime Minister. He was King Henry VIII's Lord Chancellor, confidant, and friend. On 6 July 1535, Henry VIII did one last favour for his friend. He ordered that More should have his head cut off. But for that gesture, More would have been hanged, drawn, and quartered.

More died because he believed that no earthly potentate could be head of Christ's Church. Yet the Pope, whose primacy Henry usurped, was himself an absolute monarch, one of a succession of pontiffs whose grip on earthly power was almost certainly greater than their claim on divine authority.

Little more than a century later, on 30 January 1649, another supposedly absolute monarch, King Charles I, had his head cut off by order of Parliament. In our country, now famous for its democratic tolerance, Parliament cut the head off a king in order to assert its primacy in matters of taxation.

Before the century was out, Charles's son, James II, had abandoned his throne and fled the country, driven out by opposition to his attempt to reintroduce Roman Catholicism to England. The English establishment turned to a Dutchman to succeed him and, when that line died out, to remote German cousins, minor royalty in Hanover. Queen Victoria, proudly pointing to the pictures of her "ancestors" on the walls of Windsor Castle, was corrected by the historian Macaulay. "Predecessors, ma'am", he said, "predecessors."

The longbow men who defeated the French at the Battle of Crecy in 1346 almost certainly thought of themselves as Englishmen. The nobility had a less certain grip on national identity. Europe and Christendom were synonymous and England was part of a Christendom in which alliances were made in support of dynastic claims more than national interest. The Wars of the Roses, the first great civil war in England, were as much about the alliances which were made by the opposing sides with France on the one hand and Holland on the other as about the strength of the native combatants.

With Henry VIII's Reformation came a different view of Englishness. The Reformation in England was as much a rejection of Continental encroachment as of Roman Catholicism. However venal Henry's motives, he tapped into a popular sense of England's island identity which has stayed with us ever since.

The struggle against France in the eighteenth and early nineteenth centuries, the conquest of Empire, and the rise of England to be the world's greatest naval and imperial power all enhanced that sense of identity. The belief that prevailed in the United States that Protestant faith and liberal politics went hand in hand, just as did Roman Catholicism and backwardness, was also prevalent in England. The history of the twentieth century did nothing to dent that innate sense of difference, even of superiority. When the Labour leader Hugh Gaitskell, speaking in 1962, decried the prospect of British membership of the Common Market as the denial of "a thousand years of history", he was appealing, not so much to "little England" as to the England of H. E. Marshall's *Our Island Story*, a potent mix of legend, history, and achievement. The UK had achieved a democracy that was respected and admired around the world. Our sense of national self-worth had been enhanced by World War II. We were still, just, an Empire on which the sun never set.

It is therefore scarcely surprising that British opinion was divided in the early 1960s between those, my teenage self included, who saw the advent of a EC as something exciting: a dramatic new politics which offered the prospect of peace and prosperity in Europe, and those who saw what Gaitskell had predicted, not a sharing of sovereignty but a loss of it. Part of this was rude awakening. In 1956, the Suez crisis had demonstrated the limitations of British power, especially in the face of American opposition. The Empire was coming to an end. Britain's relative prosperity was diminishing compared with her European neighbours. But to feel the winds of change was one thing. To pitch in our lot with Continental powers, some of whom had been our enemies less than two decades earlier, all of whom were considered morally and politically Britain's inferiors, was quite another.

The hard road to Britain's first application to join the EEC is easily under-stood. It is harder to analyse why, over thirty years after the 1975 referendum which confirmed Britain's EC membership, public opinion in Britain seems scarcely to have changed. The relative unpopularity of the EU in Britain is not matched, according to opinion polls, in any other member state, even those, such as Denmark and Sweden, which have a large dollop of scepticism.

"If the British Empire and its Commonwealth should last for a thousand years, men will still say 'This was their finest hour'." Churchill's words still resonate. Of course, the British Empire lasted barely another two decades. The British people had to reconcile the pride in their wartime achievement with the relative poverty in which it left us and the twilight of our role as a world power. We act out those withdrawal symptoms still, as successive British Prime Ministers strive to ensure that they are the first foreign leader to clamber onto an aeroplane to Washington to meet the new President of the United States. It is not surprising that Tony Blair calculated that, given a choice over Iraq between "old Europe" and the United States, it was better politics to choose the United States. The unpopularity of that policy had more to do with its failure than any sense in Britain that we were first and foremost Europeans and that there should be a European policy towards Iraq first and a transatlantic policy second.

Membership of the EC was always controversial. At the time that the European Communities Bill was being guided through the House of Commons in 1972, ministers did not disguise from MPs the fact that EC law would have primacy over national law, but nor did they spell it out for fear of the adverse reaction. Ted Heath could, from personal conviction, sign up to the goal of European union, political and economic, in the autumn of 1972, but his successors, Labour and Conservative, felt it necessary, for domestic political reasons, to redefine what Union meant: it became not a goal but a process. In other words, Union was watered down to be whatever the member states were doing at any one time, not what they might attain to at some point in the future. While Britain's partners reluctantly went along with that definition at the time of the Stuttgart Declaration in 1983, that was not what many of them believed or wanted. When Geoffrey Howe, resisting the idea of treaty change to achieve the Single Market, described the Treaty of Rome as the constitution of the EC, he was not doing what the opponents of the Constitutional Treaty feared some twenty years later. He was not saying that the EC had some of the characteristics of a state. On the contrary, he was saying "thus far and no further". The limits of the sharing of sovereignty had been set in the Treaty of Rome and the British government did not want to see those limits extended.

Geoffrey Howe and Tony Blair are among the very few British politicians who sought to address the issue of sovereignty. In resisting the idea of treaty change, Howe was being loyal to his brief. In reality, he had a growing sense of sovereignty, not as a finite commodity in danger of being eroded, but as an instrument to be deployed in the national interest. In other words, he shared Macmillan's view that in giving up some of our sovereignty we were not engaging in a one-way trade. We would get something back from the other countries in return. But the language of EU and talk, by Helmut Kohl among others, of a United States of Europe made it inevitable that many in Britain would see concessions on matters of EC competence, not as sensible measures for a specific purpose, but as the first steps onto a slippery slope. That was the sense of Margaret Thatcher's "No, no, no" in response to Delors's ideas on European democracy in 1990. That was why Malcolm Rifkind was able to tell his German audience in 1996 that people in Britain saw more powers for the EP, not as a welcome extension of their democratic rights, but as the embryonic arm of a federal superstate.

It is impossible to know how far successive British governments could have called the bluff of our partners by embracing some of the rhetoric of integration. From Margaret Thatcher onwards, Britain's partners could nearly always count on Britain to be first into the breach in opposition to anything that involved extending Community competence. When, with enormous self-control, Britain sat on her hands in the first weeks of the negotiations on the SEA, our reticence did have exactly the desired effect: it forced France and Germany out of the woodwork and to reveal that their objectives for treaty change were not much more ambitious than our own. After the 1997 General Election, the relatively relaxed attitude of the new British government to majority voting in some areas produced silence from the British delegation negotiating the Amsterdam Treaty where, before the election, there had been vocal opposition. This caused consternation among some other delegations who had counted on Britain, in fighting her own battles, to fight theirs as well. At Amsterdam, it was the German and Dutch Foreign Ministers who almost came to blows as Kohl was forced by domestic opinion to row back from some of the forward positions he had taken only a few weeks earlier.

Those were relatively rare exceptions to the normal British rule and the tactic was anyway not foolproof. I was one of those, scarred by my experience in the 1980s, who advised Tony Blair to go along with the idea of a Constitution for Europe, believing that there was no mileage in resisting the idea and every likelihood that we could secure a result which satisfied British interests. In that instance, it was the British Euro-sceptic press that called the government's bluff. There was nothing in the Constitutional Treaty as negotiated which involved significant extensions of competence but the title "Constitution" was a red rag to a bull and created a political whirlwind that blew the Prime Minister into his decision to offer a referendum, against his wishes and earlier resolution.

One reason why such a media firestorm can take hold is because successive British governments have done relatively little to explain to the British people what the true nature of the European project actually is.

In 1972, the issue of the primacy of EC law was soft-pedalled. At the 1975 referendum on continued UK membership of the EC, the Luxembourg Compromise, which turned out to be a rather frail crutch a few years later, was sold as a national veto. The pillared structure to the Treaties achieved at Maastricht was sold as halting the advance of the Commission, EP, and European Court. The impression was given, over many years, that the role of governments in determining European policy was what safeguarded the interests of the British citizen against the depredations of the supranational parts of the enterprise.

One of the reasons why this ultimately misleading impression was given was fear. In raising the spectre of a federal superstate, British ministers were not seeking to whip up public opinion, they were trying to assuage it. They themselves saw the danger of a federally ambitious European Commission and sought to head it off either, as Mrs Thatcher did, by setting out to slay the dragon or, as John Major did, by seeking to demonstrate that, if there had been a dragon, it had now been effectively put to sleep. As part of this effort to persuade people that Europe was "going our way", governments played up those parts of European action which were based on voluntary cooperation between governments, achieved by consensus, and played down those that involved action through the Community method (Commission initiative, majority voting, EP, and ECJ involvement).

The only speech on sovereignty by any of the three Prime Ministers who feature in this book was the one by Tony Blair quoted in an earlier chapter. It is, however, surprising that no more sustained effort has ever been made to explain that the reason for supranational institutions is to prevent potentially damaging disputes between quarrelsome countries. Without that framework of supranational institutions, the settlement of disputes would be achieved by the law of the survival of the fittest. In the absence of supranational institutions, the large are likely to bully the small and to end up pitting themselves against each other in all the fields where their national interests potentially collide. Had a consistent and persistent campaign of information been undertaken, it is possible that public opinion, knowing the reasons for the existence and powers of the European institutions, might have been more ready to recognise their role in defending important freedoms as well as to accept their inevitable imperfections.

At times, the European Commission was its own worst enemy. Jacques Delors was a brilliant Commission President. His ideas for the Single Market and for EMU were clever and far-sighted. His vision, which he shared with Kohl and Mitterrand and most of their fellow Heads of Government, was of a Europe which had to integrate politically in order to sustain the momentum of the project and in order to punch its weight in the world. That is a view I share. But, for much of the 1980s, the Commission's motivation seemed to be to treat the member states as the opposition and to contrive, with the EP, to move as much policy as possible into the sphere of Community competence, in the name of the common good and also in the interest of centralised authority. The democratic legitimacy of elected national governments, and the fact that the nation state was likely to remain the basis of that legitimacy, were often disregarded. It was provocative of Delors to put forward the notion of a Europe in which the Council of Ministers would become the second chamber of a quasi-federal government. There was every reason, in terms of trust between the Commission and the member states, for the Commission to interpret the provisions of the Single European Act on health and safety in a more conservative way. Instead, they sought to push the boundaries of interpretation and used the provision to extend their activity into social areas which may or may not have been desirable but were certainly legally and politically controversial.

I felt in the 1980s that the Commission would have been better advised to proceed more gradually and less publicly. This was not an argument for deception. It was an argument for reading the character of some member states, Britain in particular. We have, over the years, accepted the growth of competence in areas such as the environment, energy, and justice and home affairs because the motivation has been practical need and the consequence a measurably satisfactory result. It was for similar reasons that Margaret Thatcher eventually accepted the treaty changes which enabled the Single Market to come about. It has been easier to accept the political, including sovereignty, implications of practical policy proposals than the implications of more visionary ideas that confront politicians and public with the prospect of less measurable and less controllable outcomes.

Britain's position in all this was not helped by the fact that, quite often, we found ourselves in the minority. A whole series of events and attitudes compounded the problem. We were not founder members of the organisation. We joined late, with the rules already written, and almost on sufferance. The budget of the EC was constructed in a way that made us disproportionately large contributors. The CAP, which largely accounted for the budgetary imbalance we suffered, had been made in the image and likeness of French farming interests. To begin to correct that required a battle. Margaret Thatcher may have been needlessly tactless in her intransigence. But she needed to be intransigent. The unwillingness of Britain's partners to recognise, let alone remedy, an undoubted injustice was a product of collective national self-interest masquerading as concern for the Community and its values. The ensuing battle set the tone of Britain's subsequent relationship with her partners.

The budget issue illustrated a particular British problem: how to tell a positive story about Europe to the British public. Germany could point to the scope for her successful industrial exports, as well as the fact that the EC was the vehicle for her democratic rehabilitation as a leader in the European family. For France, the EC was a way of binding her old enemy tightly to her side. It also gave France's agriculture a privileged position. With the exception of Germany and the UK, for the EC member countries, the European budget was a source of net financial benefits, even for those such as Denmark and Luxembourg which, on a per capita basis, were among the more wealthy.

It is relatively easy to tell a popular story about an organisation that brings prosperity to the countries that belong to it. For the poorer member states, such as Greece, Ireland, Spain, and Portugal, the economic transfers from rich to poor represented by the structural funds played a big part in their economic regeneration. That money smoothed the path of painful adjustment to European rules and economic competition. In the case of Ireland, the structural funds represented, at one stage, 7% of GDP and were brilliantly used to fuel the growth of what became the Celtic Tiger.

Britain was never able to tell such a story. Even after the Fontainebleau settlement on the rebate, Britain remained a significantly higher net payer into the budget than France and Italy, countries of like prosperity. France's ferocious assault on the British rebate during the Blair government was a product of the fact that, for the first time ever, France was about to overtake Britain as a net payer. The declining popularity of Europe in Italy, France, the Netherlands, and Ireland can, I believe, be traced in large part to the decline in their receipts from the EU budget.

Against this background, throughout the years of our membership, successive British governments have found themselves making an essentially negative case in favour of British membership. It has been based on arguing how much worse off we would be if we were outside. The argument is entirely valid. There would be a huge loss to British interests if twenty-six other countries were taking, without us, decisions on energy, environment, agriculture, trade, industry, transport, foreign policy, and defence when those decisions would in all cases bear directly on our national interest and, in most, have to be implemented in Britain simply because we would otherwise be unable to operate in the European market place. But it is not easy to arouse popular support for Europe on that basis. Even where steps have been taken in the EU which are in our interest, we have found it hard to proclaim them or give credit to "Brussels" for them. The adversarial nature of the relationship, established in the battle of the budget, has been hard to shake off. Our own politics, based on first past the post and confrontation across the despatch box, lend themselves less to conciliation than is the case in partner countries where coalition and therefore compromise are the norm. Because all decisions taken at EU level have implications for legal competence, it has been politically easier to play down their significance, or to mask it by talk of British victory, than to explain the true situation. Victory implies an adversary. Maastricht's "Game, set, and match" was ill-judged in diplomatic terms but spot on in striking the chord that would resonate with the Red Tops.

Chris Patten has written about the frequency with which, during his five years as a European Commissioner, people would engage him in conversation with the question: "Will Britain ever join the EU?" We have been members since 1973 but the debate about the benefits of membership, regardless of EMU or the Constitution, continues in Britain as in no other EU country. No other member state has such a relentlessly hostile Press. No other country raises in the minds of its partners the question whether it will remain a member of the organisation. How far have successive British governments made that rod for their own backs? Or how far have they been driven by a lukewarm public opinion, a hostile press, and reluctance to take on a wearisome and debilitating campaign to turn things around? I think the answer is a mixture of those things. Ted Heath's enthusiasm for Europe put him ahead of public opinion. "Fanfare for Europe", the public celebrations of our entry organised by the government in 1973, did not find any echo in the public imagination. The referendum in 1975 was in part a device to get the Labour government off the hook of its own internal divisions. But those divisions were themselves a reflection of the views of a divided public.

Margaret Thatcher's fight for the British rebate, once resolved, promised calmer waters ahead. But Britain, under her leadership, put itself in a needless and ultimately unsustainable stance of opposition to the treaty change that Malcolm Rifkind was honest and perceptive enough to realise was necessary if we were serious about achieving an internal market for our goods and services. Margaret Thatcher established a track record of being in a minority and our partners eventually established a track record of manoeuvring around her. She saw Europe as a problem to be confronted and she hectored her EU colleagues as she did her British ones. She had no friends among the other Heads of Government. The scurvy treatment meted out to her paper on POCO by Kohl and Mitterrand in 1985 was an example of that. The hair's breadth by which, in 1988, she prevented the eleven others reaching an agreement on budgetary and agricultural policy without her does not mean that she was wrong on substance, but that she played the tactics to the brink. She misjudged, understandably given Kohl's professed reluctance at the time, the extent of the impulsion towards EMU. Later on, while her Chancellor of the Exchequer, John Major, saw clearly the need to accommodate the fact that eleven countries could, if they wished, go ahead with EMU without us, she saw only the folly of the eleven and the wisdom of the one and set her face against the inevitable.

Once out of office she fulfilled her declared intention to be a back-seat driver. She made herself the main parliamentary focus of Conservative opposition to the Maastricht Treaty. By doing so, she almost derailed it. Loyalty to the perceived legacy of an undoubtedly great Prime Minister and Party Leader became the touchstone of attitudes to Europe. She fostered an anti-European sentiment which had little to do with European policy and much to do with Europe as a symbol of a reality too painful to be accommodated. After all, John Major had negotiated a treaty which explicitly protected Britain's position. EMU could go ahead without us. Political Union could go ahead without us. Even if there was to be a European superstate, there was no obligation on Britain to be part of it. What irked the sceptics was the irresistibility of the European project, not in terms of the impotence of Parliament to assert British interests, but in terms of the inescapable logic for a small island such as Britain of working with other democracies as one member of a team. British governments have not always been candid in spelling out the facts and implications of decisions taken with their participation in the EU. But their lack of candour is outdone by that of many of the opponents of British EU membership who have done the British people an even greater disservice by distorting the nature of issues under debate in Brussels and by presenting a vision of an alternative world in which Britain could successfully operate without the rest of Europe or, even more insidiously, simply pick and choose at will which bits of European policy Britain chose to adhere to.

John Major sought to correct this anti-European tendency. He was honest in his appraisal of the costs and benefits to Britain of particular courses of action. He always rejected as totally un-negotiable the notion, occasionally put forward inside his government, that Britain could do a deal with her partners whereby, on any issue we disliked, we could bow out while having full rights to participate whenever it suited us. There was never any question of Britain signing up to a treaty on EMU which did not allow her an opt-out. In some ways, it was a relief when it was realised that the other eleven countries could, if necessary, make their own treaty on EMU without the participation of the UK. That saved Britain from engaging in another painful row which would have left her in a minority of one. But, with the opt-out from EMU and the Social Chapter she was, nonetheless, in a minority of one, albeit arrived at through relatively amicable agreement. Britain had, in particular, excluded herself from the most integrationist step taken thus far by the EU. John Major's government believed, correctly, that opting out of the social chapter was a significant net gain for the UK. They were not so confident in respect of EMU. A price had to be paid for Britain's opt-out/opt-in and that price was to allow the other member states to go ahead, with the possibility that the euro zone would surge forward in economic growth and other aspects of policy integration. So far, that calculated gamble by John Major, perpetuated by the Blair government, has paid off. But it is not surprising that speeches by other EU leaders then and since have, in one breath referred to the importance of the British contribution to Europe and, in the next, defined that principally in terms of our role in foreign policy and defence. They see us as excluding ourselves from other key areas of EU activity.

The power of the Euro-sceptics in the Conservative Party grew as a result of the Danish referendum result on Maastricht and the humiliating circum-stances of Britain's withdrawal from the ERM. That withdrawal, and the sub-sequent healthy performance of the British economy, made the prospect of